DEVELOPMENT
OF CONSERVATION FARMING
ON HILLSLOPES

DEVELOPMENT OF CONSERVATION FARMING ON HILLSLOPES

W. C. MOLDENHAUER, N. W. HUDSON,
T. C. SHENG and SAN-WEI LEE
EDITORS

SOIL
AND WATER
CONSERVATION
SOCIETY

SOIL AND WATER CONSERVATION SOCIETY
ANKENY, IOWA USA
in cooperation with
WORLD ASSOCIATION OF SOIL AND WATER CONSERVATION
CHINESE SOIL AND WATER CONSERVATION SOCIETY
NATIONAL CHUNG-HSING UNIVERSITY
NATIONAL SCIENCE COUNCIL, R.O.C.

Copyright © 1991 by the Soil and Water Conservation Society
All rights reserved
Manufactured in the United States of America

Library of Congress Catalog Card No. 91-8109

ISBN 0-935734-24-4

$30.00

Library of Congress Cataloging-in-Publication Data

Main entry under title:

Development of conservation farming on hillslopes / W. C. Moldenhauer...[et al.], editors.
    p. cm.
"In cooperation with World Association of Soil and Water Conservation, Chinese Soil
and Water Conservation Society, National Chung-Hsing University [and] National Science
Council, R.O.C."
Based on material presented at an international workshop held in March 1989 at National
Chung-Hsing University in Taiching City.
    Includes index.
    ISBN 0-935734-24-4 : $30.00
    1. Hill farming-Congresses. 2. Conservation tillage-Congresses. I. Moldenhauer, W.
    C. II. Soil and Water Conservation Society (U.S.) III. Kuo li chung hsing ta hsueh.
S604.3.D48   1991   91-8109
631.5'8—dc20   CIP

CONTENTS

Part 7: Case Studies

Part 8: Reports of Discussion Groups

PREFACE

In March 1989, the soil conservation community on the Island of Taiwan, Republic of China, graciously hosted an international workshop, "Conservation Farming on Hillslopes," at National Chung-Hsing University in Taichung City. This book is based on material presented at that workshop.

The event was organized by the Chinese Soil and Water Conservation Society in cooperation with the World Association of Soil and Water Conservation and the Soil and Water Conservation Society. It was sponsored by National Chung-Hsing University; Food and Fertilizer Technology Center for the Asian and Pacific Region; Council of Agriculture, R.O.C.; National Science Council, R.O.C.; Society of Soil and Fertilizer Sciences of the Republic of China; National Taiwan University; and the Department of Agriculture and Forestry and the Mountain Agricultural Resources Development Bureau, both of which are affiliated with the Taiwan Provincial Government.

The 165 workshop participants included nearly 80 representatives from 22 countries other than Taiwan.

The Taiwan workshop was a logical follow-on to an earlier workshop, "Conservation Farming on Steep Lands," organized in March 1987 by the World Association of Soil and Water Conservation and the Soil and Water Conservation Society. That earlier workshop, because of its location in San Juan, Puerto Rico, permitted considerable emphasis to be put on the development of hillslope farming systems in the western hemisphere. Notably lacking was any extensive discussion of hillslope farming methods used in the Pacific Rim region and elsewhere in the eastern hemisphere.

Taiwan has had 35 years of experience in soil and water conservation, watershed management, and hillslope farming. In spite of frequent natural disasters, such as typhoons, earthquakes, and landslides, the Taiwan experience has proved extremely successful. Workshop organizers, therefore, felt this experience could be valuable to many people confronted by similar circumstances in other countries. Likewise valuable to others, it was felt, particularly in developing nations, might be Taiwan's path toward industrialization, which has had profound impacts on land use and watershed development in the island nation.

Because of population pressures and food shortages, marginal land, especially hillslope land, is being brought into cultivation in many countries around the globe. In some of these countries, the unwise use of hillslopes has been a result of socioeconomic conditions. The need for proper policy and planning, as well as the development of appropriate infrastructure, conservation farming systems, and machinery, is imperative when hillslopes are developed for agricultural purposes. The Taiwan experience offers a successful model to emulate.

Particularly significant in the Taiwan story is that many things must occur simultaneously, with full government support, if success is to be achieved. As socioeconomic conditions change, government must respond to ensure that the agricultural sector remains viable. This point is valid worldwide, in both developed and developing nations. Without such response, years or even decades of progress might be lost.

The purpose of the workshop and this book is to give scientists and technicians examples of what has been achieved in Taiwan and elsewhere in the use and conservation of hillslope soils. It is hoped that this information will prove helpful in formulating strategies for hillslope development in other settings.

The Taiwan workshop and subsequent workshops being planned in Indonesia and Africa all build on the Puerto Rico workshop. Individually and collectively, these events seek to develop sound soil conservation policy around the world through the sharing of experiences, particularly success stories, and making materials available for study and use by scientists, technicians, program admininstrators, and government officials.

Special thanks, of course, are due all of the organizers and sponsors of the Taiwan workshop and officials of the National Science Council, R.O.C., for their financial support of this book. The workshop was a substantial undertaking by many individuals with the Chinese Soil and Water Conservation Society, National Chung-Hsing University, Council of Agriculture, and Food and Fertilizer Technology Center, and they all performed admirably.

My personal thanks go to Mr. San-Wei Lee, who contributed enormously to the organization of the workshop and served as co-editor of this book, and to Dr. S. S. Wann, who was the executive secretary of the workshop organizing committee. My co-editors, Drs. Norman Hudson and Ted Sheng, also deserve thanks for their significant contributions to the preparation of this book.

Finally, thanks are due all of the workshop participants, those who presented papers and the others who enthusiastically entered into the discussion throughout. Their contributions were essential to the workshop's success and to whatever value this book may have in promoting conservation farm development on hillslopes throughout the world.

W. C. Moldenhauer

THE TAIWAN EXPERIENCE 1

THE EVOLUTION
OF CONSERVATION FARMING
ON HILLSLOPES IN TAIWAN

C. C. KOH, M. C. LIAO, S. W. LEE, and J. D. CHENG

I n developing countries, the use of hillslopes for agricultural purposes usually starts as a result of some combination of high population density, limited arable land, rapid expansion of urbanization and industry in plains areas, and significant financial contributions to individual farmers and the national economy from hillslope farming. Taiwan, for example, has a land surface of about 3.6 million hectares. Less than one-third of the area is plains. The rest ranges from hilly to mountainous. About 340,000 hectares of hillslopes are being used for livestock or crop production.

Until recently, hillslope agricultural use had generally been profitable for farmers. Many cash crops (e.g., bananas, pineapple, tea, citrus fruits) and livestock (e.g., hogs, beef, and dairy cattle) have been produced on hillslope farms for local consumption and for export. Hillslope farming certainly played an important role in Taiwan's successful agricultural recovery in the 1950s and 1960s, which led to the emergence of industry on the island.

Hillslope agriculture is not without problems, however. Heavy rainfall, erodible soils, steep slopes, and other factors contribute to serious erosion on the cultivated hillslopes in Taiwan. Conservation practices are essential, not only to protect and enhance the on-site sustainability of productivity on hillslopes, but also to help prevent or to minimize off-site detrimental impacts.

Conservation farming on hillslopes, hereafter referred to as slopeland conservation farming, has occurred in Taiwan since 1952. The evolution of slopeland conservation farming in Taiwan is generally characterized by (a) a continuous striving for excellence in developing and delivering effec-

3

tive programs with proper institutional arrangements; (b) a pragmatic extension approach; and (c) adequate incentives to encourage farmer participation by actively promoting the use of sustainable, productivity-enhancing, labor-saving, economically viable, and environmentally sound conservation technologies through a combination of field testing, research, and experience.

The Evolution of Slopeland Conservation Farming

Institutional Structures. Slopeland conservation farming is a recognized issue of national importance. It has enjoyed firm governmental support from the beginning. In the early years, all slopeland conservation farming programs were small. With only a few people working at the national and provincial levels, slopeland conservation farming involved mainly pilot projects in key targeted districts and important reservoir watersheds. These projects were intended to demonstrate the use of selected soil conservation practices and farming systems and their potential beneficial impacts on hillslopes. A Committee for Soil Conservation was established in 1954 by the Taiwan Provincial Department of Agriculture and Forestry (PDAF) to play the lead role in conservation promotion.

From the outset, priority was given to setting up decentralized field stations. Slopeland conservation farming services should be as close as possible to where they are needed. One pilot field station was established in the northern region in 1954 and two more shortly afterward in the central and southern regions. Meanwhile, soil conservation stations were also set up in the Wusheh and Akuntien reservoir watersheds.

Establishment of the Mountain Agricultural Resources Development Bureau (MARDB) under the PDAF in 1961 marked the beginning of island-wide implementation of the slopeland conservation farming program. The MARDB has four operational divisions, namely, soil conservation, mountain agriculture, animal husbandry, and planning, which indicate its multidisciplinary nature. There were eight field stations directly under the MARDB by 1973. Another 19 soil conservation stations were attached to various county or city governments across the island. Consolidation in 1974 reduced the number of MARDB field stations from eight to six. The 19 county or city soil conservation stations also became regular units of their respective governments in 1974 with a name change from "station" to "section," suggesting formal recognition of their contributions. Meanwhile, the Soil and Water Conservation Division has become a regular unit in two reservoir administrations, Shihmen and Tsengwen.

Prior to December 1978, the Forestry Division of the Chinese-American

Joint Commission on Rural Reconstruction (JCRR) served a promotional and advisory role and provided financial and technical support for slopeland conservation farming programs. In 1979, when the JCRR was reorganized and became the Council for Agricultural Planning and Development, a Resource Conservation Division was created to assume, among other things, functions related to slopeland conservation farming programs. Meanwhile, the short-lived Bureau of Agriculture of the Ministry of Economic Affairs also had a Conservation Section to take care of matters that fell within the ministry's jurisdiction. When the Council for Agricultural Planning and Development and the Bureau of Agriculture were combined as the Council of Agriculture (COA) in September 1984, the Resource Conservation Division was reoriented and expanded to include, in addition to slopeland conservation and watershed management, the conservation of other renewable resources, such as wildlife and fisheries habitat protection.

The Statute on the Conservation and Use of Slopeland Resources of the Republic of China, first proclaimed in 1976 (3) and revised in 1986, provides the legislative basis for conservation work on officially designated slopelands. A Soil and Water Conservation Act that will extend the application of conservation practices beyond the 970,000 hectares of designated slopelands is now being considered by the Legislative Yuan (Parliament).

Survey and Classification. Detailed surveys and classifications with regard to use potentials and limitations are essential to planning land use and developing solutions for identified problems. Initially, an islandwide land use survey made in the 1953-1958 period provided the basic data for overall planning and assessment purposes (1). Later, more detailed ground surveys were made according to the requirements of specific projects, often on a watershed scale (4).

From 1974 through 1978, an aerial survey of slopelands in Taiwan was conducted to provide the data for a more detailed land classification scheme adopted in 1979 (2). The results indicated that there are 972,727 hectares of designated slopelands; these slopelands occupy about 27 percent of Taiwan's land area. Of the 459,475 hectares of slopelands classified as suitable for agricultural uses, 296,418 hectares are actually farmed or grazed. Of the 425,230 hectares of slopelands classified as suitable for forestry, 50,249 hectares are now being farmed (8).

With COA support, the MARDB is initiating an ambitious project on slopeland stability classification using a geographic information system. The preliminary results look promising. This may be a new and important step in the direction toward improved slopeland conservation and utilization by providing a better data base for planning and land use regulation.

Training and Education. The slopeland conservation farming programs originally were spearheaded by a few knowledgeable, experienced, and highly motivated people with training and education in such fields as soil science, forestry, agronomy, engineering, and horticulture. However, it was realized that entry-level and, subsequently, regular training as well as formal university educational opportunities in slopeland conservation farming should be developed and implemented in a timely fashion to meet manpower requirements for programs that were expected to increase in scope, diversity, and complexity.

The first soil conservation training class with a proper curriculum was held in 1953. That class turned out 26 graduates, many of whom are still working in conservation and related fields. MARDB established a permanent Soil Conservation Training Center in 1958 to provide training on selected topics in soil conservation, mountain agriculture, animal husbandry, and integrated planning and management of slopeland resources.

In 1964, Soil and Water Conservation Departments were established at the National Chung Hsing University with a bachelor of science program and at two other colleges with diploma programs to provide professional education in slopeland conservation farming. A master's degree (M.S.) was added in 1975 at the university and a doctor of philosophy (Ph.D.) program was recently approved. The National Taiwan University has had a program offering M.S. and Ph.D. degrees in forest hydrology and watershed management since 1975. Meanwhile, soil and water conservation and slopeland utilization courses of various levels are also available to forestry, agriculture, and engineering students at the National Chung Hsing University, the National Taiwan University, and other universities and colleges. Training and education opportunities have thus become adequate to meet the needs of slopeland conservation farming programs as well as the professional and career aspirations of individuals.

Extension. Many farmers in Taiwan may feel that they have a moral and social responsibility to protect their land from soil erosion and to avoid causing detrimental impacts downstream. However, the lack of financial resources and technical know-how were and are major barriers preventing adoption of slopeland conservation farming practices. When slopeland conservation farming programs were first initiated, it was decided that a voluntary participation approach supported with adequate technical assistance and economic incentives, would be used in the extension efforts.

Technical assistance includes many field demonstrations and training classes to help farmers acquire knowledge and techniques in slopeland conservation farming practices. Economic incentives initially included food and cash subsidies. Later, free construction equipment with experienced operators was provided on conservation projects. In recent years, a low-interest (or interest-free) loan plan has been offered to farmers for adopting slopeland conservation farming practices. In general, economic incentives are useful and required to facilitate the initial acceptance of slopeland conservation farming practices by farmers until they can understand the benefits of these practices. It is also important to have adequate mechanisms to encourage continued use of slopeland conservation farming practices and proper maintenance of existing conservation treatments and facilities. By December 1987, a total of 152,941 hectares of slopelands—about one-third of the slopelands suitable for agricultural uses—had been treated with conservation practices. The current target for slopeland conservation farming extension is about 3,000 hectares per year.

Interagency Coordination. The integrated approach to planning and implementation of slopeland conservation farming programs was adopted early to consider, in addition to soil conservation, the crop production functions and infrastructure needs in several special areas, such as reservoir watersheds (5). Conservation for conservation's sake can have difficulties in gaining farmer support; their financial means are so limited that they must give priority to measures that increase productivity and income.

In 1966, the integrated approach had been formally adopted by the MARDB in the Integrated Soil Conservation and Land Use Program. Important features of this integrated program include soil conservation, proper crop pattern and management, adequate transportation, irrigation and drainage systems, facilities for pest and disease control, farm mechanization, and the introduction of a joint operation and management system to improve land use and maximize production with reduced costs. This integrated approach has been firmly in place since 1966 for slopeland conservation farm planning and implementation on many areas islandwide. By December 1987, a total area of 137,000 hectares of slopelands has been completed under this integrated soil conservation and land use program, with full support and cooperation of farmers and many other resource management and conservation agencies. The average cost of basic infrastructure for the integrated land use program is $360 per hectare (8).

Slopeland conservation farming has been an important component of several pilot watershed management projects in Taiwan. The multidisciplinary nature of these projects requires an adequate framework for good coordination among many participating agencies. A Forestry, Water Conservancy and Soil Conservation Joint Technical Committee was established in 1963 to foster this coordination; the Taiwan Forestry Bureau, the

Taiwan Water Conservancy Bureau, the MARDB, and other agencies were members of this committee. Prior to 1982, this committee had helped to promote cooperation and coordination among various agencies in dealing with survey, planning, and other technical matters of slopeland conservation farming and watershed management.

In 1983, this committee was reorganized as the Watershed Protection and Planning Commission to provide the promotion and coordination functions for slopeland conservation farming work and watershed management in terms of setting priorities, overall program planning, and monitoring progress. At the local level, farmers actively participate in many advisory and planning committees to deal with specific problems, such as arranging local funding and required land acquisition in individual project areas.

Research and Development. Research and field tests have been conducted since 1952 to provide practical solutions to slopeland soil erosion and crop management problems in Taiwan (5). Many of these projects have been supported by the COA (formerly the Joint Commission on Rural Reconstruction and Council for Agricultural Planning and Development).

Substantial achievements have been made over the past 35 year in studies on runoff and erosion rates from slopes with various land uses, drainage and irrigation, the proper selection and use of grass species for various covers, improved design of hillside ditches, mulching, and vegetative ground-cover (6, 7). Because of a shortage of agricultural labor in recent years, efforts have concentrated on labor-saving, cost-effective slopeland conservation farming management practices to enhance profitability by increasing productivity and reducing cost. Significant advances have been made in research on the use of grass species for ground protection and nutrient enhancement; improved transportation systems; automatic irrigation systems; pest and disease control; windbreaks; gully control; and mechanization of many slopeland operations, including the development of a small, multipurpose transporter for use on slopelands and in rural areas (5).

Results of these research projects and field trials, along with erosion control and other slopeland conservation and management practices with proven effectiveness, are included in the *Soil Conservation Handbook*, first published in 1963 in an attempt to standardize extension and technology. This handbook was revised in 1973 and again in 1983.

Future Prospects and Challenges

With continued government support, slopeland conservation farming programs in Taiwan have contributed significantly to achieving the national goals of environmental protection and disaster prevention. The programs have played an important role in agricultural production for domestic needs and for export, which helped to foster the emergence of industrial development in the early 1960s. However, in the past 2 decades, socioeconomic conditions and the needs and aspirations of people have been changing rapidly. These changes include the increasing wealth among people individually and for the nation as a result of rapid industrial development and rapid growth in international trade, with a highly favorable balance of foreign exchange; a growing proportion of well-educated and environmentally conscious people; and the declining importance of agriculture in the national economy. The future problems and challenges for slopeland conservation farming and other conservation work are closely related to these changes in socioeconomic conditions.

Despite a steady increase in absolute production value, agriculture's share of the net domestic product fell from 35.9 percent in 1952 to 6.1 percent in 1987. Profitability in farming remains relatively low because of the low prices in relation to high production costs. The high production costs are associated with high labor wages for the scarce manpower still available for farming after the large migration of rural people to the fast-growing, higher paying industrial sector. More recently, because of the appreciation of the New Taiwan dollar and relaxation of import restrictions on some fruit and poultry products, the strong competition from overseas' agricultural products, particularly U.S. products, has further reduced the agricultural profitability, especially on orchard-dominated slopeland farms.

Farm families in Taiwan usually have members taking on full- or part-time jobs off-farm to supplement their incomes. On the other hand, based on the premise that a prosperous and healthy agricultural sector remains essential to the social, political, and economic stability of the country, the government also is giving considerable attention to solving farmers' problems and enhancing their welfare. Since 1973, a series of programs initiated by the government to reduce production costs and to improve farm incomes has helped raise the ratio of average farm family to nonfarm family income from 64 percent in 1971 to 73 percent in 1987. Several new initiatives, such as a health insurance program for farmers and an improved pricing system, also are being implemented or planned to improve further the welfare of farmers and rural communities.

Slopeland conservation farming and other conservation work are essential public investments—to ensure sustained development and a desirable environment with minimum adverse impacts. These programs also are capable of providing productive, diverse employment opportunities in rural communities. This can help reduce social conflicts by enhancing a more equitable distribution of national wealth. The major challenge in the future is to develop and implement appropriate policies, strategies, and programs in slopeland conservation farming and watershed management that can be integrated with the government's other efforts to improve the income and welfare of farmers and rural communities. This may indicate the need to review, adjust, or expand the current slopeland conservation farming and watershed management programs.

Some important items can be included in expanded slopeland conservation farming programs. For example, efforts could be made to formulate proper policies and amend necessary legislation to retire from production some farms with highly erodible soils and to reforest those illegally cultivated slopelands with a capability designated for forest use only. Some mechanisms can be established to provide proper amounts of financial compensation to farmers who own or cultivate those slopelands targeted for retirement. A mandatory conservation compliance provision could also be put in place, through proper legislation, so that farmers are required to develop and implement conservation plans within certain time limits and conduct necessary maintenance periodically on their erodible farms to remain eligible for some forms of government benefits, such as price and income supports, crop insurance, free or low-cost services of slopeland machinery, and free or low-interest loans.

We also will confront problems and new challenges in other aspects of slopeland conservation farming as we strive for excellence in land stewardship. For example, much remains to be accomplished in research and development of highly efficient, environmentally sound slopeland machinery and systems, as well as cost-saving, effective conservation practices. There is still much to be done in quantitatively assessing the impact of and developing solutions for the potential problems of slopeland farms as nonpoint sources of pollution and in economic assessment of slopeland conservation farming practices and programs (9). Knowledge with regard to the stability of slopelands and limitations to their proper use must be greatly improved as well. Better knowledge and technology must also be developed for making more rational decisions about how to regulate the nonagricultural uses of slopelands. Furthermore, better methods and techniques must be found for closer integration of land and water management activities on individual farms, in small watersheds, and in large drainage basins.

A society with great wealth and well-educated people, such as the Republic of China on Taiwan, can attach higher priority to and afford to invest in long-term, worthwhile projects for the future, such as slopeland conservation farming and watershed and forest management programs, without unfavorable impacts. Furthermore, because the Republic of China on Taiwan is a country with a strong sense of mission, programs to ensure economic, social, and environmental well-being of future generations are a matter of great importance and worthy of support. Nevertheless, a properly designed and implemented public information and education program is required to help create and sustain public awareness and appreciation of the need for the long-term protection of the nation's soil and water resources. After all, conservation is everybody's business. Farmers and conservationists alone cannot win the war against the loss or degradation of soil and water resources on which the future depends.

REFERENCES

1. Hsia, C. H. 1958. *Land use conditions in Taiwan.* Forestry Series: No. 5. Joint Commission on Rural Reconstruction, Taipei, Taiwan.
2. Hsu, M. C., P. W. Chien, and J. J. Lin. 1990. *Integrated soil conservation and land use programs for slopelands in Taiwan.* In *Development of Conservation Farming on Hillslopes.* Soil and Water Conservation Society, Ankeny, Iowa. pp. 17-24.
3. Koh, C. C. 1984. *Soil conservation in the Republic of China on Taiwan.* In *Proceedings, Sino-Korea Bilateral Symposium on Soil and Water Conservation of Sloped Farm Land.* National Science Council, Taipei Taiwan. pp. 1-7.
4. Lee, S. W. 1987. *Soil conservation and slopeland development in Taiwan.* In S. Jantawat [editor] *Soil Erosion and Its Counter Measures.* Soil and Water Conservation Society of Thailand, Bangkok.
5. Liao, M. C. 1976. *The evolution of soil conservation practices in Taiwan* (in Chinese). Journal of the Agriculture Association of China New Series 96: 117-122.
6. Liao, M. C. 1979. *Improvement of hillside ditches in Taiwan.* Journal of Soil and Water Conservation 34(2): 102-104.
7. Liao, M. C., S. C. Hu, and H. L. Wu. 1990. *Soil conservation research and development for hillslope conservation farming in Taiwan.* In *Development of Conservation Farming on Hillslopes.* Soil and Water Conservation Society, Ankeny, Iowa. pp. 12-16.
8. Liao, T. N. 1988. *Soil conservation practices in sloped farm land in Taiwan.* Mountain Agricultural Resources Development Bureau, Provincial Department of Agriculture and Forestry, Taichung, Taiwan. 10 pp.
9. Wu, C.K.H. 1979. *The economics of slopeland development: The Taiwan experience.* Monograph Series No. 17. The Asia and World Forum, Taipei, Taiwan. 71 pp.

SOIL CONSERVATION RESEARCH AND DEVELOPMENT FOR HILLSLOPE FARMING IN TAIWAN

MIEN-CHUN LIAO, SU-CHERNG HU, and HUEI-LONG WU

U seful information and quantitative data have been obtained from basic investigations regarding soil conservation on hillslopes in Taiwan. These results have helped to provide solutions with respect to the use and management of hillslopes in Taiwan.

Highlights of this research on soil conservation include the following:

• Studies have been conducted to determine the relative erodibility of major slopeland soils in the field. Survey and classification of slopeland soils are underway.

• Values of hydraulic conductivity for soils with various conservation treatments were determined by the constant-head method. Grass cover was found to be capable of gradually enhancing soil permeability.

• A grass or legume cover can enhance aggregate stability better than mulching. In comparison with legumes, grass is more effective in promoting the stability of aggregates.

• Effects of bahiagrass (*Papalum notatum*) cover and mulching on nutrient uptake by banana were studied with P^{32}-labeled fertilizers. Competition for phosphorus fertilizer can be adjusted by planting grass at a distance of more than 65 centimeters from banana plants and by mowing the grass.

• Inferred sources of soil erosion on agricultural watersheds were tested by identifying the characteristics of clay minerals.

• Rainfall erosion indices for Taiwan were derived, and 12 divisions were proposed based on R-index (erosivity) characters.

• Percolation and moisture movement in soils with cover crops and mulching were studied using large lysimeters.

• Characteristics of bahiagrass were studied and its germination improved.

• A dynamic model of overland flow on slopeland farms was simulated and verified for actual application in the design of drainage systems on steep cropland.

Development of Soil Conservation Measures

Bench Terraces. Three terrace types (reverse-slope, outward-slope, and level) are used in Taiwan. Because of high construction costs and inconvenience to machinery operation, terraces have not been used over large areas since 1970, except where clean-cultivated crops are grown in rows 2 to 5 meters apart. Planting or leaving suitable grass species on terrace risers can be effective in soil stabilization and good for field management (5).

In terraced orchards, farm paths and link roads are constructed between terraces for convenient farm management. After terraced orchards had been improved, more than a 62 percent reduction in transportation and labor-saving management costs were reported (6).

Hillside Ditches. Hillside ditches reduce the length of hillside slopes, which reduces sheet and rill erosion. They also provide paths for small farm machines. The width of the ditch bottom ranges from 2 to 2.5 meters. Ditch spacing is affected by landslope, soil type, rainfall intensity, and cropping pattern.

The first application of trapezoidal-shaped hillside ditches on a sugarcane plantation in 1956 resulted in lower yield. The design of the ditch was later modified into a broad V-shaped cross-section. Tests of the modified ditch by the National Taiwan University indicated the improved cross-section was hydraulically sound (3, 4). Field observations by the Taiwan Sugar Experiment Station indicated that the ditch bottom could be successfully used for planting sugarcane. Use of the ditch resulted in increased production. Furthermore, the cross-section of the hillside channel is stable, maintenance is low, and soil moisture content in the ditch is high.

The improved hillside ditch can easily be built by bulldozer, while the hillside ditch with a trapezoidal cross-section can only be constructed by human labor. The ditch bottom of the improved hillside ditch also can be used for crop production or as a farm road. Given these advantages, the improved hillside ditch was quickly adopted for large-scale use.

Cover Crop and Mulching. Grass crops and mulching are applied in two ways: covering the entire area and establishing strips of grass at intervals between fruit trees. Bahiagrass is the most recommended crop cover in Taiwan (5). Research shows that bahiagrass and mulching, combined with hillside ditches, reduces soil erosion and runoff more than other practices.

When a grass cover and mulching are used, weeding and herbicides are seldom required, and there is almost no soil contamination as a result. These factors make zero-tillage possible (7).

Drainage Systems. The drainage systems applied on slopeland farms generally consist of grass waterways, chutes, drop structures, and prefabricated flumes. Grass waterways have been used successfully on steep slopes. Planting grasses in waterways facilitates economic drainage and helps to reduce negative visual impacts. Bahiagrass, carpet grass (*Axonopus compressus*), and centipede grass (*Chrytsopogon aciculatus*) are recommended for use.

Gully Control. The best way to control gullies is to prevent their formation. In Taiwan, grass plantings along gully channels, combined with simple, cheap structures, such as sandbag dams, loose-rock dams, single-fence dams, and sausage gabion dams, have proved effective in stabilizing medium and large gullies on slopelands.

Conservation Practices for Major Crops. A variety of soil conservation practices for major crops have been recommended for use on slopelands in Taiwan. Table 1 summarizes these practices, by crop (6).

Slopeland Capability Classification

The preliminary land use classification of slopelands in Taiwan was initiated in 1954 after completion of the land use and forest survey. Based on

Table 1. Recommended soil conservation practices for major crops in Taiwan.

	Hillside Ditch with:				Bench Terraces		
Crops	Cover Crop and Mulching	Hillside Contour & Close Planting	Ditch Grass Barriers	Stubble Mulching	Reverse-Slope	Level	Outward-Slope
Citrus	XX*						X
Tea	X	X			X	X	X
Mango	XX						X
Litchi	XX						X
Pineapple		XX		XX			
Banana	X		X		X	X	X
Apple	XX				X	X	X
Mulberry	XX						
Upland crops					XX	XX	X

*XX, very suitable; X, suitable.

the cumulative cost index of conservation practices, calculated from the physical characteristics of land, the land was divided into eight classes. These classes were adopted from the United States with some modifications. The slope limit suitable for farming and pasture is 55 percent.

For slopeland planning, conservation, and utilization, the "Criteria for Land Use Capability Classification of Slopelands" was promulgated in 1977. In this new system, land is classified into six classes according to slope, effective depth of soil, degree of soil erosion, and characteristics of parent material. The first four classes (I-IV) are suitable for farming and pasture; the fifth (V) class is suitable for forestry only; and the sixth (VI) class requires intensive conservation practices. This land capability classification is treatment-oriented.

Another slopeland classification was made in 1978 using aerial photos and ground surveys. According to that survey, the slopeland area suitable for farming and pasture was 459,475 hectares—47 percent of the island's slopelands. Of this, 296,418 hectares were actually farmed or grazed.

Developing Technical Guides

The first edition of the *Soil Conservation Handbook of Taiwan* was published in 1964 (*1*). It contained 11 practices based on field experience and a few experiments. With results from later research, the handbook was revised in 1975 and again in 1983. The latest edition includes 24 practices: eight mechanical measures and their complementary treatments (hillside ditches, orchard hillside ditches, bench terraces, broadbase terraces, grassed hillside ditches, grassed risers, grass barriers, and rock barriers), five agronomic measures (contour tillage, cover crops, mulching, green manures, and windbreaks), four farm road treatments (farm paths, link road, grassed farm road, and vegetative slope stabilization), and seven drainage facilities (diversions, grass waterways, chutes, and drop structures).

The first edition of the *Soil Conservation Engineering Handbook* was published in 1984 (*2*). A series of technical bulletins also were published to introduce new techniques to conservation technicians and farmers. Some pamphlets on general conservation were rewritten from professional papers for public communities and schools to stimulate concern for conservation. Recently, these activities have met expected goals.

Future Research Needs

Substantial progress has been made in slopeland research and development for soil conservation purposes. However, many problems and issues remain that will require research attention in the future. The important research needs are as follows:

• Quantitative studies on factors affecting soil erosion as a means of developing an empirical soil conservation equation based on a modification of the universal soil loss equation.

• Developing cost-effective breeding methods for conservation plant materials—for application as cover crops, on grass waterways, and for slope stabilization.

• Evaluating the net economic benefits of soil and water conservation, both onsite and offsite.

• Developing cost-effective erosion control measures for sloping farm land, such as drainage systems and gully control.

• Developing computer programs for designing conservation structures and for technology transfer.

REFERENCES

1. Chinese Soil and Water Conservation Society. 1987. *Soil conservation handbook.* Taipei, Taiwan. 121 pp.
2. Council of Agriculture and Mountain Agricultural Resources Development Bureau. 1984. *Soil conservation engineering handbook* (in Chinese). Taipei, Taiwan. 248 pp.
3. Liao, M. C. 1976. *Effects of bench terrace and improved hillside ditch.* In Proceedings, International Symposium on Hill Lands. West Virginia University, Morgantown. pp. 404-409.
4. Liao, M. C. 1979. *Improvement of hillside ditches in Taiwan.* Journal of Soil and Water Conservation 34(2): 102-104.
5. Liao, M. C. 1981. *Conservation measures for steep orchards in Taiwan.* In Proceedings, South-East Asian Regional Symposium on Problems of Soil Erosion and Sedimentation. Asian Institute of Technology, Bankok, Thailand. pp. 341-351.
6. Liao, M. C., and H. L. Wu. 1987. *Soil conservation on steep lands in Taiwan.* Chinese Soil and Water Conservation Society, Taipei, Taiwan. 112 pp.
7. Liao, M. C., S. C. Hu, H. S. Lu, and K. J. Tsai. 1988. *Evolution of soil conservation practices on steep lands in Taiwan.* In *Conservation Farming on Steep Lands.* Soil and Water Conservation Society, Ankeny, Iowa. pp. 233-241.

INTEGRATED SOIL CONSERVATION AND LAND USE PROGRAM FOR SLOPELANDS IN TAIWAN

MOU-CHANG HSU, PI-WU CHIEN, and JIANN-JANG LIN

Over the past 40 years, the population of Taiwan increased rapidly from 6.1 million in 1946 to 19.7 million in 1987. Because of the need for more land for industrial development, as well as population expansion, over the last 20 years, farmland in the plains area has declined steadily. The demand for more land for both agricultural and nonagricultural uses has led to extensive development of slopeland.

Taiwan experiences frequent earthquakes and typhoons. The heavy rains, together with the steep slopes and weak geological formation, often expose those slopelands in agricultural uses to serious soil erosion. To secure the proper slopeland conservation and sustained use, the government has implemented the integrated soil conservation and land use program on slopelands throughout Taiwan since 1965.

Slopeland Use Status

Slopeland Capability Classification. To ensure the rational use of slopelands and to facilitate the enforcement of the Statute and Regulations on Conservation and Use of Slopelands in Taiwan, the government issued the slopeland capability classification in 1977. This classification system was based on slope, effective soil depth, degree of soil erosion, and parent material characteristics.

Under the land capability classification, slopelands are classified into one of six classes, namely, class I to class VI. Three categories exist to limit the land for a specific use, according to the land capability classification. They are (1) land suitable for cultivation and animal husbandry, classes I to IV; (2) land suitable for forestry, class V; and (3) land requiring intensive conservation practices, class VI.

Table 1 shows the slopeland distribution in Taiwan by land capability and by land use suitability.

Present Slopeland Use. According to the aerial survey made by the Agro-Forestry Aerial Survey Institute of the Taiwan Forest Bureau from 1983 to 1987, slopeland use in Taiwan was tabulated as shown in table 2.

Table 1. Slopeland distribution in Taiwan by land capability and by land use suitability.

Classification			
Land Use Suitability	*Land Capability*	*Area (ha)*	*Percentage*
Land suitable for	Classes I & II	81,619	8.22
cultivation and	Classes III, IV	367,805	37.05
animal husbandry			
Subtotal		449,424	45.27
Land suitable for	Class V	428,579	43.17
forestry			
Land requiring	Class VI	114,711	11.56
intensive conser-	Nonclassified		
vation and other land			
Total		992,711	100

Source: Aerial survey report, Agro-Forestry Aerial Survey Institute, Taiwan Forest Bureau, May 1988.

Table 2. Slopeland use statistics in Taiwan.

Land Use	*Area (ha)*	*Percentage*
Crop cultivation		
Rice	37,504	3.78
Miscellaneous food crops	20,176	2.03
Special crops	59,624	6.01
Tree fruits	154,356	15.55
Forage crops	1,885	0.19
Subtotal	273,545	27.56
Forestry and grass growing		
Woods	458.970	46.23
Bamboo	111,910	11.27
Natural grasses	43,013	4.33
Subtotal	613,893	61.83
Others	105,273	10.61
Total	992,711	100

Source: Aerial survey report, Agro-Forestry Aerial Survey Institute, Taiwan Forest Bureau, May 1988.

Table 3. Transition of slopeland use from 1956 to 1987.

Land Use	1956-1958	1975-1977	1985-1987
		%	
Rice, upland crops	30.7	22.8	12.0
Tree fruits	2.2	11.9	15.6
Forest and bamboo	50.9	51.6	57.5
Grasses and idled	10.1	4.2	4.3
Others	6.1	9.5	10.6
Total	100	100	100

Source: 1956-1958, agro-forest marginal land use investigation; 1975-1977, slopeland planning investigation; 1985-1987, agricultural resources and land use investigation.

Transition of Slopeland Use. In the last 30 years, slopeland use has changed considerably with the change in rural economic conditions, demand and supply for farm produce, and policy support by government. The most significant changes include the following:

• Cultivation of short-term, intensively cultivated crops: Except for rice under irrigation, the production of many crops, such as cassava, corn, and sweet potatoes, declined greatly.

• Cultivation of long-term tree fruits: Banana and pineapple production declined year after year because of reduced export markets. Citrus production gradually declined because of pest damage. But longan, pear, mango, peach, and plum production increased significantly.

• Cultivation of special crops: Tea and sugarcane production declined gradually, while citronella and sisal were seldom planted.

• Forestation and bamboo plantation: Tree and bamboo planting increased little by little to replace some short-term, intensively cultivated crops.

• Nonagricultural use of waste slopelands increased somewhat, and no change occurred in the use of idled slopelands.

Table 3 shows the transition of slopeland use in terms of crop cultivation as recorded by three land investigations in 1956-1958, 1975-1977, and 1985-1987, respectively.

The Integrated Soil Conservation and Land Use Program

Before 1965, soil conservation practices were applied on individual farms regardless of the drainage system and basic installation according to an overall plan. To secure effective soil conservation and profitable farm management, the government commenced to implement the integrated soil conservation and land use program in 1965.

The program's primary purposes are to undertake soil conservation, set up basic public installations, and provide farm management assistance simultaneously on the concentrated slopelands under an overall plan. Given its good early results, this program has become the major work pattern for strengthening soil conservation and the promotion of slopeland use.

The program has seven major elements:

1. Project site selection. The program has been carried out annually with separate projects at different locations. Project sites are selected by the relevant Hsien governments and Mountain Agricultural Resources Development Bureau (MARDB) work stations. The sites are concurred in by MARDB and the Council of Agriculture, according to the results of investigation and planning for the specific slopeland development areas.

Following are the conditions to be considered in site selection:

• Slopelands should be concentrated in a group with a total area of more than 50 hectares.

• Slopelands have the potential for development of crop and animal husbandry, as well as the possibility for establishing mutual or cooperative farm management.

• Local farmers are able to contribute part of the project funding and provide the necessary land for public use without compensation.

2. Planning. Preliminary planning is to be completed by the executive units with respect to soil conservation practices, field drainage system, farm road network, irrigation facilities, and gully control works, according to the physical conditions and requirements for agricultural development. The executive units submit their preliminary planning reports, including estimated work amounts and budget, to MARDB as a reference for the latter to compile the yearly program.

Detailed planning is to be done for each major project work. Topographic surveys and geological borings are included, when necessary.

3. Field work. The soil conservation treatments and auxiliary works are to be undertaken by the farmers, with technical assistance from the executive units, or performed by MARDB personnel and heavy equipment, as required. Basic public installations are to be constructed under the control of the contractor after inviting bids.

4. Farmers' organization. Prior to starting a project, the executive unit invites local farmers in the project area to set up the Project Implementation Committee. The committee's function is to assist in obtaining the land needed for the basic public installations and collecting construction funds.

In the early stages of project implementation, the executive unit helps the local farmers organize the Farm Management Discussion Class. This group periodically discusses matters related to project implementation and attempts to solve problems encountered in crop production, marketing, and maintenance of the basic public installations.

5. *Extension education and technical training.* As a part of extension education, informational materials about soil conservation, slopeland conservation and use, farm management, and knowledge of relevant laws were published and distributed to farmers. The intent was to promote their understanding of the project.

Training classes on soil conservation practices, slopeland farm planning, field survey, and work-site staking were held for technical personnel to enhance their knowledge and techniques to improve the quality of work.

6. *Grant and loan.* For reducing the pressure caused by labor shortages and for reducing the farmers' expenses, grants were made available for construction of auxiliary soil conservation works, cover grass planting, and farm management. For such works as hillside ditching, bench terracing, and link-road construction, mechanical operation services were provided by MARDB with government subsidies. For large works, such as farm road construction, irrigation systems, and gully control, the central and provincial governments provided grants of up to two-thirds of the work expense, while local governments and farmers shared the remaining one-third.

To cope with investment difficulties, the central government and the provincial government commenced the Slopeland Conservation and Use Loan Program and the Slopeland Development Fund Loan Program, respectively, in 1974 and 1977 to provide long-term and short-term loans for farmers for soil conservation treatments, basic public works construction, and farm management improvement. By 1988, the total amount of loans made to farmers exceeded NT$1,416 million.

7. *Mechanical operation services.* In the early years, soil conservation treatments were performed manually on the farm. Because of the shortage of farm labor in rural areas, a result of rapid economic development after the late 1960s, MARDB began, in 1969, to use small- and medium-sized equipment to carry out soil conservation and basic installation works. MARDB now has 32 bulldozers and 4 excavators doing mechanical operation services. These services help farmers to accomplish soil conservation practices on about 1,800 hectares and to construct about 120 kilometers of farm and link roads annually in a total of about 30,000 working hours. The mechanical operation services include land preparation, ditch digging, slope shaping, and related tasks. The service charge, which is made on a working-hour basis, averages about NT$430 per hour.

Work Accomplished, Expenses, and Benefits

From 1965 to June 1988, the program accounted for soil conservation treatments on 83,586 hectares in 524 areas (149,840 hectares). Adding the acreage treated under individual treatment programs since 1961, the total area with soil conservation practices reached 155,829 hectares—35.3 percent of the entire 441,787 hectares of slopeland suitable for cultivation and 72.8 percent of the 213,990 hectares of slopeland now cultivated.

Table 4 summarizes the major soil conservation works completed in the 1961-1988 period.

Table 5 lists the soil conservation works completed and the amounts of money expended in the 3 most recent years (1986-1988).

As shown in table 5, the expense for soil conservation works on 9,670 hectares of slopelands totaled NT$716.5 million, an average of NT$74,100 per hectare. Farmers contributed additional funds or labor. Generally, the government supported 60 percent of the soil conservation expense, while farmers contributed the remaining 40 percent.

The program not only has yielded significant soil conservation on slopelands but also has provided considerable benefits in labor-saving farm management. An investigation by the MARDB's Third Work Station on the Chiayi Farm showed that the labor expense saved was NT$69,000, or 138.2 man-days on the treated land in the citrus orchard, and NT$44,000, or 88 man-days on the treated land of the bamboo plantation (Table 6).

The labor-saving effect was brought about chiefly with convenient and effective transportation as a result of the construction of farm and link roads under the program. In general, farm road density is 20 meters per hectare and link road density is 50 meters per hectare.

Conclusion

In Taiwan, slopeland is an irreplaceable natural resource. This resource needs to be used sustainably. It was for this purpose that the Integrated

Table 4. Major soil conservation works completed in Taiwan, 1961-1988.

Work Items	Unit	Under Integrated Program	Under Individual Treatment	Total
Soil conservation treatment	ha	83,586	72,243	155,829
Field drainage	m	1,241,643	287,822	1,529,465
Farm road	km	1,696	-	1,696
Link road	km	2,346	-	2,346
Irrigation facility	place	2,115	45	2,160
Gully control	place	3,711	180	3,891
Cover-grass planting	ha	1,195	-	1,195
Road-surface grass planting	m²	1,653,375	-	1,653,375
Hill-slope grass planting	ha	4,354	-	4,354
Farm pond	place	1.076	181	1,257
Water tank	set	12,559	6,144	18,703

Table 5. Soil conservation works completed and the amounts of money expended in Taiwan in 1986-1988.

| Year | Amount Expended (NT$1,000) | Major Work Items | | | | |
		Soil Conservation Treatment (ha)	Field Drainage (m)	Farm Road (km)	Gully Control (place)	Irrigation Facility (place)
1986	249,436	3,665	101,705	32.3	293	322
1987	233,850	3,117	101,633	28.2	254	319
1988	233,245	2,888	81,114	27.6	257	315
Total	716,531	9,670	284,452	88.1	804	956

Table 6. Labor-saving investigation under the integrated soil conservation and land use program (man-day/ha)

Cropping Labor Requirement	Cultivation	Farm Supplies Transportation	Farm Produce Transportation	Total
Citrus orchard				
Before the program	135.0	35.0	40.0	210.0
After the program	52.2	9.0	10.0	71.2
Labor-saving (%)	61.3	74.3	75.0	66.1
Bamboo plantation				
Before the program	76.0	8.0	40.0	124.0
After the program	29.0	1.0	6.0	36.0
Labor-saving (%)	61.8	87.5	86.0	71.0

Slopeland Conservation and Use Program was implemented—and with excellent results over the past 20 years.

The success of the program can be attributed to well-prepared planning; the full cooperation between farmers and the executive units of government; and, most of all, steady support by the government. Putting land conservation and use on an equal basis may be the best way to deal with slopelands when they are to be developed.

A SOIL CONSERVATION AND LAND USE PROGRAM FOR THE RELEASED NATIONAL FOREST LAND IN TAIWAN

TANEU LIAO and JU-SHIUNG WU

From 1945 into the 1960s, agriculture was a main sector of Taiwan's economy. Agriculture shifted to the hills and mountains because of the fast-growing population and limited farmland in the plains. Production changed increasingly to profitable upland crops, such as citronella, sisal, tea, bananas, pineapple, and other upland fruit trees. A large area of slopelands were reclaimed for agriculture in this process. Much national forest land gave way to agricultural use, especially land in gently to moderately sloping areas and land adjacent to the plains.

National forest land was transformed by being rented for reforestation but used illegally for agriculture. Farmers who used the land without title were generally unwilling to invest in proper land use and cared little about soil conservation. Most of this land was extensively abused, resulting in soil depletion, soil erosion, landslides, low water retention, heavy sedimentation in reservoirs, floods, and drought and a threat to people and property in downstream areas.

To encourage soil conservation and promote slopeland development, the government released 68,098 hectares of severely abused national forest land on gentle and moderate slopes to farmers through land leasing and sale. In 1969, a comprehensive program of land treatment, soil conservation, and land use for this land was presented by the Executive Yuan.

Principles for Soil Conservation and Land Use

Principles for management of the released national forest land were as follows:

• Land suited to farming or animal husbandry was to be sold to the present cultivators. The sale price was to be paid by the purchaser in 20 equal installments over 10 years.

• Land suited to farming or animal husbandry had to be treated with soil conservation practices before the purchase. Title to the land would only be given after full payment of the sale price. If the necessary soil conservation treatment was not completed in the time prescribed, the purchase right was withdrawn and the land sold to another farmer. The amount paid by the farmer was not refunded.

• Land suited to afforestation was to be leased to the present cultivators. But some afforestation-suited land could be sold to the present cultivators, along with the sale of land suited to farming and/or animal husbandry.

• Several organizations were involved in different stages of the operation. The organization responsible was to plan any required infrastructure and retain necessary land for this purpose before sale or leasing. After sale or lease, this organization was to supervise the farmer in undertaking soil conservation practices, provide planning and subsidy assistance, and give the deadline for finishing the work.

• The limit for finishing conservation work was not to exceed 3 years.

• With respect to the necessary soil conservation expenses, the government was to provide the whole grant or partial subsidies on the public installations and furnish specific subsidies for individual soil conservation practices.

• After the land was sold or leased to the farmers, the organization responsible was to provide assistance in land development, improving farming techniques and establishing demonstration areas for better conservation and use of slopeland.

Work Procedures and Executive Organizations

The responsibility for different aspects of the plan fell on various units of provincial and local governments:

• Delimitation of land to be released: by the Taiwan Forestry Bureau (TFB).

• Land survey and mapping: by the Taiwan Land Administration Bureau (TLAB) and related local governments.

• Land investigation (including investigation on land use right and on land use classification): by TLAB, the Mountain Agricultural Resources Development Bureau (MARDB), and related local governments.

• Identification of land categories and grades: by TLAB and related local governments.

- Land overall registration: by TLAB and related local governments.
- Planning of public installations: by MARDB and related local governments.
- Land sale and leasing: by TLAB, TFB, and related local governments.
- Soil conservation planning and related assistance: by MARDB and related local governments.
- Land use planning and related assistance: by MARDB, TFB, and related local governments.

Land Survey, Investigation, and Planning

The work of land survey, investigation, and planning of land use and soil conservation under the program were to be completed in 3 years by TLAB, TFB, MARDB, and related local governments.

- Land survey and registration: According to the land survey made by TLAB, there were 67,123 parcels of national forest land to be released, totalling 53,467 hectares. These parcels were distributed in 13 forest work districts over the island.
- Land capability classification: The released national forest land was classified as 41 percent suitable for farming, 57 suitable for afforestation, and 2 percent suitable for roads and buildings.
- A survey of land use showed 49 percent was being cultivated, 41 percent was in tree and bamboo plantations, and 10 percent was in other uses.
- Planning for soil conservation and land use:

Soil survey. The soil characteristics under survey included pH, organic matter content, soil texture, soil permeability, soil porosity, etc. These are the basic data for planning in soil conservation, land use, and farm management.

Soil conservation planning for land suited to farming. This included examining the land on which conservation practices were pending, the practices planned, and setting up the in-field drainage systems.

Preliminary planning of public installations. Preliminary planning was done for the road network, irrigation systems, prevention of sedimentation, and gully control.

Sale and Leasing of the Released National Forest Land

According to the Land Treatment, Soil Conservation, and Land Use Program for the Released National Forest Land, land suited to farming was to be sold or leased to cultivators; those areas suited to afforestation were to be leased for that purpose. From the program's start in 1974 to 1988, there were 30,934 hectares in 30,686 pieces of farming-suited land sold, 1,617 hectares in 3,712 pieces of farming-suited land leased, and 10,032 hectares in 9,814 pieces of afforestation-suited land leased.

As stipulated in the Statute for Conservation and Use of Slopeland Resources, the provincial government could set up a slopeland development fund for development and conservation of slopelands.

Contributions to the slopeland development fund came from special funds appropriated by the government, revenue from the woods felled and sold after releasing the national forest land, the sale and rent of the released national forest land after deducting management expenditures, and other income.

By May 1988, the total revenue from land sales and rental and woods felled and sold after release amounted to NT$294 million—equivalent to half of the total income in the slopeland development fund.

The fund was used mainly for preferential low-interest loans to slopeland farmers in farm management and soil conservation. Part of the fund also was used for loans to local farmer organizations for constructing farm roads, irrigation facilities, farm produce collection stations, etc.

Major Work Accomplished

The program was conducted after 1973 with budgets earmarked by the government. Major work included application of soil conservation practices, improvement of slopeland farming conditions, and improvement of slopeland farm management. These tasks were undertaken preferentially in the concentrated slopeland areas under systematic regional planning.

The major work accomplished can be summarized as follows:

• *Application of soil conservation practices.* There were 13,414 hectares treated with soil conservation measures among 15,276 hectares of released land requiring treatment—a treatment rate of 88 percent. The completed farm drainage ditches amounted to 250,330 meters—representing 94 percent of the total of 266,933 meters originally planned. Most soil conservation practices were applied on the basis of unit land groups under regional planning and in compliance with the layout of farm roads and irrigation facilities.

• *Improvement of slopeland farming conditions.* Improving slopeland farming conditions was undertaken to facilitate farm management and reduce production costs on slopeland. Work completed included 381,530 meters of road construction and establishment of irrigation facilities at 202 locations. It was estimated that an average of 20 meters of farm road was provided for every hectare of slopeland. Irrigation facilities that supplied water for both spraying and irrigation helped a great deal to increase farm production and to improve quality of farm produce.

• *Improvement of slopeland farm management.* Measures to improve slopeland farm management included encouragement of planting suitable economic crops, such as tree fruits and tea, and providing subsidies for farm produce collection and marketing installations.

Generally speaking, with the release of the improperly used national forest land, the farmers who had the right to use the land by leasing for afforestation or who owned the land for farming after purchase were more interested in investment and management. Farmers' income increased and better soii conservation and land use were attained as a result.

THE APPLICABILITY OF TAIWAN'S EXPERIENCE IN SOIL CONSERVATION IN DEVELOPING COUNTRIES

TED C. SHENG

Т he paper by Koh and associates (*I*) describes the evolution of conservation farming on hillslopes in Taiwan since the 1950s. Because Taiwan's soil conservation program is so successful, one could ask the question: Is Taiwan's experience applicable in other developing countries?

Being a co-worker from the early 1950s to late 1960s in Taiwan and thereafter working in other developing countries in United Nation's Food and Agriculture Organization projects, I will attempt to answer this question and to provide a basis for discussion of this important topic.

A Brief Analysis of the Taiwan Experience

Koh and associates (*I*) analyze the Taiwan experience well. In brief, there are three program elements used by Taiwan that are important, if not essential, to success:

1. *Expand the program gradually.* Before Taiwan launched a national program, hundreds of small demonstrations were established to obtain farmers' clear understanding and support (*6*).

Institutions were built from the bottom up. County and city field offices were set up over several years. The Mountain Agricultural Resources Development Bureau (MARDB) was institutionalized later in the 1960s when the need was identified for an agency responsible for overall development and conservation of slopeland resources. Taiwan's experience shows that interdisciplinary teamwork is essential to such a program.

Effective services and incentives also were provided. Field offices were given the best technicians, with vehicles, instruments, equipment, and sufficient expense and support for effective service to farmers. Service was concentrated in important watersheds or special project areas; in other areas, service was given on a first-come, first-served basis. No farmers were left out. Cash subsidies or food were supplied at the outset of the program. Emphasis gradually shifted to loan programs.

Training of technicians was continuous and the supply of manpower was emphasized. More than 5,000 people have gone through various courses (*1*).

2. *An integrated approach.* An integrated approach was essential. Integrated Soil Conservation and Land Use Pilot Areas were established prior to 1974 totalling 18,000 hectares; by 1987, 137,000 hectares were included (*1*). Farm machinery, crop storage, marketing, and processing arrangements were carefully made (*2*). This approach proved economically feasible and beneficial to agricultural development (*5*).

Joint planning for watersheds and special projects was conducted. Close coordination and a joint planning strategy among related organizations were emphasized (*1, 4*). For the development of special crops or special areas, local development committees were organized with seven to nine farmers as board members. Committees helped in planning, implementation, local funding, and acquiring land (*6*).

Practical research on runoff and soil erosion rates under various land uses, waterways, vegetation, and transportation systems was carried out by agricultural and forestry research institutes, universities, colleges, or local experiment stations and readily applied (*3*).

3. *Steady support from the government.* Firm policy was obtained. The Joint Commission on Rural Reconstruction (JCRR), which later became the Council of Agriculture (COA), gave priority to hillslope development and operated at the national level (*1*). The provincial government recognized mountain watershed management and flood control as its first priority. Taiwan did not start its program with legislation. Rather, with a firm policy and local support, the work was carried out smoothly.

Adequate supporting resources were provided. There must be sufficient qualified personnel to do the work. Taiwan has 500 technical people in the field to carry out hillslope conservation and development, as well as watershed rehabilitation programs. The total annual allocation of funds is $100 million at present.

Is the Taiwan Experience Applicable?

Some Unique Conditions. The foregoing provides only a brief account of Taiwan's successful experience in soil conservation. An overall picture would not be complete without discussing the unique conditions that helped its conservation program. These conditions include the following:

• Farmers have a long tradition of building, maintaining, and using conservation structures, particularly rice terraces.

• Most of Taiwan's farmers are well educated and hard working.

• The mountainous terrain and heavy population pressure make hillslope development essential.

• The disaster-prone environment constantly reminds the people in Taiwan of conservation's importance.

• Organizations like JCRR and COA, which embrace policy formulation, research, extension, and funding in one body, greatly enhance the promotion and guidance of the program.

• Recent industrialization and the rise in living standard have profound impacts on land use changes and resource conservation demands that benefit the overall soil conservation program.

Socioeconomic conditions and institutional structure vary from country to country. Other countries do not necessarily need to follow the pattern of Taiwan. However, Taiwan's experience and background provide a case for developing countries to examine.

General Constraints in Developing Countries. Many developing countries have serious constraints in their soil conservation programs. The common ones are as follows:

• Lack of manpower or experience or both.

• Shortage of funds, vehicles, and equipment to support the field work.

• Inadequate service to farmers and poor coordination among agencies to undertake an integrated approach.

• Lack of incentive schemes to help farmers who are willing to join a soil conservation program.

• Inconsistency in policy or lack of policy.

It is not fair to say that Taiwan has had no such constraints. It has, but to a lesser degree because of the steady government support. Its conservationists have struggled since the 1950s to alleviate such bottlenecks.

What is Really Applicable? Developing countries that are about to launch or have started a national soil conservation program could learn from Taiwan. While there is no universal answer to the diversity of conditions, some basic approaches used in Taiwan are applicable in other settings:

• Gradual expansion of a program is the safest approach, not only because farmers' acceptance is gradual, but also because institutions need time to build. Taiwan's experience shows that such a program should only grow as fast as trained personnel are available and as farmers are receptive.

• An integrated approach is the right approach, which Taiwan adopted at the initiation of its program. Soil conservation for conservation's sake only will not win people's support. The productivity of any conservation program, together with infrastructure needs, should be emphasized.

• A well-supported field operation is essential because soil conservation is a field-oriented program. Technical service and incentives must be available to all farmers who are willing to join the program. Delegating authority to the field offices and involving local farmers in planning and implementation processes are equally important.

• Applied research is necessary to solve problems arising in the field. With proper coordination, the work can be carried out without setting up special research organizations. Taiwan has done its research in soil conservation quite cost-effectively, and the results have been used extensively and promptly in the field.

• To be successful, a soil conservation program must, first, have a commitment from government to maintain a firm policy and, second, to give the program continuing support. Taiwan's experience shows just that.

The Upshot

Taiwan has become highly industrialized in the past decade, and its people are more and more concerned about their environment. The emphasis in the soil conservation program on hillslopes has shifted to disaster prevention and watershed rehabilitation. Nevertheless, the path and experience of Taiwan can be a good example for other countries.

REFERENCES

1. Koh, C. C., M. C. Liao, S. W. Lee, and J. D. Cheng. 1990. *The evolution of conservation farming on hillslopes in Taiwan.* In *Development of Conservation Farming on Hillslopes.* Soil and Water Conservation Society, Ankeny, Iowa. pp. 3-11.
2. Lee, S. W. 1987. *Soil conservation and slopeland development in Taiwan.* In S. Jantawat [editor] *Soil Erosion and Its CounterMeasures.* Soil and Water Conservation Society of Thailand. Bangkok.
3. Liao, M. C., S. C. Hu, and H. L. Wu. 1990. *Soil conservation research and development for hillslope farming in Taiwan.* In *Development of Conservation Farming on Hillslopes.* Soil and Water Conservation Society, Ankeny, Iowa. pp. 12-16.
4. Sheng, T. C. 1959. *Present soil conservation program in Taiwan.* Journal of Soil and Water Conservation in India 7: 69-78.
5. Wu, C.K.H. 1979. *The economics of slopeland development, the Taiwan experience.* The Asia and World Forum. Taipei, Taiwan.
6. Yiu, P. C. 1984. *Soil conservation extension on sloping farmlands in Taiwan.* Mountain Agricultural Resource Development Bureau. Nantou, Taiwan.

COUNTRY PERSPECTIVES 2

MANAGEMENT OF HILLSLOPES FOR SUSTAINABLE AGRICULTURE

DIMYATI NANGJU

Hillslope farming, known also as steepland agriculture or mountain agriculture, is generally defined as the growing of food and perennial crops on land with a slope exceeding 36 percent (20 degrees) (*14*). This form of agriculture is an important but neglected sector of Asian agriculture. Recently, however, it has received considerable attention from policymakers, environmental specialists, and resource scientists because of its increasing importance and its impact on downstream areas. In Asia, where about 40 percent of the world's people live, hillslope farming has increased rapidly because of population pressures and the rapidly growing demand for food, fuel, and fodder. The widespread expansion of steepland agriculture is invariably accompanied by environmental degradation of mountain habitats as well as downstream areas.

Steepland Agriculture: An Overview

In Asia, steepland agriculture is most widely practiced in the Hindukush-Himalaya Region, which covers parts of Afghanistan, Bangladesh, Bhutan, Burma, the People's Republic of China, India, Nepal, and Pakistan. It is home to many of the world's major river systems, including the Ganges, Indus, Bhramaputra, Mekong, and Yangtze. Directly and indirectly, steepland agriculture in this region affects more than one-third of the world's population.

In these areas, farmers commonly grow food crops, such as maize, finger millet, barley, and buckwheat. They also raise livestock on land with slopes between 30 and 70 percent. Steepland agriculture is practiced to a lesser

35

extent in other parts of Asia as well, including the tropical highlands of Indonesia, the Philippines, Malaysia, Thailand, and Taiwan.

Steepland areas are generally characterized by the following:

- Rapid rates of population growth, ranging from 2.5 to 5 percent a year.
- Widespread poverty, with per capita income ranging from $50 to $150.
- Long histories of settlement and dense populations (200 to 500 people per square kilometer); people generally prefer to live in the highlands rather than the lowlands because of the more favorable climate, low disease incidence, and other factors.
- Highly variable rainfall and soil types.
- Strong interrelationships between crop production, livestock production, and forest areas.
- Subsistence farming.
- Poor marketing, transportation, and communications infrastructure.
- Low labor productivity.
- Lack of off-farm employment.
- Isolation from national political processes.

Although most crop production textbooks recommend that steeplands not be used for growing food crops because of soil erosion and stormwater runoff, hillslope farming has increased in Asia, particularly in the Himalayas. This is due to rapid population growth, coupled with the low productivity of agricultural labor and the limited availability of flat land. In the Himalayas, increased population growth leads to increased the demand for basic needs, such as food, fodder, and fuelwood. These increased demands, in turn, lead to reduction in forest density and the eventual conversion of forestland to shrubland, overgrazed communal pasture, or cropland. In some countries, such as the Philippines, Thailand, and Indonesia, forest destruction is aggravated by uncontrolled commercial exploitation of forest products. As fuelwood shortages grow, animal manure, which is used to maintain soil fertility, becomes a source of energy. As a result, crop yields decline; soils deteriorate; landslides, gullying, and soil erosion increase; siltation in major rivers increases; floods become worse; and groundwater supplies decline.

Pressure to expand the cultivated area and increased demand for fuels and fodder are the prime causal factors in deforestation (6, 10). In Nepal, forest degradation, rather than complete loss of forest cover, seems to be the typical effect on forest resources. Landslides in the Himalayas, however, are not only caused by deforestation but also by road construction. As forest cover is lost and forested land is converted to cropland or common grazing land, soil erosion increases. This leads to low soil productivity and flooding in downstream areas. Overgrazing of common land is a major cause of soil erosion, not only in the Himalayas, but also in Latin America and Africa (9).

Improper Hillslope Development: The Nepal Experience

Uncontrolled hillslope development can cause severe environmental degradation. Both on-site and off-site effects of hillslope farming have been documented by research and observations in Nepal (8).

About 800,000 hectares or 54 percent of the hillslope farms in Nepal are in level terraces. Level terraces in the country are probably among the most impressive and intensive in the world. They are monuments to the industry, resourcefulness, and self-reliance of Nepali farmers in steepland areas. Despite these terraces, hillslope farming in Nepal has become a major concern.

On-site Effects. The major crops grown on hillslopes in Nepal are paddy, wheat, maize, finger millet, barley, buckwheat, and oilseeds. Paddy and wheat are generally grown in the valleys, where water is more readily available. Maize, finger millet, barley, buckwheat, and oilseeds are grown on steepland under rainfed conditions. From 1970-1971 to 1985-1986, yields of all cereal crops, except wheat, declined. The yield reductions, which ranged from 22 percent to 30 percent, were attributed to the effects of soil erosion and, to some extent, also to the lack of chemical fertilizer applications (8, 9).

As crop productivity declines, farmers are forced to open new land for cultivation of food crops to feed the rapidly growing population. During the 1970-1971 to 1985-1986 period, the cultivated area in Nepal's hillslope areas increased about 90 percent, from 800,000 hectares to 1.5 million hectares (15).

This increase in cultivated area was accompanied by the destruction of valuable forest resources. Over the 15-year period, the area under forests in Nepal declined 33 percent, from 6.4 million hectares to 4.3 million hectares (16, 17).

The decline in per capita food availability, coupled with lack of alternative employment opportunities in the hills and mountains, forced many hill people to migrate to the Terai of Nepal and neighboring countries, such as India and Bangladesh, in search for employment.

Off-Site Effects. The off-site effects of agricultural activity on steepland areas are equally severe. These effects include the high costs of operation and maintenance of roads and irrigation projects, seasonal flows of rivers and streams, flooding in the lowland areas, and the loss of hydropower potential (*16*).

A Strategy for Hillslope Management

A few countries in Asia, such as Taiwan and Malaysia, have successfully minimized the adverse effects of hillslope farming by developing appropriate approaches and strategies for agricultural development. Taiwan is a mountainous country with abundant rainfall. Only 900,000 hectares of the island nation's total area of 3.5 million hectares—26 percent—is cultivated. In spite of a high population density (about 550 persons per square kilometer) and steep slopes, agricultural production has not caused serious environmental effects. Taiwan's success in developing and protecting hillslopes has been attributed to the following factors (*3, 13*):

• An ability to increase crop productivity and cropping intensity in lowland areas through irrigation development, soil and water conservation practices, a high level of fertilizer and insecticide application, and the adoption of high-yielding varieties and multiple-cropping practices. Yields of most crops are among the highest in the world.

• An ability to develop the country's industrial sector, thereby providing alternative employment opportunities for people in rural areas, while at the same time supporting agricultural development through forward and backward linkages. Between 1952 and 1986, agriculture's contribution to Gross Domestic Project declined from 35.1 percent to 5.7 percent; the number of people employed in the agricultural sector declined from 56.1 percent to 16.8 percent as more people obtained employment in the industrial sector.

• Reforestation in the hills and mountains has been given top priority by government. Large areas have been replanted with various species, in line with the government's policy to conserve forest resources.

• Farmers are industrious and innovative, with strong farmers' organizations.

• The government has emphasized development of strong agricultural extension and education, research, and rural community development efforts and provided various incentives, including land reform, low-interest loans, modern marketing systems, and adequate supplies of farm inputs.

Malaysia has also been successful in minimizing the environmental effects of hillslope development. This was mainly achieved by promoting the cultivation of perennial crops, such as oil palm, rubber, cocoa, and coconut. Of a total cultivated area of 4.3 million hectares, tree crops (perennial crops) account for about 3.3 million hectares, 77 percent of the total.

Tree crops cause much less erosion than annual crops, and high productivity of tree crops on Ultisols and Oxisols has been achieved in Malaysia through research by government and in the private sector (*11, 12*). In 1987, the country earned about $3.2 billion from the exports of rubber, oil palm, and cocoa. This represented about 36 percent of the total export value (*5*). Although population growth in Malaysia is rather high (2.8 percent per annum), unemployment in the rural area has been kept relatively low by industrial development.

Nepal is a rugged, mountainous, and landlocked country. In contrast to Taiwan and Malaysia, it has had severe environmental problems resulting from uncontrolled development of hillslopes and widespread deforestation. A number of factors have contributed to these environmental problems. First, the development of hillslopes has been based on the promotion of annual crops, rather than perennial crops. This is partly due to the fact that rubber, oil palm, cocoa, and coconut cannot be grown in Nepal because of the low annual rainfall, low temperatures, and unsuitable soils. Cultivation of tea, which is widely practiced on the hillslopes of India and Sri Lanka, has only been promoted in recent years.

Second, the industrial sector is not developed sufficiently to provide alternative employment opportunities for the rural poor.

Third, the government's institutions responsible for providing support services (e.g., research, extension, etc.) are generally weak.

Fourth, government policies do not spell out clearly the priority and strategy for developing the hilly and mountainous areas.

Finally, high population growth and widespread poverty have offset what progress has been made in alleviating environmental problems in the remote hill and mountain areas. The experiences of Taiwan and Malaysia are not directly applicable to Nepal as a result.

The major concern in Nepal and other countries in the Hindukush-Himalaya Region is whether steepland agriculture can be sustained and its environmental effects, which undermine agricultural productivity, can be contained. Steepland agriculture has suffered a serious decline in crop production in recent decades. In most parts of the hill and mountain areas where steepland agriculture is practiced, there is a widening gap between the demand and supply of both land resources and subsistence products. The available data clearly show that this has serious consequences for both the mountain population and the people downstream in the plains because the economies of the two areas are closely linked.

In the past 2 decades, many projects financed by the government and external donors have been implemented to improve the natural resource base and the environment in the Himalayas. Despite these efforts, steepland agriculture continues to deteriorate. The failure of these projects can be attributed to an approach based on curative, piecemeal solutions, rather than on confronting the real issues (7).

The Asian Development Bank has recently approved technical assistance to the International Centre for Integrated Mountain Development for a study of strategies for the sustainable development of mountain agriculture. The center, which was established in 1983, is the first international center devoted to mountain area development. The main objective of the technical assistance is to support the center in an examination of the factors affecting mountain agriculture in order to identify the elements needed for sustainable development.

The strategy for tackling environmental degradation in the Hindukush-Himalaya region depends on government policies with respect to steepland agriculture. In this regard, the government has three choices:

• To develop mountain agriculture on the basis of an integrated rural development concept involving agroforestry, horticulture, hill irrigation development, applied research to increase productivity of hill crops, soil and water conservation, construction of farm roads, reforestation, and development of more efficient pasture production. This approach is likely to bring only marginal returns to investments because soils in the hills and mountains are poor and highly dependent on unreliable rainfall distribution, the infrastructure is inadequate, and any improvement will take years to produce meaningful results.

• To discourage any development in the hills and mountains so people in these areas will be persuaded to move to lowland areas. This approach may take the form of well-coordinated migration and family planning programs in order to reduce population pressures to a manageable level.

• To develop mountain agriculture while, at the same time, carrying out a coordinated migration and family planning program to reduce population pressures (a combination of the first and second approaches above).

The third approach is highly recommended because it would be more politically acceptable to the government and more likely to be successful in alleviating the environmental problems in the Hindukush-Himalaya region. These environmental problems are partly recent and caused mainly by rapid population growth. If population density in the region can be kept at a low level, in equilibrium with the natural resources in the mountains and the hills, the soil degradation and deforestation problems can at least be minimized to allow for sustainable agriculture, albeit at relatively lower productivity levels than in lowland areas. The success of this approach would be assured if the government adopted policy measures that are being prepared under a Forestry Master Plan Study with the assistance of the Asian Development Bank, and a study on natural resources management for sustainable development, which is being done with assistance from the World Bank and the Overseas Development Administration, a funding agency of the United Kingdom.

Role of Donors

Multilateral and bilateral donor agencies, such as the Asian Development Bank and the World Bank, should play an important role in addressing the problems of steepland agriculture; they can provide the required technical and financial assistance. Over its 21 years of existence, the Asian Development Bank has had considerable experience in agricultural and rural development projects. It is, therefore, in a position to provide the necessary assistance in this area if requested by the developing member countries. From 1968 to 1987, the Asian Development Bank's cumulative lending had reached $21.8 billion for 793 projects in 29 developing member countries, of which $4.7 billion or 21.7 percent of the total were in the agricultural sector (4). Agriculture remains the most important sector of the Asian Development Bank's operations (1). Environmental impact assessment has been given a major emphasis in considering a project to be financed by the Asian Development Bank (2).

While environmental impact assessment is an effective tool for integrating environmental issues in project planning, it is still piecemeal in terms of addressing regional environmental concerns. The Asian Development Bank has recently published a document entitled "Guidelines for Integrated Regional Economic-cum-Environmental Development Planning" that demonstrates the multidisciplinary approach required in designing sustainable agricultural development. The Asian Development Bank also is pursuing a study on economic policies for sustainable development. This effort will demonstrate the effect of agricultural and economic policies on the environment and recommend an approach for sustainable development.

REFERENCES

1. Asian Development Bank. 1985. *Agriculture in Asia: Its performance and prospects and the role of ADB in its development.* Staff Working paper. Manila, Philippines. p. 238.
2. Asian Development Bank. 1986. *Environmental planning and management.* Proceedings, Regional Symposium on Environmental and National Resources Planning. Manila, Philippines. p. 259.
3. Asian Development Bank. 1988. *Agricultural research in the Asian and Pacific Region: Current situation and outlook.* Staff Working paper. Manila, Philippines. p. 520.
4. Asian Development Bank. 1988. *Annual report 1987.* Manila, Philippines. p. 187.

5. Asian Development Bank. 1988. *Key indicators of developing member countries of ADB.* Manila, Philippines. p. 383.
6. Bajracharya, Deepak. 1983. *Fuel, food or forest? Dilemmas in Nepal villages.* World Development 12: 1,057-1,074.
7. De Boer, A. John. 1988. *Sustainable approaches to hillside agricultural development.* U.S. Agency for International Development, Kathmandu, Nepal.
8. Department of Food and Agricultural Marketing Services. 1987. *Agricultural statistics of Nepal.* Kathmandu, Nepal.
9. Fleming, W. M. 1983. *Phewa Tal catchment management program: Benefits and costs of forestry and soil conservation in Nepal.* In L. S. Hamilton [editor] *Forest and Watershed Development and Conservation in Asia and the Pacific.* Westview Press, Boulder, Colorado.
10. Griffin, D. M., K. R. Shepherd, and T.B.S. Mahat. 1988. *Human impact on some forests of the Middle Hills of Nepal. Part 5. Comparisons, concepts, and some policy implications.* Mountain Research and Development 8: 43-52.
11. International Board for Soil Research and Management. 1987. *Management of acid tropical soils for sustainable agriculture.* Proceedings, IBSRAM Inaugural Workshop. Bangkok, Thailand. p. 299.
12. International Board for Soil Research and Management. 1987. *Soil management under humid conditions in Asia.* Proceedings, First Regional Seminar on Soil Management Under Humid Conditions in Asian and the Pacific. Khon Kaen, Phitsanulok, Thailand. p. 466.
13. Koh, C. E., M. C. Liao, S. W. Lee, and J. D. Cheng. 1990. *The evolution of conservation farming on hillslopes in Taiwan.* In *Development of Conservation Farming on Hillslopes.* Soil and Water Conservation Society, Ankeny, Iowa. pp. 3-11.
14. Lim, J. S., Y. K. Chan, and K. F. Loh. 1987. *Soils on steepland in peninsular Malaysia.* In *Proceedings of the International Workshop on Steepland Agriculture in the Humid Tropics.* Mardi, Kuala Lumpur, Malaysia.
15. National Planning Commission. 1987. *Program for fulfillment of basic needs.* Kathmandu, Nepal.
16. Sharma, C. K. 1988. *Natural hazards and manmade impacts in the Nepal Himalayas.* Printing Support Pvt. Ltd., Kathmandu, Nepal. p. 142.
17. Water and Energy Commission Secretariate. 1987. *Fuelwood supply in the districts of Nepal.* Kathmandu, Nepal.

SOIL AND WATER CONSERVATION IN KERALA STATE, INDIA

V. K. SASIDHAR, K. VISWAMBHARAN, and G. BALAKRISHNA PILLAI

K erala is one of India's southern states. Soil erosion is severe because most of the cultivated area in the state is on undulating or steep land. Nearly 2 million hectares, of the state's 3.9 million hectares, are vulnerable to erosion.

About half of the cultivated area in the state is on hillslopes, which, according to the land capability classification, are unsuited to cultivation. Increasing population pressure necessitates cultivation even on steep slopes. This pressure, coupled with heavy rainfall (as high as 5,000 millimeters in some areas), and the fact that the latest recommended land management practices are not followed, causes severe soil erosion. Denudation of forests and poor watershed management lead to frequent drought, in spite of the high rainfall.

History of Soil Conservation Activities

Concerted and systematic efforts to control soil erosion were made toward the end of the first "Five Year Plan" with establishment of a separate Soil Conservation Department in 1954 in what was then Travancore Cochin State. In 1956, with the formation of the present Kerala State, the Soil Conservation Department was moved into the Department of Agriculture. The Soil Conservation Department became a separate department once again in 1963, then was merged again with the Department of Agriculture in 1969, where it remains today. The Kerala Land Development Corporation is also responsible for certain land development work as part of the reclamation of waterlogged areas.

Land Development Act of Kerala

Soil conservation is provided for in the Kerala Land Development Act of 1964. This act has amended and unified the laws and regulations relating to land development, soil conservation, development of soil resources, and reclamation. Under the act, the district collector has the power to enforce soil conservation even if landowners object.

A Watershed-Based Soil Conservation Program

The concept of organizing soil conservation programs on a watershed basis is of recent origin in Kerala State. With its 44 major rivers, the state receives an average annual precipitation of 3,300 millimeters. Geomorphological conditions, soil characteristics, and the existing drainage system render the land highly susceptible to erosion, floods, and drought. Planning and implementation on a watershed basis would help avoid frequent drought and flooding.

Nature of Soil Conservation Activities

Soil conservation practices are recommended on a watershed basis by the Soil Conservation Unit. These practices are broken down into engineering, cropping, use of grasses, and forestry.

Engineering Practices. Contour bunds are recommended on steeper slopes because of the shallow soil, and, particularly, because of the stability of the lateritic stones used for bunding. Stone-pitched contour bunds are more durable and stronger than earthen ones. Over a period of years, the bunds become a series of terraces.

The vertical intervals recommended for contour bunds are as follows: up to 15 percent slope, 2 meters; 16 to 35 percent, 3 meters; 36 percent and above, 4 meters. The recommended heights of stone-pitched contour bunds are as follows: up to 5 percent slope, 50 centimeters; 6 to 10 percent, 70 centimeters; 11 to 35 percent, 100 centimeters; 36 percent and above, 150 centimeters. A height of 1 meter applies in most areas. A foundation of 15 to 22 centimeters deep is necessary for a 1-meter height.

The specifications for stone-pitched bunds included the following: top width, including pitching, 45 to 50 centimeters; thickness of pitching, 15 to 22 centimeters; side slope (uphill side of earth packing), 1.5:1; downhill side of pitching, 5:1; and foundation, 15 to 22 centimeters.

For general conditions in Kerala State—high rainfall areas and slopes up to 33 percent—bench terracing is a suitable practice. However, the initial cost of bench terraces is high compared to contour bunding, which is a great disadvantage to a majority of farmers who are too poor to afford this high initial cost. Moreover, bench terracing is not suitable for shallow soils. Because of these constraints, bench terracing is recommended only in certain areas.

Recommended specifications for contour trenches are as follows: top width, 1 meter; depth and bottom width of trench, 0.5 meter; and side slope, 2:1, vertical to horizontal. Graded trenches are not widely used in Kerala State.

Diversion channels, check dams, drop pits, and water harvesting structures are constructed in conjunction with contour bunding programs on some hillslopes. But these have not received much publicity among farmers. However, because of recurring drought, farmers have begun to use water conservation measures, which also ensure soil conservation.

Cropping Practices. The important agronomic practices recommended for soil conservation in Kerala State include contour cultivation, crop rotation, cover cropping, mixed cropping, application of organic matter, zero tillage, mulching, strip fallowing, and stripcropping. These practices are not common because, unlike contour bunding, farmers are not given any financial assistance for doing them. Also, the Soil Conservation Unit has no machinery for implementing these practices.

Use of Grasses. Steep slopes are best suited to grass, but they are being cultivated because of heavy pressure on the land. The Soil Conservation Unit thus recommends grass only on top of contour bunds and on sides of drainage channels and gullies. Turfing on contour bunds provides a binding effect that provides greater durability. *Congosignal* and guinea grass (*Panicum maximum*) are recommended for bunds, but Vetiver grass (*Vetiveria zizanioides*) has proved best for gully sides and channel linings.

Forestry Practices. The forest resources of Kerala State have been indiscriminately cut, and steep slopes cannot be replanted using existing afforestation practices. However, boundaries of farms and lateral bunds can be planted to trees. Recommended species are eucalyptus, acasia, subabul, and glyrecidia. Subabul is the best for making a hedge along the contour.

Again, while the contour bunding program has been accepted by farmers, the others have not. To attain an integrated approach to soil conservation, therefore, appropriate, site-specific technologies must evolve through development of appropriate technologies and intensive extension activities.

Some Research Results

A field experiment was conducted in 1979-1980 by Kerala Agricultural University to study the effect of various practices on runoff and soil loss

Table 1. Runoff and soil loss as affected by different treatments before and after harvest of intercrop.

	Runoff (mm)				Soil Loss (t/ha)		
Treatments	Before Harvesting Intercrop	After Harvesting Intercrop	Total	Percent of Total Rainfall	Before Harvesting Intercrop	After Harvesting Intercrop	Total
T_1	77b†	23b	100b	15b	23.5b	10.6b	34.2b
T_2	37c	17c	54c	8c	2.6c	4.3c	6.9c
T_3	19d	8d	27d	4d	2.3cd	1.9d	4.1d
T_4	12e	5e	18e	3e	1.7d	1.4d	3.2d
T_5	140a	52a	193a	28a	39.5a	37.9a	77.4a

*T_1-Tapioca alone in mounds.
T_2-Tapioca in mounds with peanut intercrop.
T_3-Tapioca alone in ridges across slope.
T_4-Tapioca in ridges across slope with peanut intercrop.
T_5-Uncultivated bare fallow (control).
†Numbers in each column followed by the same letter are not significantly different.

Table 2. Total runoff and soil loss as affected by different treatments during the period of observation.

Treatments	Runoff (mm)	Soil Loss (t/ha)
T_1*	311a†	93.3a
T_2	236b	78.5ab
T_3	248b	91.7a
T_4	82d	11.0c
T_5	236b	71.8b
T_6	104c	12.7c
T_7	234b	70.4b

*T_1-Tapioca alone on ridges.
T_2-Uncultivated bare fallow.
T_3-Tapioca on ridges along the slope with cowpeas as intercrop.
T_4-Tapioca on ridges across the slope with cowpea as intercrop.
T_5-Tapioca alone on mounds.
T_6-Tapioca alone on ridges across slope.
T_7-Tapioca on mounds with cowpea as intercrop.
†Numbers in each column followed by the same letter are not significantly different.

Table 3. Runoff and soil loss as influenced by intercropping and nitrogen levels.

Treatments	Runoff (mm)	Soil Loss (t/ha)
T_1*	13,279ab†	30.8a
T_2	13,495a	29.5a
T_3	13,090b	22.3b
T_4	13,036b	21.5c
T_5	13,040b	21.2c
T_6	13,111b	22.2b

*T_1-Tapioca alone at 50:50:50 kg N, P_2O_5, and K_2O/ha.
T_2-Stylosanthes alone at 10:30:20 kg N, P_2O_5, and K_2O/ha.
T_3-Tapioca + Stylosanthes at 50:50:50 + 10:30:20 kg N, P_2O_5, and K_2O/ha.
T_4-Tapioca + Stylosanthes at 50:50:50 kg N, P_2O_5, and K_2O/ha.
T_5-Tapioca + Stylosanthes at 35:50:50 kg N, P_2O_5/ha.
T_6-Tapioca + Stylosanthes at 20:50:50 kg N, P_2O_5, K_2O/ha.
†Numbers in each column followed by the same letter are not significantly different.

under cassava on a 15.3 percent slope. Results show that peanut intercropping or planting cassava on contour ridges can reduce soil and water losses considerably (Table 1).

Another study was conducted during the heavy rainfall season on a hillslope to assess the effects of various agrotechniques on soil loss, surface runoff, and soil moisture storage. The study showed (Table 2) that cassava planted on contour ridges, with cowpea as the intercrop, was effective in reducing soil and water losses (2). It was also found that cassava alone on contour ridges was not effective in controlling soil losses because the ridges usually break during heavy rainfall.

Another experiment was conducted to study the effectiveness of cassava-stylosanthes intercropping in reducing soil erosion. The results (Table 3) show that intercropping cassava with stylosanthes was effective in controlling soil and water losses from sloping land (1).

Conclusion

On the basis of research findings, action is being taken to reorient conservation programs to become more effective in fulfilling their objectives. It is urgent that soil conservation be done as soon as possible on 2 million hectares. During the past 32 years, only 87,150 hectares have been adequately treated. At this rate, more than 700 years will be required to complete the job.

REFERENCES

1. Anilkumar, P. 1983. *Nitrogen economy and soil conservation in tapioca-stylo inter-*

cropping system. Masters thesis. Kerala Agricultural University, Kerala, India.

2. Menon, A. K. 1984. *Effect of agro-techniques on soil loss, surface runoff and soil moisture storage in hillslopes-Part II*. Masters thesis. Kerala Agricultural University, Kerala, India.

3. Viswambharan, K., and V. K. Sasidhar. 1983. *Influence of conservation practices on runoff and soil loss under tapioca in hillslopes*. Agricultural Research Journal, Kerala 21(1): 9-16.

AGRICULTURAL DEVELOPMENT
OF SLOPELANDS IN MALAYSIA

GHULAM MOHD HASHIM

Malaysia is comprised of three
distinct geographical regions: the Malay peninsula, also known as Peninsular Malaysia; Sarawak; and Sabah. The land areas of these regions are
13.04 million hectares, 12.25 million hectares, and 7.75 million hectares,
respectively. The land can be divided into two broad categories, upland
and alluvial areas. If one considers all uplands (nonalluvial areas) as slopelands, they amount to roughly 80 percent of the country.

Soils too can be divided into two broad groups: upland soils and alluvial
soils. The upland soils are formed in inland areas on a variety of rock material. These deeply weathered soils, mostly Ultisols and Oxisols, are usually
associated with slopes. The alluvial soils occur mainly in coastal plains
and along river valleys. On the west coast of Peninsular Malaysia, the coastal
alluvium may extend 60 kilometers inland.

Accessibility and high fertility have made the coastal alluvial areas the
choice land for agriculture. The areas are now largely exhausted, and agriculture has spread rapidly to upland areas. Agricultural production is targeted to increase further through both higher production from existing land
and an expansion in cultivated area. This expansion must involve slopelands.

Soil erosion is an important phenomenon associated with the use of
slopelands for agriculture. Annual rainfall is high. In Peninsular Malaysia,
it ranges from 1,625 millimeters in the extreme northwest to 3,750 millimeters
in the northeast. Annual rainfall in Sabah ranges from 1,780 millimeters to
3,800 millimeters and in Sarawak, from 3,048 millimeters to 5,588
millimeters. Intense rainstorms are a common feature of the rainfall regimes
in all three regions.

Present Land Use

Various tree crops dominate slopeland agriculture in Malaysia. A crop mix of rubber, oil palm, and cocoa is common on large plantations. Fruit crops are grown also on a smaller scale. On smallholdings, a single crop species, either rubber, oil palm, or cocoa, is common. However, during the immature phase of these crops, shorter duration crops, such as banana, papaya, groundnut, or maize, may be grown in the interrows.

There also are mixed-fruit farms. These are usually small. The average size of orchard per farm family in 1975 was 0.1 hectare, and there were 250,000 orchards in Peninsular Malaysia. Fruits cultivated in Malaysia can be broadly classified as seasonal or nonseasonal. The former includes durian, rambutan, mangosteen, duku langsat, and mango. The latter includes banana, papaya, pineapple, watermelon, and jackfruit. The total acreage in fruits is relatively small, however.

In Sarawak and Sabah, shifting cultivation is important. About 2.9 million hectares of land in Sarawak is shifting cultivation (3). This practice is a relatively safe form of land use when small areas are cleared and fallow periods are long. In both regions, however, the lengths of fallow periods are declining rapidly. In some areas in Sarawak the fallow periods are as short as 3 years. The yield of hill rice, which exceeded 1,000 kilograms per hectare when primary forest was first cleared, has declined to 300 to 400 kilograms per hectare (3). A similar downtrend in length of fallow period in Sabah is being accompanied by lower crop yields, a decline in soil fertility, and increased erosion, siltation, and forest fire hazard (10).

More intensive land use is being practiced in some high-altitude areas. One example is the Cameron Highlands in Peninsular Malaysia where subtropical and temperate crops are cultivated. Altitudes exceed 900 meters. Tea, flowers, citrus, and other fruits, and 25 types of vegetables are grown on about 5,000 hectares. Most cultivated areas are on slopes ranging from 18 percent to 70 percent, and terracing is common (6). Severe soil erosion occurs, however. The off-site effects of erosion in the Cameron Highlands are well-known. About 382,000 cubic meters of sediment are dredged annually from the various intakes and rivers in the catchment of the hydroelectric dam that is downstream from the major fruit and vegetable areas.

Land Use Factors in the Uplands

Tradition and climate seem to be important factors governing land use. Economics are also a major consideration. In private companies with large land holdings, the allocation of land for various crops is sometimes dictated by the need to have sufficient acreage of each crop to make it economically viable. But where land area is not a limitation, allocation takes into account crop suitability according to soil and topography. For example, where the crop mix is rubber, palm oil, and cocoa, rubber is relegated to the steeper land and cocoa is usually planted in the most fertile areas. Rubber is the least demanding of the three crops in terms of soil fertility and topography, while cocoa requires highly fertile, well-structured soils (*11*).

Land use planning for rubber takes into account such factors as steep slope and shallow soil. For example, in rubber planting recommendations, the suitability of various clones for steep terrain are rated as suitable, acceptable, or unsuitable (*9*). Factors considered include resistance to wind damage and high-yielding characteristics.

For relatively small plantations that cultivate oil palm in addition to other crops, there must be enough palm fruit production to support an oil mill. In these cases, oil palm might even be planted on slopes that are normally allocated to rubber only. In areas where slopelands consist of relatively fertile and well-structured soils, as in some parts of Sabah, relatively steep slopes may even be planted to cocoa.

Agricultural Land Expansion

An aerial survey in 1974 and 1975 showed that at that time a large proportion of the agriculturally suitable land in Peninsular Malaysia was planted to various crops. The cropped area of land has since increased even more. For example, land in oil palm increased from 486,800 hectares in 1974 to 879,900 hectares in 1980. There were similar increases in the land area in cocoa, fruits, and other crops.

In the Fifth Malaysia Plan period, 1986 to 1990, the Federal Land Development Authority alone will open 175,500 hectares, mainly to grow cocoa, oil palm, and rubber (*2*). Several other federal and state agencies also will develop land for agriculture.

The area under fruits is expected to increase. The government sees potential in 14 fruit types and plans to encourage their production. A large part of the uplands will thus be converted from forest to agriculture.

Problems Related to Land Clearing

The native vegetation of Malaysia is tropical rainforest, which is characterized by many strata of trees, floor herbs, and leaf litter. The topsoil under forest has a good open structure and is almost completely protected from accelerated erosion and other degradative forces. However, when native vegetation is removed to make way for crops, erosion and other forces set in. Even in mature tree crop stands with a closed canopy, relatively large soil losses are observed (Table 1).

Land clearing commonly involves heavy machinery. Manual clearing is slow and requires a large labor force. Economics and ease of management also dictate that large pieces of land be cleared at any one time. In areas developed by the Federal Land Development Authority, clearing is carried out in 2,000-hectare parcels of land. The use of heavy machines inevitably causes great soil disturbance because trees are pushed and uprooted in the operation. Topsoil is thus rendered more susceptible to erosion. The repeated movement of machines over the area compacts the soil, leading to lower infiltration rates. A complete coverage by leguminous creepers takes at least 3 to 4 months after sowing. The disturbed and compacted soil is, therefore, exposed for a considerable period and subjected to high erosion rates during heavy downpours.

Table 2 shows the results of soil erosion and runoff measurements on the east coast in Peninsular Malaysia in 1985. All of the areas concerned had a good aerial cover of tree canopy and a good surface cover of leaf litter. But in cases one to three, clearing of forest trees by machines had taken place, and the resulting disturbance and erosion left a surface soil with poorer structure than in cases four and five where the original forest trees remained. Consequently, runoff and erosion were much higher in the former areas. In spite of differences in slope gradient, the large difference in erosion was partly attributable to the disturbance of the original topsoil in the cropped areas. Assuming that the relation $E \propto S^2$ (5), where E is erosion and S is slope gradient, holds for all five situations, soil erosion from the cropped areas, in comparison to that from the forested areas, was much higher than what could be attributed to slope gradient differences alone.

In the land-clearing process, tree felling is followed by stacking and burning. It is often difficult to get a good burn, however. Adverse weather conditions that affect field operations are common. All these delay the sowing of cover crops, thus prolonging the period when the soil is vulnerable to

Table 1. Suspended load in streams from three catchments with different land use (1).

Land Use	Suspended Load ($m^3/km^2/yr$)	Ratio
Undisturbed jungle	31	1
Mature rubber and oil palm (small catchment)	46	1.5
Mature rubber and oil palm (large catchment)	87	2.8

Table 2. Soil loss and runoff in the March-December period with different vegetative cover.

Description of Vegetative Cover	Soil and Slope	Soil Loss (t/ha)	Runoff (mm)	Soil Bulk Density (g cm⁻³)	Organic C Content (%)
Mature cocoa, Gliricidia, closed canopy, leaf litter.	Padang Besar series. Plinthic orthoxic tropudult. Sandy clay loam to clay loam surface. 22%.	2.6	117	1.41	1.54
Mature cocoa, Gliricidia, closed canopy, leaf litter.	Padang Besar series. Plinthic orthoxic tropudult. Sandy clay loam to clay loam surface. 11%.	2.5	119	1.33	1.48
Mature cocoa, Gliricidia, closed canopy, leaf litter.	Apek series. Oxic dystropept. Silty surface. 11%.	3.2	34	1.40	1.33
Logged rainforest, closed canopy, leaf litter.	Padang Besar series. Plinthic orthoxic tropudult. Sandy clay loam to clay loam surface. 11%.	0.3	5	0.92	2.22
Logged rainforest, closed canopy, leaf litter.	Padang Besar series. Plinthic orthoxic tropudult. Sandy clay loam to clay loam surface. 11%.	0.5	1	0.86	2.90

Source: Ghulam M. Hashim, unpublished data.

erosion and degradation.

Most crops have a limited economic life. The economic life cycle for rubber in plantation, for example, is 30 to 35 years. Therefore, clearing of cultivated slopelands is carried out repeatedly. Without strict conservation measures, disturbance and erosion of topsoil occur with every clearing operation. The consequent exposure of poorer structured subsoil leads to high rates of runoff and erosion, which continues even after crops mature.

Soil Conservation Practices

Bench terracing and establishment and maintenance of leguminous cover crops are two of the most important soil conservation measures being practiced. Terraces are normally used when the slope exceeds 8 percent. There are slight variations in the types constructed, depending on soil depth, soil type, slope, and other considerations. Normally, however, terraces are 2 meters wide and have an inward slope of 30 centimeters. Cross or stop bunds are constructed to check lateral erosion. Terracing involves displacement of large quantities of soil. Terraced land is very susceptible to erosion during and immediately after construction when there is no vegetative cover.

While terracing is a straightforward matter on gentle slopes, problems are encountered in steeper areas, especially where the local geology is dominated by shale and sandstone. Here, the soil is often shallow, and the terrace cuts are in parent material. This problem is less common in areas with granitic material.

Individual platforms allow better root proliferation than terraces. Mohd Noh Jalil (8) found this in the case of coconut on slopeland. However, platforms pose problems for in-field movement and transportation of crops, such as rubber and palm oil.

Use of legumes as ground cover is a good soil conservation practice. Legumes also bestow many other benefits to the soil and crop. One of the disadvantages of legume cover crops, however, is their high cost of establishment and maintenance. Smallholders usually prefer to plant short-term cash crops in the interrows of tree crops during the immature phase. The timing of cover crop seeding in relation to the rainfall pattern also is very important because it takes 3 to 4 months before legumes provide a complete surface cover. Furthermore, in the cultivation of mango, for example, in areas with a dry season, there is controversy associated with cover crops. First, excessive accumulation of nitrogen through fixation by legumes encourages excessive vegetative growth. Second, cover crops raise the microhumidity, which, in turn, discourages flowering. Third, legumes die during prolonged drought and become a fire hazard.

Another important practice is straw mulching. Under mature oil palm, pruned fronds are systematically arranged to help control erosion. Lim (7) discussed erosion control under mature palms by various methods of placement of pruned fronds and found that evenly spread fronds are more effective than fronds concentrated in heaps. In one orchard, coconut husks and empty oil palm bunches were used with wire mesh to hold the mulch in place.

Farm Transportation

Transportation of farm produce and agricultural inputs is an important consideration on slopelands. In steep areas especially, a well-planned, efficient road system is critical. The roads serve collection points, factories, and processing centers and are usually suitable for motorized transport. The layout of the road system must not contribute to runoff generation and sediment transport.

Terraces serve as footpaths and aid in movement within farms. In rubber and oil palm plantations, terraces are preferred over platforms to enable workers to move about easily.

In some instances, a good transportation system is required not only to reduce labor but also to ensure the quality of the produce. On some highland farms, vegetables are placed in large baskets that are then transported through a system of overhead cables. A similar arrangement may be necessary for such farm products as bananas in order to reduce handling and thus lower the chances of damaged or bruised fruit.

Conclusion

Present trends show that more slopelands will be used for agriculture in the future. It is important that a thorough knowledge and understanding of the nature of forested slopelands be obtained to enhance their use and management. More studies are needed on soil management and erosion control during and immediately after clearing.

REFERENCES

1. Daniel, J. G., and A. Kulasingam. 1974. *Problems arising from large-scale jungle clearing for agricultural use: The Malaysian experience.* In Paper, International Expert Consultation on the Use of Improved Technology for Food Production in Rainfed Areas of Tropical Asia-Hydrabad, Khon Kaen and Kuala Lumpur, November 24-December 13, 1974. Food and Agriculture Organization, Rome, Italy.
2. Government of Malaysia. 1986. *Fifth Malaysia plan, 1986-1990.* Kuala Lumpur.
3. Hatch, T., and Y. L. Tie. 1979. *Shifting cultivation in Sarawak and its effects on soil fertility.* In Proceedings, Malaysian Seminar on Fertility and Management of Deforested land. Society of Agricultural Scientists, Sabah, Malaysia. pp. 9-16.
4. Hudson, N. 1971. *Soil conservation.* BT Batsford Ltd., London, England.
5. Hudson, N. W., and D. C. Jackson. 1959. *Results achieved in the measurement of erosion and runoff in southern Rhodesia.* In Proceedings, Third Inter-African Soils Conference. Compte Rendus 3, Dalaba.
6. Ko, W. W., A. R. Syed, N. Mohd Shukor, H. Safruddin, and J. A. Azhar. 1987. *Agriculture in the Cameron Highlands.* In Proceedings, International Conference on Steepland Agriculture in the Humid Tropics. Malaysian Agricultural Research and Development Institute, Kuala Lumpar.
7. Lim, K. H. 1988. *A study on soil erosion control on mature oil palms in Malaysia.* In Proceedings, Fifth International Soil Conservation Conference. Department of Land Development, Bangkok, Thailand.
8. Mohd. Noh Jalil, Musa Mohd Jamil, and Abdullah Othman. 1987. *Influence of slope on root distribution and yield of coconut.* In Proceedings, International Conference on Steepland Agriculture in the Humid Tropics. Malaysian Agricultural Research and Development Institute, Kuala Lumpur.
9. Rubber Research Institute of Malaysia. 1986. *Planter's bulletin no. 186.* Kuala Lumpur, Malaysia.

10. Sinajin, J. S. 1987. *Alternatives to shifting cultivation in Sabah, East Malaysia.* In Proceedings, International Conference on Steepland Agriculture in the Humid Tropics. Malaysian Agricultural Research and Development Institute, Kuala Lumpur.
11. Smyth, A. J. 1975. *Soils.* In G.A.R. Wood [editor] *Cocoa.* Longman Group, London, England.
12. Webb, W. E. 1973. *Sabah forest inventory.* Forestal Int. Ltd., Vancouver, Canada.

INTEGRATION OF TRADITIONAL AND MODERN CONSERVATION METHODS ON HILLSLOPES IN SRI LANKA

J. S. GUNASEKERA

Sri Lanka has a favorable climate and sufficient rainfall because of two monsoons. The island, with an area of about 64,000 square kilometers and a coastline of 1,700 kilometers, consists of three sharply defined altitude zones: the lowest with an average altitude of 30 meters above sea level; the middle with an altitude of some 300 meters; and the highest with an altitude of 1,500 to 1,800 meters. Some peaks reach to 2,400 meters. Many valleys and gorges radiate from the center of the island toward the coast in all directions. This results in a number of river basins, the largest of which is the Mahaweli.

The Upper Mahaweli Catchment

The Upper Mahaweli catchment forms that section of the Mahaweli drainage basin above the Minipe anicut (wier), where the new right-bank transbasin canal takes off near the old left-bank canal built more than 1,000 years ago. Here, the rugged, dissected topography of the Upper Mahaweli River Basin ends abruptly, becoming undulating plains toward the east and northeast. From here the catchment extends southward, southeastward, and southwestward, encompassing the region referred to as the Central Highlands. It includes the Kandy and Nuwara Eliya administrative districts of the Central Province and the greater part of the Badulla administrative district of the Uva Province. Several tributaries feed the Mahaweli in its descent to the plains, the more important being the Kotmale Oya, Maha Oya, Hulu Ganga, Atabage, and Nilambe Oya.

Three major reservoirs built were under the Accelerated Mahaweli Program: the Katmale in the upper reaches, the Victoria in the middle reaches, and the Randenigala in the lower reaches. A number of other lakes, such as Nuwara Eliya and Kandy, are included, as are several other smaller tanks and wewas.

The climatic year in Sri Lanka can be divided into four main periods: the Southwest and Northeast Monsoons and two intermonsoonal periods. The island has been divided into three rainfall and climatic zones—the Wet Zone, the Dry Zone with a Transition Zone, and the Intermediate Zone.

Natural Vegetation

The original vegetation consisted mainly of grass, forests, and wetlands. The forests include the Montane, at high elevations; the Wet Zone, at middle elevations; the Intermediate Zone; and the Dry Zone on the boundary with the lowland plains. The grasslands include the Wet Patna of the high plains; the Dry Patna of the Central Highlands, mid-country, and Uva; and the Kekila fernlands of the Wet and Mid Zones.

Early Settlement Patterns and Conservation Strategy

The first settlements were associated with tank-based agriculture in the lowlands and on gently sloping land. Here, paddy was confined to the valley bottoms and flatter land, while adjacent highlands were developed as homesteads and mixed gardens. The land with gentle slopes was developed under shifting cultivation, locally referred to as "chena." This is a pattern of multiple cropping with only a partial clearing of the jungle, causing little disturbance of the soil, and leaving crop residue and stubble after harvest.

The main conservation measure on rice land consisted of level bench terraces with risers. These were maintained and repaired as necessary after each season. The paddy land was also irrigated by a system of canals from anicuts or wiers constructed across streams. These traditional conservation methods withstood the test of time. The practices continued from generation to generation and even extended into modern times with some modifications.

Closely associated with the paddy land are the homesteads, settlements, and mixed gardens. These provide the main habitat for the vast majority of the population. The mixed gardens provide food, oils and fats, fruit, sugars, fibers, fuel, timber, and medicines. They meet the basic requirements of the people, but at a subsistence level. From the conservation aspect, this pattern of land use provides a dense vegetative canopy. Litter covers the ground, intercepts rainfall, promotes infiltration, and controls erosion.

In some locations, land further upslope was used under a system of rotational shifting cultivation with a multiple cropping system. Crops included closely spaced cereals, such as finger millet (*Elucine corocana*), with wider spaced vegetable crops. However, as population pressure increased, the resting periods decreased. A significant aspect of this system was that, originally, the land in the remainder of the catchment, particularly in the upper slopes, crests, and land forming headwaters and sources of rivers, were under dense forests. Aside from minimizing the hazards of soil erosion, the land use system ensured a source of water for both the upper catchment and downstream areas, including the lowland plains.

Land Use Changes and Influence on Conservation

Changes took place with the advent of plantation farming, first under coffee, then under tea. Extensive areas of steep land, hitherto under forest, were cleared for tea. These areas included the headwaters and sources of main streams. At that time, tea did not give adequate land protection, and serious erosion resulted. Subsequently, however, conservation measures were developed. These consisted of contour or graded drains. These were fed into natural drainageways or into artificial waterways provided for this purpose. The other conservation measure was the stone terrace. These terraces reduced the length of slope and controlled surface runoff.

Biological conservation measures included planting tea on the contour at relatively close spacings, along with high-density vegetative material. Selective weeding, reduction in size of weeding implements, and chemical weed control also were adopted. These measures acted to furnish shade and canopy interception at high, medium, and low levels, as in forest conditions and mixed gardens.

On sloping land in rubber, conservation measures consisted of contour platforms combined with contour planting. Ground cover consisted of *Puraria javanica, Centrocema pubescens, Calapagonium mucinoidia,* and *Desmodium ovalifolium.*

On coconut plantations, the main conservation measure was ground cover, mainly grass. Also, on steeply sloping land, the individual coconut trees were provided with individual, crescent-shaped terraces using coconut husks. Other measures were contour or graded lock-and-spill drains on moderately sloping land and narrow-based contour bunds on gently sloping land. More recently, nitrogen-fixing plants on the contour have been adopted for conservation as well as for improvement of fertility.

The establishment of plantations on what was once peasant land and the hiring of expatriate instead of peasant labor made it inevitable that peasants would move to and cultivate steep, unstable, land. This has resulted in severe erosion. Conservation has been limited to mechanical measures, such as lock-and-spill drains and stone terraces. However, by themselves, these measures do not give adequate protection against erosion.

More recently, attempts have been made to use a system of alley farming, where double rows of a nitrogen-fixing shrub, such as *Gliricidia*, is grown on the contour at specified intervals to act as a stop-wash buffer. The shrub is also used for green manure, as a mulch, and for fuelwood, in addition to providing partial shade. Areas between the rows are used for growing seasonal crops with grass strips between. Permanent crops, such as coffee and coconut, are then grown at specified intervals.

Diversification of plantation crops on sloping land is another strategy. Tree crops, such as cloves, nutmeg, coffee, and pepper, are common, especially when conditions are marginal, submarginal, or uneconomic.

The constraints imposed by limited land resources and a high-density and growing population leave no alternative to the use of steeply sloping land, but the danger of degradation can be reduced by the adoption of an overall strategy of applying an integrated land use and conservation plan. This requires a combination of traditional and modern conservation methods, together with improved land use. The conservation measures include physical works on cultivated land, such as the various forms of terraces, bunds, and drains described, and other conventional works, such as gully control, stabilization of streambanks and roads, the safe disposal of runoff into stable channels and waterways, stabilization of areas subject to mass movement, and measures to control sedimentation in lakes and rivers. Conservation forestry will also be part of such a plan (1).

On plantations, physical conservation works need to be combined with developing and maintaining a good vegetative cover, diversification from monocropping into the traditional pattern of mixed tree-crop garden, and the possibility of alley cropping. Increased production and more high-value cash crops are to be encouraged (1). The principle of this integrated approach to a land use and conservation plan is accepted and is being put into practice in certain small watersheds in the Upper Mahaweli, such as Hapuwela Naran Ela, including the provision of a monitoring system for measuring streamflow and soil loss.

REFERENCE

1. Hudson, N. W. 1989. *Soil conservation strategies for the future.* In Sanarn Rimwanich [editor] *Land Conservation for Future Generations.* Department of Land Development, Ministry of Agriculture, Bangkok, Thailand.

DEVELOPMENT OF HILLY LAND IN THE NORTHERN REGION OF THAILAND

SANARN RIMWANICH

Hilly land development in Thailand has occurred in both upland and highland zones and under the auspices of different Thai government agencies, for example, the Department of Land Development, the Royal Forestry Department, the Land Cooperatives Department, the Department of Agriculture, and the Public Welfare Department. In addition, special projects created by His Majesty the King of Thailand have been launched in many hilly areas of the northern and other regions of the country to solve the welfare problems of the hill tribes, the narcotics problem, the insurgency problem, and the natural resources endowment problem. Land development activity is an important part of the integrated development program conducted in part to solve these problems.

Development Strategies

At present, the potential for water catchment and forestry production in the mountains cannot be realized because of the destruction of forested areas by the extensive slash-and-burn cultivation. This cultivation form is practiced by the indigenous hill-tribe mountain farmers and by Thai peasants who are moving onto hilly, marginal land, away from the severe population pressure in some lowland areas of the country, particularly in the North. To tackle the problems, the Thailand government wrote national strategy guidelines for the highlands or hilly land development, as follows:

• Stabilize existing highland populations where they are through the provision of secure means of producing subsistence needs, plus a modest cash income conditional on the relinquishment of opium production by the highland populations.

• Resist any further migrations into highlands for the time being.

• Fully develop the forestry potential of the highlands.

• Proceed to further develop the agricultural potential of the highlands and allow further settlement only if and when the requirements of forest management and watershed protection allow.

For the highland development project to be successful, careful planning and implementation is necessarily at every stage. There are six phases of development:

1. Soil Survey and Land Suitability Classification Approach. To achieve the development goal through intensive farming, nondamaging, and permanent agricultural practices, the soil survey and land capability interpretation are first conducted in the project areas to collect soil and land information considered as limiting factors for permanent crop production in the highland areas. Soils found in the areas vary in characteristics and properties. The soils occur in an intermingled pattern, very difficult to delineate for a single or individual series on the map. Existing soil survey techniques and land suitability classification used in Thailand are thus oriented toward the needs of lowland, irrigated, and rainfed cultivation. As such, they are not suitable for the needs of permanent highland cultivation. The systematic soil survey is generally not feasible for the highland areas. The highland development project as a result has adopted the land suitability classification system based on potential suitability, where the main improvement is the implementation of soil conservation measures. In upland and highland areas of North Thailand, slope is the most dominant soil characteristic. Major slope phases are delineated as follows:

• Zero to 2 percent—land suitable for any type of land use if soils are not very shallow or very rocky or stony. No erosion control structures needed.

• Two to 35 percent—land suitable for any type of land use, provided the applicable erosion control structures (in possible combination with water retaining structures) are installed prior to the production of crops involving soil disturbance and/or the introduction of livestock.

• Thirty-five to 85 percent—land suitable for production of crops not involving soil disturbance. Some erosion control structures may be needed in combination with tree crop production on some soils.

• Greater than 85 percent—land not suited to any form of commercial production, with or without erosion control structures.

According to the National Forestry Policy issued in 1985, land with slopes greater than 35 percent is not recommended for general crop production. This land will be preserved as forest for watershed protection.

2. Soil and Water Conservation Approach.

2. Soil and Water Conservation Approach. Soil erosion is a serious natural resource hazard in Thailand. Soil, the foundation of agriculture, is being lost at an alarming rate. The Department of Land Development, in a 1980 publication entitled "Soil Erosion in Thailand," pointed out that about 17 million hectares, widely distributed throughout the country, had rates of soil erosion ranging from a medium to high degree of severity. The severity of soil erosion increases in highland or slopeland areas of North, Northeast, and Central Highlands of the country where shifting cultivation is widely practiced. Suspended sediment from all watersheds is estimated to be 27 million tons annually.

Soil erosion in Thailand threatens to be a more serous problem in the future. Population pressure and a land shortage in the lowlands of the country, particularly in the northern region, have resulted in a spontaneous movement of people to the uplands and highlands of the region. In northern Thailand it is estimated that destruction of forests has occurred at an annual rate of 3.6 percent over the last 5 years.

Because of the severe soil erosion problem in highland areas, soil and water conservation is an important part of the integrated development program. Careful consideration is given to ensure that conservation measures are appropriate, well-designed, and constructed to the highest possible standards. Structural measures are designed for all situations in the project areas because it is not possible to rely on farmers using suitable management practices, particularly in the initial years after development.

Many conservation structures are used in highland development projects:

• Graded banks of conventional design are used on all soil types, on slopes of 3 to 20 percent to divert runoff into natural waterways. On areas with a 10 to 15 percent slope, alternative designs are used, for example, small cross-section banks at close spacings.

• Level banks are constructed when adequate water disposal areas are not available. These banks are generally suitable only on permeable soils up to 10 percent slope because runoff disposal is by infiltration into the soil.

• Gully control structures are built to prevent further erosion of gullies and to act as silt traps. These structures often have the added advantage of storing surface water for livestock or domestic purposes.

The spacing of contour banks on 3 to 10 percent slopes is based on the vertical interval (VI) formula: for areas with annual rainfall less than 1,200 millimeters, $VI = 0.38$ [(slope %/2) + 2] m; for areas with annual rainfall greater than 1,200 millimeters, $VI = 0.30$ [(slope %/2) + 2] m.

• Bench terracing is one of the most important soil conservation practices in the hillslopes. There are two distinct types of bench terraces in Thailand. The first is the bench terrace constructed for vegetables, flowers, and short-term crops. The second is constructed for tree crops or orchards. Bench terracing is commonly practiced in the hilly land of northern and southern regions. In the South, bench terraces are constructed for rubber plantations. In the North, they are common for vegetables and on tea plantations. This type of soil conservation structure has not been accepted by the hill-tribe people because construction is rather costly and time-consuming.

• Hillside ditches are used together with natural and/or leguminous cover in orchards and areas of tree-crop cultivation. Spacings depend on the cultural practices required and types of tree crops grown. However, the gradient is usually 0.5 to 1 percent. The width of the hillside ditch may vary from 1 to 2 meters.

• Farm ponds form an integral part of the highland development program. The capacity of pond construction varies with topography, but on average is 5,000 to 10,000 cubic meters. The farming community uses these ponds for stock water and as a source of water for spray application of herbicides and pesticides during the cropping season. In addition, these ponds trap sediments from upslope to avoid sedimentation in river courses and reservoirs in the lowland areas.

In addition to the engineering measures, agronomic measures for soil conservation are used in the highland development project. These include cover crops and mulching. Cover crops are commonly used in orchards and on tree-crop plantations, including Para-rubber, mango, rambutan, and others. Leguminous plants are chosen because they fix nitrogen, as well as add organic matter and improve soil structure. The most common legume species used as covers on rubber and fruit tree plantations are *Pueraria phaseoloides, Centrosema pubescens,* and *Calopogonium mucunoides.*

Mulching is another measure for soil erosion control. It serves as groundcover for reducing runoff and soil loss, suppressing weeds, increasing organic matter in soils, supplying varying amounts of nutrients as the mulch decomposes, and increasing the moisture-holding capacity of the soil. In Thailand, mulching is often practiced by farmers using materials obtainable on their farms, but very definitely carried out in vegetable and fruit crops, like strawberries in northern Thailand.

3. Crop Management Approach. The purpose of crop management is to minimize soil loss and maximize soil fertility in terms of organic matter. The studies on crop management in the highland development areas have concentrated largely on the traditional crops, including upland glutinous rice, peanut, maize, soybeans, mungbean, sesame, and castorbean. Increased productivity can be achieved through a combination of the following:

• Raising individual crop yields through the use of better varieties, pest and disease control, improved weed control, attention to time of planting, plant population and plant distribution, legume innoculation, and more strategic use of fertilizers, as well as other crop culture changes.

• Increased unit-area production through intercropping.

• Increased seasonal production through a combination of relay or double-cropping in association with intercropping.

From research findings conducted by different agencies in northern Thailand, it can be concluded that stripcropping of rice-peanut or rice-sorghum causes less erosion than monocropping. It has also been found that stripcropping of peanut-rice using 10-meter-wide strips on 3 to 5 percent slopes can replace contour banks. In addition, a recommendation was made by scientists of the Land Development Department that a cropping system of upland rice followed by mungbean, combined with grass strips, can effectively control soil loss. The grass strip also provides mulch and/or animal feed. Alternatively, all kinds of useful perennial crops, particularly tea, coffee, and some fruit trees, can be cultivated within established grass strips. However, both soil conservation techniques and the choice of cropping system are currently matters of discussion for the parties involved in highland agricultural development. There are already many examples of soil conservation measures in the northern highlands, and it has been found that either grass or *Leuceana* strips have proved to be the most effective soil erosion control measures. From the standpoint of cropping systems, fruit trees and temperate plants are being evaluated, and a combination of fruit trees and annual cropping systems need to be investigated to determine effective and appropriate long-term systems that incorporate sound conservation techniques.

4. Woodlot Development Approach. Areas with slopes greater than 15 percent, or where soils are unsuitable for annual cropping, are normally allocated to woodlot development for fuel wood and charcoal production. Village woodlot associations are set up wherever the need is recognized, and farmers are requested to contribute their labor for planting the seedlings and to maintain the woodlot areas. The project develops the woodlot areas for the farmers.

There are two basic types of development:

• Full clearing and plowing to control regrowth, followed by the planting of superior tree species. Although relatively expensive, this method allows young seedlings to establish rapidly in the absence of competition from regrowth species.

• Enrichment that is normally practiced on areas considered to be too steep for normal clearing, or where the existing vegetation can be left and enriched by planting other species. The method is not suited to situations where competition from the existing vegetation can inhibit the establishment of the new seedlings.

The main genera planted to date are *Eucalyptus, Acacia,* and *Leucaena,* all of which are rapid-growing and suited to relatively infertile soils. A natural development of the woodlot program will be the introduction of fruit tree crops in areas where soil types and climatic conditions are favorable.

5. Extension Approach. Extension is an important aspect of the development package because of the wide range of activities undertaken by the project and the necessity to work closely with the farming community at all times during the planning, development, and follow-up stages. The extension staff is responsible for briefing farmers on the proposed development work, including discussion of the concept plan for a particular area. The extension staff also is responsible for helping farmers to understand all aspects of the development package and to make best use of their resources following development by using recommended soil conservation measures, seed, cultural practices, and others.

Activities undertaken by the project extension staff include:

• Collection and review of survey and research information.

• Conduct of farmer meetings for briefing, liaison, and coordination of the development program.

• Coordination between the research team and farmers regarding farming problems and possible solutions.

• Specific extension programs designed to overcome particular farming problems.

• Liaison with institutions, such as credit banks and the Department of Agricultural Extension, to ensure continuity in post-development years.

6. Research Approach. Research related to soil conservation is being focused on the following aspects:

• Experiments to test the formula currently being used for spacing banks.

• Crop management practices, such as stubble mulching, reduced tillage, and no-tillage. These are being investigated for their soil conservation benefits in Thailand.

• Crop management and soil erodibility factors in order to adapt the universal soil loss equation for soil loss prediction under different conditions in Thailand.

- The effect of plant spacings on soil erosion reduction.
- Conservation and land management practices as alternatives to mechanical earthworks, such as graded banks.
- Soil structural stability as affected by management practices, both during and after development.
- Revegetation methods for earthworks.

Research pertaining to soil fertility is concentrated on the increase of soil organic matter and deficiencies of nitrogen, phosphorus, and sulfur, which may occur in some soils of the project areas.

Agronomic research is directed at the immediate, practical problems of agricultural production in the development areas. The major emphasis is on collaborative experiments. These are planned in conjunction with farmers and implemented by farmers on their own land. The program includes:

- Varietal evaluation of upland rice, peanut, mungbean, and corn.
- Weed control using preemergence herbicides on maize, rice, and peanut.
- Fertilizer response of maize and rice cultivated on major soil series.
- Disease and pest control in cultivated crops.

Conclusion

The problem on the hilly land of Thailand, as in many parts of Asia with a similar agroenvironment, is that land pressures because of population increases have resulted in a spontaneous movement of people from the lowlands to the uplands and highlands of the country. In northern Thailand it is estimated that the forested area has been destroyed at an annual rate of 3.6 percent over the last 5 years. This causes loss of other natural resources, particularly soil resources, in the highland areas. In addition, there are problems related to narcotics, insurgency, and welfare of hill-tribes in the highlands as well, which the Thai government must urgently confront by formulating an integrated development plan. Therefore, land development works, including soil and water conservation practices on hillslopes, play an important role and are given high priority in the development program.

CONSERVATION HILLSLOPE FARMING IN AUSTRALIA

W. A. WATKINS

Conservation farming in Australia, particularly in hillslope areas, occurs mainly in the coastal plains and tablelands of the island continent. Wheat production especially presents a serious threat of land degradation, primarily because of soil erosion and soil structural decline. Over the last 10 years, however, increasing attention has been paid to steeper slopes. The principles of conservation farming are now being applied to hillslopes used for grazing and for horticultural crops, such as tropical fruits, nuts, and grapes.

Australia in Context

Although Australia is a large country—approximately 8 million square kilometers, 80 percent of its people live in urban centers, mainly on the coastline. The population is approaching 17 million.

The climate is arid; 70 percent of the land area is too dry for agriculture; and only about 10 percent is suitable for regular farming under natural rainfall. Irrigation is important in some of the major river systems (Figure 1).

The better watered areas used for farming are along the coast, the tablelands, and the slopes of the hinterland. These areas comprise the eastern sections of Queensland, New South Wales, Victoria, and Tasmania along the eastern seaboard of Australia (Figure 2). Other hillslope farming areas of lesser extent are located in South Australia and in the far southwestern corner of the continent.

In all of these areas, rainfall is the main agent of erosion. For agriculture, rainfall is typically unreliable and increasingly so as one moves from a temperate climate across southern Australia to a tropical climate in the north. Rainfall intensities in excess of 100 millimeters an hour are not uncommon, which lead to a severe erosion hazard on many cultivated soils and steep slopes.

Much of the inland is arid, with annual rainfall less than 250 millimeters. The drier parts of the country are used for pastoral grazing of sheep. Wind erosion is the main form of land degradation in these extensive areas.

Australia is an old landscape. Its soils have been subject to weathering and erosion for thousands of years. They are generally low in both chemical and physical attributes for productivity. Because of the arid climate, the soils are also low in organic matter by world standards and often are highly erodible as a result. Many subsoils are dispersible because of the strong influence of exchangeable sodium in their formation, which also contributes to their high erodibility.

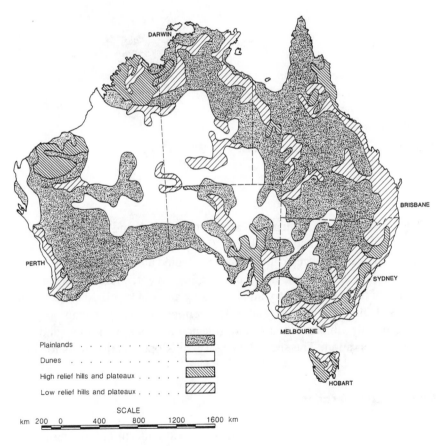

Plainlands . . . .

Dunes . . . .

High relief hills and plateaux . . . . .

Low relief hills and plateaux . . . . .

SCALE

km 200   0   400   800   1200   1600   km

Figure 1. Major landform groups of Australia.

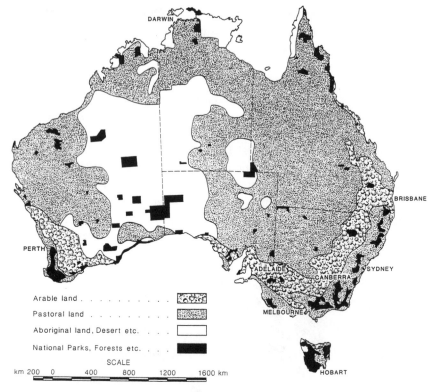

Figure 2. Major land use in Australia.

Hillslopes in Australia

The following broad categories are proposed to define the general land uses occurring: plains and lower slopes, 0-10 percent, cereal cropping, mixed farming, or grazing (sheep/cattle) in better watered areas and extensive grazing (sheep) in drier areas; hillslopes, 10-30 percent, grazing (sheep/cattle), natural timber, or forestry and increasing areas of specialist crops (such as vines, fruit, nuts, and vegetables); steep terrain, greater than 30 percent, generally timbered and often protected as catchment areas and for nature conservation. The second category, hillslopes, is the focus for this chapter.

Conservation Farming

Conservation farming in Australia is a broad concept embracing practices that aim to achieve the conservation of soil, water, and energy resources.

It involves using the land according to its capability and includes such practices as contour farming, reduced tillage, stubble retention, crop rotation, stripcropping, conservative stock and pasture management, and the installation of soil and water conservation works as appropriate.

The concept has been applied strongly to cereal growing, which is a mainstay of Australian agriculture. Because this use occurs mainly on sloping land (0-10 percent), it represents a potential for widespread soil erosion. Hence, the application of conservation farming has involved the use of structural works, combined with contour farming principles, reduced tillage, and the retention of crop residues (stubble), which have traditionally been burned.

However, the principles of conservation farming, as developed in the wheatlands, also apply to the areas of hillslope farming that involve more specialty crops and intensive grazing. These principles revolve around minimum disturbance of the soil and maximum retention of vegetative material to protect and improve it. These apply equally to extensive cropping, to intensive (specialist) cropping, and to grazing management. In Australia, conservation farming has now spread into areas of hillslope agriculture. It is proving to be of long-term benefit, both in terms of farm productivity and the control of land degradation.

Hillslope Farming in Australia

Most hillslope farming in Australia is carried out along the eastern tablelands, 50 to 250 kilometers inland from the coastline (Figure 1). The slopes involved are generally between 10 and 30 percent, although in the case of some specialty crops, such as vines or orchards, much flatter slopes are often used. The upper limit for cereal growing is in the region of 10 percent because of the erosion hazard and difficulty of machine operation. Above this limit, therefore, land is typically considered capable of grazing only, possibly with occasional cultivation or specialty cropping with intensive soil conservation protection by way of structural works and/or special practices.

Rainfall in these hillslope areas, which is more reliable than in the cereal-growing regions, typically ranges up to 1,200 millimeters or more near the coast and down to 600 millimeters on the inland side of the ranges. Hillslope soils vary widely, but because of the special needs of the more intensive farming systems in operation, they are frequently more chemically and physically fertile than those in the cereal belt. Basaltic soils (e.g., rhodic and humic ferralsols on the "Soil Map of the World") are often deep and well-structured, meeting the needs of many vegetable and fruit crops. Soils with podzolic features (e.g., Haplic and Luvic Yermosols and some Nitosols and Luvisols on the "Soil Map of the World") are also common on these slopes and widely used for less intensive farming operations.

Land Uses Involved

A variety of land uses are common on hillslopes typical of the Australian hinterland. These uses can be categorized by the type of farming or by the crops grown. In all cases, however, they require reliable rainfall, generally in excess of 600 millimeters, to be economically successful for temperate crops and in excess of 1,000 millimeters for tropical crops.

• *Vegetable crops.* While many of Australia's vegetable supplies are grown on alluvial soils, certain types, such as potatoes, are also widely grown on hillslopes. The widening variety of vegetables coming onto the market reflects the increasing use of hillslopes with good rainfall for growing these important foods.

• *Vines.* Australia has a number of premium wine grape-growing areas that are situated in hillslope regions. A wide range of soils and slopes may be involved, giving variety in character to the resulting wines.

• *Nuts and tropical fruits.* The number of tropical fruits grown on Australia's coastal hillslopes is increasing each year. Bananas, mangoes, paw-paws, avocadoes, pineapples, and macadamia nuts are among the main types grown.

• *Sugar cane.* Growth of cane on hillslopes is mainly carried out in Queensland because of the requirement for the right combination of soils, rainfall, and temperature.

• *Orchard crops.* Fruits, such as citrus, pome, and stone fruits, are grown in localized areas where a combination of soils, topography, aspect, and climate suit each individual fruit. Oranges, lemons, grapefruit, apples, pears, cherries, and plums are popular types.

• *Pasture grazing.* Sheep and cattle grazing would be the most widespread uses of hillslope areas, occurring from the drier parts to the coldest and wettest upland areas. Sheep are grown for wool and meat, while cattle are grown exclusively for meat.

• *Agroforestry.* This is a farming system that combines the growth of timber as a crop with other, more conventional agricultural activities, typically grazing.

• *Dairying.* Although predominantly a coastal hillslope activity, because of better rainfall occurrence, there are localized areas on the tablelands, favored by suitable soils and other factors, where dairying is carried out quite efficiently. The main product is fresh milk for human consumption or processing.

Land Degradation on Hillslopes

The main forms of land degradation on Australian hillslope areas are soil erosion by water; soil structural decline; and, in some cases, soil acidification. Tree decline also has been a problem in some tableland areas where natural ecosystems have been unduly disturbed. Ecological disturbance by overclearing on these hillslopes has also given rise to changes in the hydrological regime of discrete catchment areas, resulting in the occurrence of dryland salinization further downstream on lower slopes.

Soil erosion is, however, the main concern. It has been particularly severe on the steeper slopes and more erodible soils. Farming operations involving cultivation are especially responsible for serious soil losses due to erosion. Where topsoils are subjected to sheet erosion, nutrient losses can also be high, leading to reduced yield potential on the soil concerned. As well as these on-site effects, the movement of soil from slopes frequently results in off-site damage to fences, streams, and reservoirs in the form of sedimentation and/or eutrophication. The quality of surface water supplies also can be adversely affected. Overall, the value and productivity of the land is reduced by erosion, and the hillslope contribution to a stable catchment and water supply area is diminished.

In some regions of particular climate/geology/landform/soil combinations, landslips are a serious problem on steep hillslopes. These represent an extreme form of erosion that is difficult and expensive to treat. In most instances, the land concerned is best allowed to return to its original forested condition.

Soil structural decline results from over-cultivation of the soil for cropping. Some soils have little resistance to the aggressive effects of tillage implements and their over-use; therefore, their natural aggregation is quickly destroyed under a cropping system. This results in lower infiltration of rainfall, poor root aeration and penetration, and the tendency for soil surfaces to seal. Plant growth is retarded and the erosion hazard is increased. The way to overcome this problem is to reduce the intensity of cultivation through use of less aggressive implements and fewer tillage operations. Crop residues should be retained and crop-pasture rotations encouraged in order to protect the soil and improve its organic content. An adjunct to these practices is the application of herbicides for weed control.

Soil acidification is a problem that is often quite natural in better rainfall areas because of normal leaching effects. However, in many tableland regions under improved pasture management, pH levels have dropped by one unit or more over approximately 50 years. Many Australian soils are deficient in phosphorus, and yearly additions of phosphorus fertilizer over this period of time have assisted the acidification. Many farmers with hillslope enterprises are now liming to improve pH levels; in some soils a pH of 5.0 or less seriously affects pasture growth. This leads to lower animal production and increased soil erosion.

Broad Conservation Strategies

The broad approach to soil and land conservation in Australia aims to combine the principles of conservation farming with those of total catchment management. Total catchment management is a concept whereby land use and management, including management of soil, water, and other biophysical resources, is integrated on a catchment basis. Such management is achieved by the coordination of policies and activities of relevant departments, authorities, companies, and individuals who have responsibilities for the management of land within catchments. In this way, and through land resource planning according to capability, sustainable land use can be achieved, along with the protection of soil, water, vegetation, and environmental quality generally. Flow-on benefits are achieved for wildlife, species diversity, and landscape aesthetics.

This approach achieves substantial and material benefits for the community and for the individual landholder. Not only is land degradation in local areas controlled, but also the stability and productivity of whole river catchments is assured for the future. Clean water supplies are guaranteed, and maintenance costs of roads, communication corridors, reservoirs, and harbors are reduced. The quality of life in whole regions is enhanced.

The secret to success is community involvement—the integration of the actions of the individual land manager with those of community groups and various levels of government. Our example is the current action being taken in the Murray-Darling catchment in southeastern Australia (Figure 3). This area comprises more than 1 million square kilometers of agricultural land in the most populous part of Australia, which produces about one-third of the country's agricultural output. It involves four states and the Australian Capital Territory in a joint plan to address a wide range of land degradation issues in an integrated fashion. The plan hinges on major community involvement (at local and regional levels) to complement the major actions that can only be taken by governments. Examples of government actions are tree-clearing controls, major salinity control works, and the implementation of subcatchment soil conservation schemes. Another key element in the plan is a major initiative to encourage more tree planting on farms, particularly where dryland salinity is a problem.

Specific Conservation Farming Solutions

Conservation farming techniques are applied to various land uses in hillslope areas:

Vegetable Crops. The main problems associated with vegetable growing on slopes are the frequency of bare ground; the use of the rotary hoe, which gives a highly erodible seedbed; and the requirement for up-and-down cropping to allow weed control or hilling (e.g., for beans, peas, potatoes). These factors all give rise to a high erosion hazard.

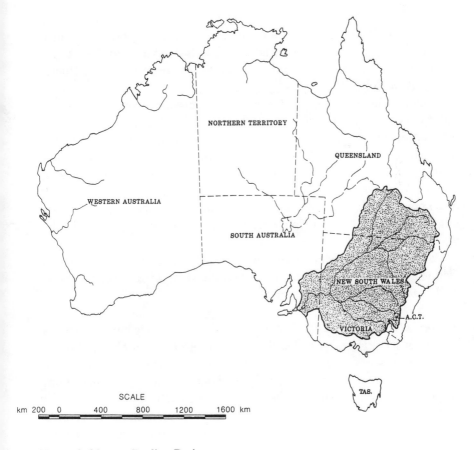

Figure 3. Murray-Darling Basin.

In concert with the principles of conservation farming, the following practices have been developed to restrict erosion in vegetable cropping areas:

• Use of grass-lined diversion channels between cropped areas to carry runoff away.

• Use of green manure crops, which are worked into the soil between cropping phases.

• Virtual elimination of cultivation by the use of black plastic sheet mulch to control weeds, usually in conjunction with drip irrigation.

• Use of advanced seedlings to reduce the number of cultivations required and exposure to erosive rains.

• Use of lime to counteract the acid soil problem is economically feasible in vegetable crops because of their typically high value.

• Use of semipermanent sod culture in small, highly intensive enterprises.

• Herbicide use for weed control, thus reducing need for cultivation.

Vines. Grape production for wine-making is a major agricultural industry in New South Wales and South Australia. The vines are grown on a range of soils and slopes, but emphasis here is on hillslope vineyards. These are particularly significant in the Barossa Valley, South Australia, and the Hunter Valley, New South Wales.

Development of the contour principle is the basis of conservation farming in hillslope vineyards. Contour layout is now at a highly advanced stage that can be adapted to a range of situations or landholder requirements. Strict contours can be varied to achieve straight vine rows, allowing easy maintenance and mechanical operations, but still achieving proper erosion control. Waterways and contour banks to dispose of runoff safely can each be combined with roads for easy access to all parts of the vineyard. Grass strips between vine rows help reduce runoff and erosion. Mulching of the vines is encouraged.

Many vignerons prefer to cultivate along the rows, however. This is facilitated by having straight rows across the slope or true contour rows as dictated by a site's topography.

Tropical Fruits and Nuts. The increased interest among banana growers in soil conservation is typical of the concern for the environment of many new entrepreneurs in the expanding area of tropical fruit production. Site selection and planning of the plantation layout is seen as particularly important. Again, the contour principle is important; it forms the basis of the design of access and operations within the plantation. Bananas typically are grown on steep slopes and in high rainfall areas. Surface runoff management is essential on these areas. Appropriately graded roads are used to convey surplus water across a slope and into stable watercourses, which are maintained in a vegetated condition. Care with clearing prior to plantation establishment is essential so maximum vegetative cover is retained.

Mulching between tree rows is encouraged, and despite plant disease problems, legislation has now been changed to allow for ground-cover plants to be grown to a maximum height of 30 centimeters. Legumes, such as *Vicia villosa* and *Dolichos lablab*, have been grown for this purpose, as have some clovers and the dwarf peanut *Arachis pintoi*.

Other tropical fruit trees have special requirements that must be integrated with sound conservation management. Mulching is always regarded as desirable; it aids soil and moisture conservation and improves soil organic matter content. Some tree crops benefit from a bare soil surface being maintained around each tree or from being grown on a mound. These particular requirements have to be integrated with conservation farming principles in the design and operation of the plantation. Drainage is especially important for some fruit trees, and contour rows may not be acceptable for this reason. Vegetative methods then must be introduced, and interrow management becomes all the more important. Harvesting requirements for some fruit trees may also impose constraints on a conservation farming system.

Sugar Cane. Sugar cane in New South Wales is grown on alluvial flats; however, in northern Australia cane extends on to hillslopes. On these hillslopes, minimum tillage, supplemented with herbicide application for weed control, is being promoted. Conservation farming techniques have been promoted on their cost-saving advantages primarily, with improved soil structure as an added benefit.

The Mackay region in Queensland provides a good example of conservation farming of sugar cane on hillslopes. Soil erosion is a major problem on sloping canelands in the Mackay region. Cultivation practices have contributed to a gradual but accelerating deterioration of soil structure, leading to increased runoff and more erosion. Crop residue retention and reduced cultivation practices are seen as means of reducing and controlling the problem.

Because the problem of erosion was greatest on newly planted cane and fallow paddocks, it was decided to concentrate on ratoon cane for four reasons: (1) It occupied 70 percent of assigned caneland; (2) crop residue was available after harvest; (3) change in farm management would be less radical; and (4) new techniques would be more readily adopted by farmers.

Crop residue retention and reduced cultivation are based on machinery that has been developed to work through trash, leaving it on the soil surface, while applying fertilizer and breaking up compacted soil layers.

Initial success was supported by better herbicide technology—spray equipment and application technology. Adoption levels in ratoon cane are high. Since commencement of the conservation farming program in 1984, 75 percent of Mackay sugar cane farmers now retain their crop residues, 80 percent practice minimum tillage, and 25 percent use reduced tillage.

Green cane harvesting will be promoted in the future. Now, however, it is impeded by sugar quality problems during milling, physical limitations of harvesters, and problems associated with specific varieties.

Orchard Crops. Fruit crops, such as apples, oranges, and cherries, have been grown under conservation farming conditions for many years in Australia. Traditional ideas of maintaining a cultivated tilth between the trees meant that in erosion-prone areas trees had to be planted on the contour and banks installed every few rows to control runoff during heavy rains. These banks led the runoff into a grassed waterway, which then conveyed it safely down the slope into a dam or silt trap. Any surplus runoff is allowed to flow laterally into a stable watercourse.

The advent of slashers and drip irrigation saw a form of sod culture become popular in many orchards. A ground cover between trees improves soil conditions and also helps to control soil erosion; this way is more consistent with a conservation farming approach. The cover must be kept short by slashing to limit water use and promote ground coverage.

Pasture Grazing. The most widespread use of hillslope areas in Australia is for grazing of native or semi-improved pastures by sheep or cattle. The principles of conservation farming are applied to these areas mainly by pasture improvement and stock management.

Pasture improvement on hillslopes is carried out by introducing more productive grass species in a sod seeding operation or by aerial sowing. This involves sowing the new seed mixture directly into an existing sward with minimum soil disturbance. The sward typically is grazed down hard and possibly reduced in vigor by applying a herbicide prior to seeding. Fertilization of pastures is important, particularly where grazing is intensive. Where acidification of soils is a problem, regular liming is necessary to maintain top productivity. Regular slashing also may be necessary to keep the herbage in a palatable condition and to encourage new growth.

Stock management from a conservation viewpoint involves stocking at rates or in a manner that encourages maximum coverage of the soil by vegetation. This may mean modest numbers of sheep or cattle per hectare for long periods, depending on climatic conditions, or larger numbers for a shorter, more intensive grazing phase. The latter method ensures that pasture is grazed more uniformly and thus kept more vigorous. However, it must be managed carefully so that overgrazing does not occur. This normally is achieved by use of a rotational system.

Another important aspect of conservation grazing is that pasture land should not be overgrazed when soils are wet. This tends to damage soil structure and reverse the positive effects of pasture on soil physical conditions. A prudent grazing manager will ensure that stock is moved to the better drained locations during and after long periods of soaking rain.

Agroforestry. This farming system, carried out increasingly in hillslope areas, combines the growing of commercial timber with normal agricultural practices. It may involve the commercial use of native trees as well as the planting and management of quicker growing trees, such as *Pinus radiata.* Native Gums (*Eucalyptus* spp.) and wattles (*Acacia* spp.) are increasingly popular as well because they also provide wildlife habitat.

Agroforestry is often combined with a grazing enterprise. With appropriately spaced tree plantings, land can be used for grazing and timber production at the same time. From a conservation viewpoint, this achieves the soil stability associated with well-managed pasture land, the protection of stock and soil provided by trees, and the hydrologic balance required for the prevention of salinization on lower slopes. Economically, it provides a guarantee of both short-term and long-term financial returns.

Dairying. Dairying is carried out on the more productive hillslopes on the coastal side of the tablelands, where rainfall is reliable and adequate to maintain pasture growth throughout much of the year. As with other grazing areas, under good management dairying is a conservative land use, requiring that much of the land remain under vigorous pasture cover for most of the time. In a conservation farming context, therefore, management aims to preserve that cover and, when necessary, replace it using minimal soil disturbance techniques.

Dairying is an intensive land use. Because many coastal soils are highly acid, the tendency for further acidification is strong in a number of areas. Balanced fertilizer application and careful monitoring of soil pH are thus important for the modern dairy enterprise.

Some Conclusions

The wider impacts of land degradation and the implications of conservation farming in hillslope areas come sharply into focus when considered in a catchment context. These hillslopes are frequently the critical upper slopes of important water supply catchments, and their stability against degradation may, therefore, be just as important as their productive use. The concept of total catchment management seeks to ensure the compatibility of these two attributes—catchment stability and long-term productivity. The control of land degradation on hillslopes is vital because of its possible influence on lower areas through sedimentation, salinization, and adverse effects on water quality. On-site effects also are important because many of the land uses on hillslopes are intensive and produce high-value crops. Degradation can, therefore, give rise to significant physical as well as economic damage to these hillslope enterprises.

Conservation farming is an integral part of a total catchment approach to the management of a wide range of agricultural operations in hillslope country. Relying as it does on the improvement of the soil through the use of vegetation, reduced disturbance, and the contour principle for layout and operations of farming enterprises, it provides the basis for productive use of hillslopes consistent with conservation of the environment associated with them.

Individual farmers on the hillslopes can benefit from conservation farming provided they are prepared to come to terms with the higher level of farm management that may be required to implement it fully. Prolonged land and soil degradation lead to lower yields, lower land values, increasing difficulty of farm management, and higher farming costs. Conservation farming, carefully and intelligently applied, can reverse these trends toward increased productivity and conservation of the environment for future generations.

However, for these high ideals to be fully achieved, individuals must see the broader implications of conservation farming from a community perspective. They must join with their neighbors to address wider issues, such as land salinization, water pollution, tree decline, and the loss of native flora and fauna. These require joint action, and community groups must interact with and lobby government bodies in an effort to get appropriate levels of funding, coordination, and expertise focused on the problems to ensure that they are solved to the benefit of the community as a whole.

HILLSLOPE FARMING
IN KOREA

IN SANG JO

Korea is a mountainous penin-
sula extending southeast from Manchuria. Most of the cultivated land, paddy,
and upland are in sloping areas, except for broad alluvial plains and tidal
land. Rational use of limited land is important because the population density
is high. Efforts have been made to extend arable land by reclaiming slopeland
and tidal land. Rice sufficiency was achieved recently, and the people's food
pattern is changing quickly by improvement in the social environment.
Therefore, interest in upland farming must focus on vegetables, fruits, and
other high-income crops.

Agricultural Land

Agricultural land in Korea is 2.1 million hectares, 21.6 percent of the country's area. Paddy land is 13.6 percent of the total, upland 8.0 percent. Forest
is targeted for conversion to increase the area for agriculture and industry or
housing (Table 1). Only 26.7 percent of the arable land is level, and this contains mostly paddy soils. Upland is located primarily on slopes of 7 to 15 percent. Almost 40 percent of the cultivated land is on slopes of more than 7
percent (Table 2). More than half of the arable land is less than 100 meters
above sea level (Table 3). Some soils are at an altitude of 500 meters or more.

Slopeland Reclamation

Soils have been classified as suitable for upland, orchard, or grassland
by considering various soil characteristics. Each soil could be recommended

for many kinds of land use, but the most favorable land use must be chosen on the basis of economic, social, or political considerations.

Vegetables are recommended only for slopes up to 7 percent; cereals and root crops for slopes up to 15 percent; orchard, mulberry, and intensive grassland for slopes up to 30 percent; and only grass or fruit trees on slopes exceeding 30 percent.

Contour cropping (up to 7 percent), contour stripcropping (7 to 30 per-

Table 1. Utilization of national land area in Korea, 1987 (11).

| Land Use | Arable Land | | | | | |
	Paddy	Upland	Total	Forest	Other	Total
Area (1,000 ha)	1,352	791	2,134	6,516	1,258	9,917
Ratio (%)	13.6	8.0	21.6	65.7	12.7	100.0

Table 2. Distribution of cultivated land (1,000 hectares) by slope (2).

| Land Category | Slope (%) | | | | | | |
	<2	2-7	7-15	15-30	30-60	>60	Total
Paddy	530	478	215	45	-	-	1,268
Upland (nonirrigated)	78	260	339	169	20	2	868
Orchard	18	29	42	25	4	-	118
Grassland	3	24	40	18	15	1	101
Total	629	791	636	257	39	3	2,355
Ratio	26.7	33.6	27.0	10.9	1.7	0.1	100.0

Table 3. Distribution of arable land (1,000 hectares) by altitude.

| Land Category | Altitude (meters above sea level) | | | | | | |
	<100	100-200	200-300	300-400	400-500	>500	Total
Paddy	935	206	73	30	16	8	1,268
Upland	504	171	86	52	21	34	868

Table 4. Land use recommendations for reclaimable land (2).

| | Surveyed Area | Reclaimable land | | | | Forest |
		Upland	Orchard	Grass	Total	
Area (1,000 ha)	3,828	221	294	1,610	2,125	1,703
Ratio (%)	100	5.8	7.7	42.0	55.5	44.5

Table 5. Reclaimed area (hectares) of slopeland (12).

1957-70	1971-75	1976-70	1981-85	1986-87	Total
151,183	15,098	18,112	5,834	3,528	193,755

Table 6. Criteria for classification of upland soil types in Korea.

Criterion	Well Adapted	Sandy Textured	Heavy Clayey	Newly Reclaimed	Plateau	Volcanic Ash
1) Soil productivity	High	Very low	Low	Moderate	Moderate	Low
2) Topography	Coastal Plains Alluvial plains Valleys and fans Lava plains	Coastal Plains River sides Hilly Mountain foot	Old alluvial terraces Mountain foots Hilly Lava plains	Valleys and fans Mountain foots	Plateau	Lava terraces Cinder cones
3) Soil requirement						
a. Drainage class	Well Moderately well	Somewhat excessively well	Well Moderately well	Somewhat excessively well	Well	Well
b. Texture family	Clay loam Loam Sandy loam	Sand Skeletal	Clay Clay loam	Clay loam Sandy loam Skeletal	Clay Clay loam	Silty clay loam
c. Soil color	Brown	Brown	Brown Red	Brown Red	Very dark Black	Very dark Black
d. Available depth	>50	<50	>50	<20	<20	<20
e. Slope degree (%)	<30	<30	<30	<30	<30	<30
Area (ha)	358,970	190,975	122,562	164,168	2,508	20,354
Percent	41.8	22.2	14.3	19.1	0.3	2.3

cent), and terracing (30 to 60 percent) are recommended for soil conservation (*14*).

Reclaimable land was found to be 2.13 million hectares as a result of a detailed soil survey. This is mostly recommended to be grassland, but 221,000 hectares of upland and 294,000 hectares of orchard also are important resources for the country's population (Table 4).

Slopeland reclamation was actively conducted by public or private interests in the 1960s, and it continued to 1980. Then it began to slow. A reclamation area of 193,755 hectares is not small compared to the total cultivated land of 2.1 million hectares (Table 5).

Upland soils are classified in six general classes according to dominant characteristics (Table 6). It is difficult for farmers or extension workers to understand the 377 soils series, but they can easily remember the type of soil. Each type of soil is described by soil characteristics and thus has meaning to farmers and extension workers when related to recommended improvement practices. Well-adapted farming soil amounts to only 358,970 hectares. Sandy, heavy clayey, newly reclaimed, and volcanic ash soils have more than one limiting factor.

Organic matter and base saturation in reclaimed soils are generally less than half of the values in cultivated land; available phosphorus is less than one-tenth of that in cultivated land (Table 7).

Sloping soils have low moisture retention because of their thin surface

Table 7. Soil properties by management type (*1*).

Management Type	pH	O.M. (%)	Available P_2O_5 (ppm)	Base Saturation (%)	Available Water (%)	Strength (MP)*	Texture	Plow Layer (cm)	Bulk Density (g/cm³)
Reclaimed soil	5.3	0.9	11	26	10	1.17	SL	7.5	1.5
Cultivated land	5.7	2.0	114	60	15	0.63	L	12.5	1.4
Ideal value	6.5	3.0	200	80	20	0.47	L	20.0	1.3

*Megapascal.

Table 8. Changes of soil characteristics by the slope in soybean fields.

Slope (%)	Plow Layer (cm)	Available Soil Depth (cm)	Strength (MP) Topsoil	Strength (MP) Subsoil	Available P_2O_5 (ppm)
A (0-2)	12.8	47.4	0.10	0.30	104
B (2-7)	11.8	48.5	0.18	0.43	99
C (7-15)	10.9	38.9	0.18	0.44	78
D (15-30)	10.3	37.5	0.20	0.45	64

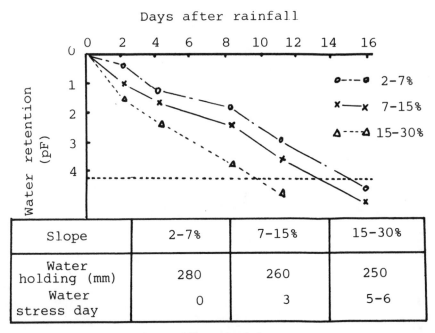

Figure 1. Soil water retention on different land slopes.

layer and compact structure. The penetration of rainwater into the deep soil is limited, and plants are easily damaged by drought (Figure 1) (*13*). Plow layer, available soil depth, and available phosphorus are lower, but soil strength is higher with increasing land steepness (Table 8) (*8*).

Soil Improvements

Physical Improvements. Plant growth is affected by soil physical and chemical properties, such as soil bulk density, strength, pH, and available soil depth.

The plow layer was found to be a most important factor in controlling the plant growth of red pepper (*6*), soybeans (*8*), and rice (*7*). Deep plowing prepares for deep root development and higher yields (Table 9).

Physical properties of subsoils from different treatments after soybean harvest and the yields are shown in table 10. The check plot had a bulk density of 1.49 and 0.73 megapascals in strength. Porosity increased and strength decreased by soil layer improvement, such as chiseling, trenching, and vertical mulching. Soybean and barley yields increased as physical properties improved.

Table 9. Soil physical and chemical properties and plant growth in red pepper fields.

Growth	Plow Layer (cm)	Available Depth (cm)	Root Zone (cm)	Bulk Density		Strength (MP)	pH	Phosphorus (ppm)	Organic Matter (%)	Stem Length (cm)	Stem Diameter (cm)
				Topsoil	Subsoil						
Very well	15.1	91	29.7	1.06	1.22	0.41	5.2	1,051	2.67	99.5	1.55
Well	13.9	89	28.5	1.06	1.26	0.42	5.4	702	1.94	87.1	1.38
Medium	12.2	88	26.3	1.09	1.32	0.50	5.1	722	2.38	77.0	1.24
Poor	9.9	49	23.7	1.13	1.38	0.60	4.9	487	2.27	70.8	1.14
Very poor	9.7	45	22.4	1.15	1.38	0.68	4.9	267	1.94	55.6	0.90
Average	12.2	72.4	26.1	1.10	1.30	0.52	5.1	646	2.24	78.0	1.24

Table 10. Physical properties of subsoil after soybean harvest (4).

Treatment	Bulk Density	Porosity (%)	Strength (MP)	Yield (kg/ha) Soybean	Barley
Check	1.49	44.0	0.73	1,814	2,248
Grass band	1.44	45.9	0.54	2,009	2,439
Chiseling	1.35	49.1	0.40	2,282	2,824
Trenching	1.30	51.1	0.35	2,212	3,063
Vertical mulch	1.34	49.4	0.35	2,182	2,822

Table 11. Soil loss by cropping system.

	Bare Soil	Corn	Wheat + Soybean	Barley + Corn	Upland Rice	Barley + Soybean	Grass
Soil loss (t/ha)	128	54	53	51	45	31	5

Soil loss was more affected by slope percentage than by slope length in barley and soybean farming (Figure 2). Soil loss increased gradually with increasing slope, except that the soil loss from a slope 10 meters in length was not greatly different than from slopes between 10 and 20 percent.

Soil loss is controlled by physical improvement. Chiseling reduces soil loss to half, a grass strip to one-third, mulching to one-seventh, and trenching plus mulching to only one-tenth (Figure 3).

Table 11 compares soil loss for different cropping systems (9). There

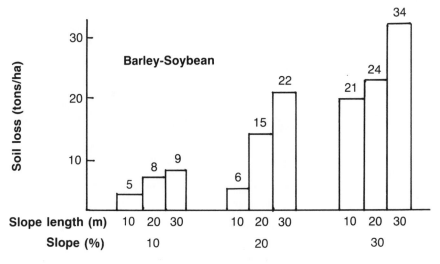

Figure 2. Soil loss of different slope and slope length.

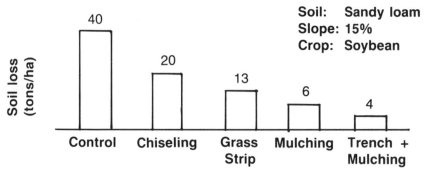

Figure 3. Soil loss and runoff from different soil management.

were no great differences between cropping systems. But the barley-soybean system and especially grass reduced soil loss.

Integrated Improvement. Various crops were cultivated on slopeland under gradually increasing soil improvement factors (*10*). Yields increased from 71 to 200 percent by integrated improvement (Table 12). The effects were greatest in the order of soybean > sesame > sweet potato > corn.

Since 1984, the Agricultural Sciences Institute has investigated the rate of maturation on newly reclaimed soil (*5*). Major upland crops were planted on loam soils with a 20 percent slope after one of the following improvements—deep plowing, compost, liming, phosphorus, and integrated

Table 12. Effect of soil improvements on the yield of various crops in newly reclaimed soil.

	Crop Yield (t/ha)						
Treatment	Soybean	Corn	Sweet Potato	Sesame	Barley after Soybean	Barley after Sweet Potato	Wheat
1. Standard (NPK)	1.08	2.82	17.40	0.23	1.46	1.91	1.89
2. Lime	2.35	2.58	20.08	0.43	2.43	3.76	2.55
3. Heavy-fused phosphate*	2.44	4.20	26.10	0.54	3.06	4.04	2.24
4. Lime + phosphate	2.42	3.76	25.98	0.49	3.13	4.34	2.89
5. Lime + phosphate + compost	2.81	6.04	31.58	0.68	3.83	4.26	4.05
6. Lime + phosphate + compost + plowing	2.90	6.49	32.58	0.57	3.95	4.40	3.23

*Heavy-fused phosphate was applied equivalent to the phosphate absorption coefficient of soil.

Table 13. Effects of integrated soil improvement factors on crop yield, 1984-1988.

Treatment Crop	Control Percent (Yield)		Deep Plowing	Compost	Lime	Phosphate	Integrated Improvement
Soybean	100	(1.64 t/ha)	118	108	118	115	129
Barley	100	(3.43 t/ha)	101	116	102	108	115
Sesame	100	(0.60 t/ha)	113	110	107	107	116
Buckwheat	100	(0.64 t/ha)	110	119	102	110	136
Radish	100	(50.8 t/ha)	148	144	130	114	174
Jobs tear	100	(1.45 t/ha)	134	116	122	128	149
Corn (silage)	100	(35.1 t/ha)	184	124	153	158	226
Sweet potato	100	(20.5 t/ha)	148	132	122	153	159
Garlic	100	(2.59 t/ha)	163	132	149	190	224

Table 14. Recommendations for soil improvement on different soil types.

Soil Improvement	Well Adapted	Sandy	Heavy Clayey	Newly Reclaimed	Volcanic Ash
Deep plowing	•	-	•	•	•
Compost	•	•	•	•	•
Lime	•	•	•	•	•
Micronutrient	-	-	-	•	•
Additional P, K	•	•	•	•	•
Area (ha)	358,970	190,975	122,562	164,168	20,354

improvement with all the above treatments (Table 13). Among the individual factors, plowing was most efficient for increasing yields when followed by phosphorus, lime, and compost. Crop yields were increased 15 to 126 percent by integrated improvement.

From the various research results, soil improvement recommendations for upland soil types were established (Table 14). Compost, lime, and additional phosphorus and potassium are needed on all upland soils.

In Summary

In Korea, 39.7 percent of all cultivated land has a slope exceeding 7 percent; 32.6 percent of the arable soils are at an altitude higher than 100 meters above sea level; and 2.13 million hectares of mountain land have been recommended for reclamation.

Crop growth was greatly influenced by plow-layer thickness and bulk density of the soils. Physical and chemical improvements, such as deep plowing, compost, lime, and phosphorus, were very beneficial for crop growth. Integrated soil improvement increased crop yields 15 to 126 percent.

Soil water balance and soil erosion control also are important in slopeland farming. Recommendations for soil improvement of upland types, and climatical zone grouping for cropping systems are very useful for improved farming.

REFERENCES

1. Agricultural Sciences Institute. 1978. *Major experiment research achievements and research target.* Suweon, Korea.
2. Agricultural Sciences Institute. 1983. *Detailed soil survey results of Korean soils.* Suweon, Korea.
3. Agricultural Sciences Institute. 1985. *Soils of Korea.* Suweon, Korea.
4. Im, J. N., Y. K. Cho, and D. H. Kim. 1978. *Studies on soil erosion control in newly reclaimed soil.* Research Report. Rural Development Administration, Suweon, Korea, 27(2): 11-20.
5. Jo, I. S., B. H. Hur, and K. H. Han. 1988. *Early maturing practices of sloped land.* Agricultural Sciences Institute, Suweon, Korea. pp. 145-153.
6. Jo, I. S., B. K. Hur, L. Y. Kim, Y. K. Jo, and K. T. Um. 1987. *Soil physio-chemical properties of redpepper fields and plant growth.* Journal of the Korean Society of Soil Sciences and Fertilizer 20(3): 205-208.
7. Jo, I. S., B. K. Hur, S. K. Kim, T. K. Cho, K. T. Um, and M. S. Kim. 1986. *Soil physical properties of the nationwide high-yielding paddy fields.* Research Report. Rural Development Administration, Suweon, Korea, 28(2): 1-5.
8. Jo, I. S., L. Y. Kim, and K. T. Um. 1988. *Relation between soil physico-chemical properties and growth soybean in upland soils.* Research Report. Rural Development Administration, Suweon, Korea, 30(2): 1-5.
9. Koh, M. H., P. K. Jung, and K. T. Um. 1982. *Determining the soil loss under different cropping system.* Agricultural Sciences Institute, Suweon, Korea. pp. 357-372.
10. Lee, C. S., and I. S. Ryu. 1975. *Study on the development of hillside soils.* Agricultural Sciences Institute, Suweon, Korea. pp. 125-135.
11. Ministry of Agriculture, Forestry and Fisheries. 1988. *Statistical yearbook of agriculture, forestry and fisheries.* Seoul, Korea.
12. Ministry of Agriculture, Forestry and Fisheries. 1988. *Yearbook of land and water development statistics.* Seoul, Korea. pp. 556-557.
13. Park, C. S., D. S. Oh, K. T. Um, and S. H. Kim. 1985. *Survey on soil water changes at different slope.* Agricultural Sciences Institute, Suweon, Korea. pp. 135-149.
14. Rural Development Administration. 1974. *Farming technics of newly reclaimed land.* Suweon, Korea.

POLICY AND STRATEGY

3

EFFECTIVE RESOURCE CONSERVATION ON HILLSLOPES

S. A. EL-SWAIFY

The necessary elements for planning and implementing effective conservation for sustainable agriculture on hillslopes are technological (biological and physical), economic, social, and political. Technological elements include appropriate selection of land uses to match site characteristics, design and use of protective management systems to preserve the stability of the vulnerable resource base, and placing strong emphases on productivity-enhancing agronomic practices to assure short-term benefits as well as long-term sustainability.

Economic, social, and political elements are more complex and interactive than are technological elements, and they are not so easily differentiated as a result. They include adopting a clear national strategy and enforceable policies for appropriate land use designations, increasing community awareness of erosion causes and impacts, improving land tenure systems, extending appropriate technologies effectively to farmers, assuring the necessary coordination among the various institutions involved in development projects, and maximizing community involvement during all phases of project design, implementation, and evaluation.

Long-term benefits of effective conservation can be realized by preventing or reversing the well-documented on-site and off-site impacts of soil erosion. Losses of soil depth, physical quality, chemical or nutritional quality, and biological quality (soil organic matter and beneficial organisms) have clear and predictable effects on crop productivity. Highly weathered tropical soils are more vulnerable to these effects than are temperate soils. When these soils lie in upland catchment areas, an overall degradation ensues in the quality and performance of the watershed. Excessive runoff and sediment generation causes economic losses in the form of water wasted for agriculture and power generation as well as the flooding and burial of lowlands; siltation and reduction in the storage capacity and hydropower-generating value of dams; destruction of life, roads, and property; deterioration in the quality of surface water supplies, fisheries, and reefs; and other downstream damages.

Short-term effects may arise from any of the above phenomena when catastrophic rainfall and runoff events cause the rapid acceleration of erosional processes. However, the more insidious, but continuous, loss of valuable water as uncontrolled surface runoff, which is unavailable for use by crops, causes major short-term damage to farming systems, particularly under rainfed conditions. Preventing or reversing this effect by using conservation practices that enhance maximum water infiltration and storage in the root zone or harnessing excessive runoff for recycling have been shown to pay handsome and rapid dividends to farm productivity. Furthermore, research has shown that the efficiency of stored soil-water use by crops increases with subsequent increases in productivity.

Design Elements for Effective Conservation

Technological Elements. A clear and preferably quantitative understanding of the physical and biological factors that cause the manifestation of excessive runoff and erosion is important for planning preventive measures and for designing monitoring programs to evaluate the performance of these measures. In general, these factors can be divided into two categories: baseline site characteristics and management strategies.

Baseline Site Characteristics. Climate, soil, and topography combine to determine the (maximum) erosion potential—the erosion expressed without control practices—at a given site. Models are available for predicting soil loss when quantitative values are provided for the aggressiveness of climatic agents (rainfall, runoff, wind), the susceptibility of soil, and the induciveness of topography (steepness, length, shape, and complexity of slope).

Unfortunately, most information available for quantifying these parameters is site-specific. Similarly, the available models recommended for their application are empirically derived and designed for temperate, "conventional" cropland. Thus, the data base for the critical factors of rainfall-runoff erosivity, soil erodibility (detachabilty, transportability, entrainability, rillability, gullying or mass-wasting potential, and depositional potential), and influences of topography are scarce, at best, for hilly areas in general and for those in the tropics and subtropics in particular. Similarly, few validations have been made of predictive empirical or process models in such areas. The lack of reliable quantitative tools for predicting and controlling runoff and erosion has often led to the adoption of imported, untested technologies and remains the strongest technical limitation for prescribing effective conservation practices on harsh landscapes.

Deficiencies in the technical information base have also perpetuated the excessive dependence on what seem to be universal but actually are site-specific and arbitrarily prescribed engineering practices, rather than application of sound scientific principles. Recent trends in the formulation of process-based erosion models promise to rectify some of the deficiencies inherent in empirical models. Ideally, a compromise is needed to reconcile the two approaches and assure that existing information is not abandoned altogether but used effectively in new initiatives. It is now also increasingly recognized that the interactions among a site's climate, soil, and topography are not universally uniform and that the role of productivity-enhancing crop and soil management practices may be more important than structural measures in imparting long-term sustainability and assuring farmer acceptance and cooperation.

Management Alternatives. Potential erosion hazard for a given site, as discussed above, is the erosional loss occurring in the absence of any land use (i.e., with bare and fully vulnerable soil) as determined by the collective interactions among climate, soil, and topography at the site. These are the very factors that determine the site's potential for supporting agricultural development. Should runoff and erosion hazards be low, no special provisions may be needed for reducing water and soil losses to acceptable limits. In other words, any form of agricultural use may theoretically be feasible. This is not a likely situation with hillslope farming, particularly in the tropics, where erosion potential can exceed tens or hundreds of tons of soil loss per hectare per year. In this case, the selection and design of cropping systems, land management systems, and water management systems must be tailored to attain effective runoff and erosion control.

• *Cropping systems:* Systems that need evaluation for use on hillslopes include conventional food crops (grown as sole crops, relay crops, ratoons, sequentially, in rotation, or as intercrops), agroforestry systems (including alley-cropping or other perennial hedge-row systems), pasture-animal grazing systems, and combinations of these. Selection and design of a land use system must be compatible with conservation needs (runoff and erosion hazard) as well as the need to meet the food, feed, fiber, fuel, and cash requirements of the community. Assuring high productivity by adopting wise agronomic practices (crop and soil husbandry) also assures efficient resource use and effective soil and water conservation.

Including perennial vegetation in cropping cycles is necessary, particularly in unirrigated, marginal rainfall regions, to ensure year-around protection by continuous cover and to provide degradation-preventing, year-around biological activity within the soil. Other known benefits of such vegetation result from specialized use as living sediment traps or barriers; sources of soil organic amendments; and, with trees, improved soil anchoring by deep root penetration.

Rapidly growing cover crops, preferably legumes, can be strategically used to provide direct soil protection, and soil enrichment where applicable, in combination with annual crops. Strategies for use of crop residues should include optimal return of residues to the soil for direct protection against erosional losses, reduced loss and improved storage of soil water, maintenance of adequate soil organic matter levels and fertility, and long-term buildup of soil structure. Tree-dominated cultures, such as fruit or nut orchards, in which ground-cover vegetation cannot thrive because of excessive shading, must be subjected to a deliberate strategy of organic residue management. Recycling of animal waste, where available, can achieve similar benefits.

• *Land and soil management:* Practices that require evaluation, aside from overcoming chemical and infertility constraints, include the manipulation of soil surface configurations, selection of appropriate tillage systems, and modification of soil structure. As with cropping systems, selection and design of such practices must be compatible with climatic and soil characteristics and based on both productivity benefits and runoff-erosion control considerations. For instance, land surface configurations intended to maximize water infiltration (e.g., contour bunds or terraces) may pose a serious erosion hazard because of breaching in structurally nonstable soils. Ridge-furrow or terrace configurations intended to control runoff may expose infertile or impermeable layers of certain soils and, as a result, reduce overall productivity. This may ultimately increase runoff and erosion in comparison with flat cultures. Similarly, intensive inversion primary tillage intended for improving the crop root environment may increase the silt content of surface layers and exacerbate surface sealing, crusting, and runoff generation potential in soils with coarse-textured surface layers and argillic B horizons (e.g., Alfisols).

Where soils have not degraded structurally, particularly with abundant, available crop residue, the adoption of reduced tillage systems may be encouraged.

• *Water management:* In association with appropriate tillage and land surface configurations, the overall field design must take advantage of watershed-ecosystem concepts to provide for the control and efficient management of rainfall and runoff. Continuing cognizance of all components of the water balance is particularly critical in rainfed regions and more so in marginal rainfall areas (e.g., semiarid, subhumid, or other regions with strictly seasonal rainfall). Minimum waste and efficient use of water by the crop is an important component of strategies aimed at sustained productivity. The safe disposal of excess runoff through stable intracatchment (interterrace) waterways is critical for overall stability. Waterways and drainageways should possess a capacity, slope gradient, and length that are adequate to cope with the prevailing rainfall regime and generated runoff. In marginal rainfall areas, the harnessing of excess runoff and/or development of other water sources may be necessary for life-saving supplemental irrigation. Water storage structures (tanks, reservoirs) must be properly sealed and means of recycling and optimally using stored water for irrigation devised.

The likelihood of successfully harvesting water in this manner, or from dedicated catchment areas, must be assessed using long-term probability analysis of rainfall patterns and runoff models. It is critical to remember that the likelihood of harvesting runoff for use during dry spells diminishes with increased frequency of such spells. The total catchment concept applies to groundwater mining as well. This source of water is more likely to provide evenly distributed amounts of water (less seasonal fluctuations) for use in periods when surface runoff is diminished.

A major feature of water harvesting and ponding in small reservoirs is the potential utility for aquaculture applications.

Socioeconomic and Policy Elements. Increasing concern with erosion problems, global recognition that natural resource degradation in many countries is nearing the point of no return, and the urgent need to sensitize and secure commitments from all members of the international community led to the adoption in 1982 of a World Soils Charter by the Food and Agriculture Organization of the United Nations. The charter sets forth principles for wise, productive, and protective land use to assure the welfare of future generations. This important and necessary declaration, however, will be of limited value if individual countries, relevant institutions within them, and land users themselves are not supportive or remain uncommitted to carrying out needed changes in land use or the enactment of protective laws and strategies.

Very often, the first and most important step in securing such support and commitment is to convey to land users and policymakers a clear understanding of the causes, extent, and impacts of erosion. Such increased awareness can now be amply supported by quantitative data and models that are available for addressing concerns based on all three aspects.

In addition to this educational or informational element, several other socioeconomic elements are needed to assure conservation-effective land use. These include the availability of a thorough land resource inventory and a clear national policy on land use priorities; adequate land tenure systems; reduced fragmentation of land due to inheritance or other owner-ship patterns; reduced cost and risk of adopting improved technology; availability of effective extension services for guiding designs for protective land use; efficient enforcement of land use policies; sufficient incentive for sustained adoption of erosion-preventing practices; meaningful involvement of all levels, particularly grass-root levels of the farming community (e.g., farmers), in developing conservation technology; and a strong commitment to the regular monitoring of erosion and its indicators to assure the continued stability of the natural resource base.

Benefits of Effective Resource Conservation

On-Site Impacts. The major on-site benefits of effective conservation on hillslopes include reduced resource losses by runoff, surface erosion, or mass movement (landslides); maintained soil qualities for high, stable, and sustained productivity; and preserved efficiency of critical upland and highland catchments for serving as watersheds in the region's vital river-basins. Most of these impacts are quantifiable and have been documented in the published literature. Some examples follow:

• *Productivity and stability benefits.* Soil erosion is the most important determinant of productive and sustainable farming in tropical environments, particularly on hillslopes. Physical, chemical, and biological soil attributes that favor crop growth and yield are subject to diminution by erosion. In rainfed areas, water loss as uncontrolled runoff also represents a serious threat to productive farming. Where conservation-effective farming is practiced and runoff and erosion are effectively controlled, less inputs of fertilizer, tillage, and supplemental irrigation will be needed to compensate for lost water, nutrients, and organic matter; to improve the soil's structural and hydrologic properties in the root-zone; and, thus, to sustain productivity. In the extreme, it goes without saying that avoiding severe erosion is critical to the very existence of the soil resource base or, at a minimum, avoiding irreversible changes in soil productivity.

Considerable evidence also exists to show that the efficiency of resource (input) use is higher for noneroded than for eroded soils. For instance, data on Hawaii's Oxisols and Aridisols show improved water-use efficiency and fertilizer-use efficiency in maize production with reduced erosion. Both result from a favorable water balance, particularly improved water storage, and superior root proliferation in less-eroded soils.

Although the impacts of soil erosion on productivity are generally presumed to be long-term in nature, dramatic short-term benefits of effective conservation have been demonstrated in tropical environments. This is partly because of the high erosion potential in these environments, the high vulnerability of well-weathered soils to erosion-productivity changes, and the immediate returns from reducing and harnessing excessive runoff for supplemental irrigation in rain-fed areas, particularly those with marginal rainfall (e.g., semiarid tropics). In such areas, crop performance is restricted by nutrient deficiencies as well as frequent drought stress. The concept of permissible losses, therefore, should be applied very conservatively and extended to include both soil and water losses.

• *Sustainability and community welfare benefits.* The maintenance of adequate, stable productivity patterns in hillslope areas will provide a much needed incentive for farmers to invest in correcting the problems encountered with shifting cultivation, or perhaps forego this practice altogether in favor of settling to practice sustained farming on the same land. Because land used for shifting cultivation is getting more scarce and the recovery periods within shifting cycles are becoming progressively smaller, this would be a welcome trend for enhancing farmers' commitments to good land husbandry and improving the welfare of the farming community as a whole.

Development projects targeted to the stabilization of agriculture in upland regions achieve only limited and short-term success if effective soil and water conservation practices, including sound farm husbandry, are not integrated into implemented management systems.

Off-Site Impacts. The major off-site benefits of effective conservation arise from the avoidance of detrimental physical, chemical, and biological changes in downstream areas as a result of catastrophic erosional events in upper catchment areas. Uncontrolled runoff in the form of floods represents a loss of valuable, nonstorable water resources as well as destruction or damage to human life and property. Sediments carried downstream may play a beneficial role in enriching low-lying agricultural land. This function, however, is highly debatable in tropical environments, particularly with catastrophic events. Such events are often very destructive and result in massive burial of productive lowlands with sediment derived from nutrient-deficient sources (exposed subsoils). Where dams and hydroelectric power generation plants have been built, both the water storage capacity and the power generation efficiency diminish. Available evidence shows that the actual, useful longevity of such structures in erosion-prone areas is almost always less than planned.

Sediment-induced changes in water quality downstream may reduce the stability and efficiency of stream channels and water conveyance structures, degrade the fishery resources in destination areas, and accelerate the chemical pollution and eutrophication of low-lying water bodies by sediment-associated nutrients, pesticides, and other compounds. Practicing effective conservation on farms in hillslope portions of catchment areas prevents the manifestation of undesirable off-site impacts, protects the properties and economic investments downstream, and reduces the costs to society of correcting these impacts when necessary.

In Conclusion

The technological and socioeconomic elements of conservation-effective farming on hillslopes are well understood but not easily quantified for the climates, soils, and topographies that prevail on the hillslopes, particularly in tropical regions. The benefits of effective conservation to the stability, productivity, and sustainability of the resource base and to the quality of downstream environments are convincing. Policymakers, land use planners, and other public agents should encourage immediate incorporation of available conservation elements into land management technologies for hillslope regions and support selective research for improved erosion prediction and conservation application in these regions.

SOIL MANAGEMENT
ON HILLSIDES
IN THE HUMID TROPICS

N. AHMAD

Steepland is land with slopes exceeding 17.6 percent (10°), and humid tropics encompass all areas 10° north and south of the equator receiving more than 1,200 millimeters of annual precipitation. Farming on such land has been traditional in different parts of the world, for example, during the Mayan and Incan civilizations in Central and South America and in the Philippines and Java at the present. Interestingly, in all of these cases, elaborate terracing systems were built as anti-erosion measures. In contrast, present-day hillside farming in such areas as Ethiopia, Central Africa, South America, and the Caribbean, where farming is on a shifting basis, results in striking soil wastage and serious damage to the environment.

The rapidly increasing tendency worldwide for small farmers to farm on steep hillsides is due to population growth, which leads to a steady increase in landless farmers and the use of flatter land for export crops and urban development. In many parts of the world, squatters with no incentives for appropriate soil management occupy the steeplands.

Uncontrolled exploitation of steeplands is leading to important ecological changes, greater runoff and soil erosion, and a rapid lowering of soil productivity. With these changes, agricultural production declines greatly, leading, in time, to abandonment of holdings and clearing of new areas. The vegetation that succeeds in these former clearings is essentially scrub and poor quality grasses, known as tropical, man-made savannas. The restoration of land once affected in this way is extremely difficult and beyond the means of many tropical countries.

Changes in vegetation lead to greater rainfall runoff, less storage, slower rates of aquifer recharge, and even to incursion of sea water in some cases. The most disastrous effects, however, are flash floods in the lowlands caused by increased runoff and landslides in the higher areas. These hazards and devastations can be prevented by appropriate management at all levels.

Advantages and Disadvantages of Hillside Farming

While there are no alternatives to farming on hillsides for many farmers, for others it may be done by preference. Elevation and climatic difference facilitate the growing of subtropical fruits, vegetables, and even flowers, which can be highly profitable. The slopes provide alternative areas for the cultivation of some vegetable crops during the wet seasons when the flatter lowland areas are too wet.

Disadvantages of steepland agriculture include problems of access and difficulty in machinery use. As a result, such inputs as fertilizers and other soil amendments are only sparingly used. Harvested produce must be manually transported, which further limits the crops grown, not only because of bulkiness but also mechanical damage. For these reasons, traditional hillside farmers tend to specialize in crops of small bulk but high value.

Soil Erodibility

A state-of-the-art position on soil erosion by rainfall was presented by El-Swaify and associates (4). These researchers agreed that soil erodibility is important but difficult to assess. The relative ease with which soil aggregates disintegrate on raindrop impact indicates reasonably well a soil's erodibility. Soils developed on basic igneous rocks and red soils on limestone are strongly aggregated because of the cementing effects of iron oxides. Soils developed on fragmentary volcanic materials that have andic properties are resistant to erosion.

Soils formed on shales, schists, phyllites, and sandstones are highly erodible. These rocks produce soil in which either the sand or silt fraction is high, and there is not enough clay-size material and iron oxide for cementing to produce a stable-structured soil. Many of these parent materials also are rich in muscovite, which can occur in all particle-size fractions of the soils. These soils are particularly weak-structured. The clay fraction is easily water-dispersible, and the weak aggregates are easily disintegrated by raindrops. The mica flakes settle on their flat axes in the film of water on the soil surface. This leads to soil crusting, which restricts entry of water into the soil (2). Water runoff is much greater as a result, causing further disintegration of soil aggregates and transport of colloidal soil material.

Table 1. Effect of soil parent material on soil erodibility and soil loss.

Soil	Slope (degrees)	Dispersion Ratio	Suspension Percentage	Soil Loss (t/ha)	Depth of Soil Lost in One Year (cm)
Goldsborough clay (volcanic tuff)	10	10.0	7	121.6	2.16
(Aquic Hapllustalfs)	20	9.1	7	170.4	2.95
BloodyBay (phyllite/schist)	10	21.2	11	212.8	3.81
(Typic Eutropepts)	30	25.0	12	180.8	3.18

Table 2. Effect of vegetative cover on soil loss and run-off from Maracas series (Orthoxic Tropudults), Trinidad (7).

Vegetative Cover	Soil Loss		Percentage of Rainfall Lost in Runoff
	Tons/Hectare	Centimeters	
Bare soil	58	0.9	50
Vegetation 1*	32	0.5	29
Vegetation 2*	21	0.3	25

*Vegetation 1, maize planted at 41,500 plants per hectare; vegetation 2, maize planted at 62,000 plants per hectare.

Actual infiltration into a crusted soil may be no more than one-fifteenth that in the same soil with some protective surface mulch. The crust causes mechanical impedance to seedling emergence and also restricts gaseous exchange, which leads to anaerobic conditions, denitrification, and toxic effects due to ethylene production.

There are relatively few measurements of soil loss from the two types of soils as influenced by slope steepness. In table 1, some values for soils in Tobago are shown. The data indicate greater erodibility and actual loss from bare phyllite/schist soil compared to that formed on volcanic tuff and breccia. Clearly, the rate of soil deterioration in the two instances is related to soil parent material. The amount of soil that can be lost in any one year can be enormous. This explains the fact that in Tobago, in the earlier part of this century, food crop cultivation was very important. But the soils used then have been abandoned because of erosion to bedrock. This situation is more the norm than the exception in many Caribbean territories (1). The same applies also to Central and South America (6) and, from my personal experience, in various parts of tropical Africa as well.

Even for highly erodible soil on steep slopes, there is a marked effect of vegetative cover on soil loss. Table 2 presents some runoff and soil loss data from Maracas series of phyllite schist parent material, on a 47 percent slope, as influenced by different plant densities (7).

For the small subsistence farmer who is probably in the majority of hillside farmers in the humid tropics, anti-erosion measures should take into account soil erodibilty.

Concerning soil differences, Andisols and Oxisols have different erosion properties than Ultisols, Alfisols, or Inceptisols. This can be illustrated by the Caribbean experience. In Jamaica, on a 31 percent slope, Sheng (8) measured over a 5-year period on an Ultisol soil loss of 104 tons per hectare per year. That is more than a 1-centimeter depth of soil. On the same slopes in the Windward Islands, (St. Vincent, St. Lucia, Dominica) and on soils with andic properties, soil erosion is not a problem. In fact, on these islands, banana is being grown on 58 percent slopes with no catastrophic soil loss. In St. Vincent, where the soils are particularly andic in behavior, annual crops, like sweet potato and edible aroids, are produced on very steep slopes with soil disturbance at both planting and harvesting.

In St. Lucia, Ahmad and Sheng (3) proposed three classes of steepland soils based on erodibility as follows: stable soils—Andisols, Mollisols, some Inceptisols, and some Alfisols (Oxisols are included in this group if they are present); less stable soils—Ultisols, some Alfisols, some Inceptisols, and some shallow Mollisols—and fragile soils—Vertisols.

If the soils are separated in this way, different levels of treatment can be prescribed for each group on comparable slopes. Also, different crops, cropping systems, and settlement can be prescribed. The problem is that in many tropical countries the soils have not been mapped in the detail required for this type of approach. But where the information is available, it should be used.

Another aspect that has special significance is soil depth. This is applicable in land restoration and in prescribing treatments. There is a difference in soil depth and effective soil depth because of the nature of the soil parent material and parent rock. If the parent rock is indurated, such as igneous and metamorphic rocks and limestones, the depth of soil is critical because of the sharp contact between the hard rock and soil. If the parent material is soft, such as shales, alluvial and colluvial deposits, or fragmentary volcanic materials, it can easily be reconstituted into productive soil by land shaping and reforming using heavy machinery. The effective depth of the soil includes some of this material also. Roots grow into these soft parent materials, which contribute to sustenance of the crop. For these soils, such simple techniques as maintenance of soil cover; reduced tillage; grass barriers on the contour; and, in some cases, contour drains, step drains, and grassed waterways may be adequate control depending on slope.

By comparison, on more erodible soils and on soils developed on hard parent rocks, a different approach to soil conservation is needed. Because of the difficulties in maintaining anti-erosion installations by small farmers, cultural techniques must be emphasized, with a certain minimum of mechanical installations. Every advantage must be taken of what the farmer can do to reduce soil loss. It is up to the soil conservationist, working in close association with the soil scientist and extension worker, to prescribe appropriate conservation measures.

Another form of soil erosion that is facilitated by farming on steeplands and that also is influenced by parent materials is land slipping. The end result may be the same, caused by accumulation of water in the subsoil, but the way the phenomenon occurs may be different in particular situations. On soils formed on phyllites and schists, the boundary between the soil and the rock is often abrupt. Because the rock can be layered and fine-grained, tree roots have difficulty growing into it. With the absence of connecting roots to stabilize the soil, and the effect of slope, water that percolates through the soil and accumulates at the sharp rock/soil contact serves as a lubricant on which the soil above can slide. Land clearing and agriculture can influence this process, especially early in the wet seasons when the cleared soil wets faster because of the lack of vegetation. Then, as the wet season advances, the soil above the rock becomes supersaturated and slips result. This form of land wastage can be disastrous and lead to serious dislocations and soil ruination, in addition to crop loss and destruction of mechanical anti-erosion practices. Slippage of this type is quite active on land that has been cleared for agriculture for the first time because of the drastic change in hydrologic conditions.

Land slips also occur in soils developed on clay sediments. These are mostly in Vertisols, the parent materials of which have well-developed slip faces. In the dry seasons, these soils develop wide, deep cracks. In the wet seasons, before swelling and sealing can occur, free water can enter and accumulate between these natural slip faces and cause land slippage. These slips can be massive and result in damage to agricultural land, roads, and buildings. Farming can hasten the slippage rate of these soils by causing excessive soil desiccation and cracking in dry seasons due to little or no vegetative cover. This provides more avenues for water to gain rapid access in the ensuing wet seasons.

Gullying is another form of erosion that occurs on steepland. This is common on more porous materials, such as the sandy soils in Eastern Nigeria, or on porous soils developed in volcanic materials, as in Ethiopia, the Caribbean, and South America. This is also an important form of soil erosion on Vertisols. In this case, water gains rapid entry into the soils, which results in supersaturation. The material then breaks off, leading to gully formation. Once again, farming activities often encourage this type of soil erosion by enabling the soils to wet rapidly at the beginning of wet seasons. Even soils not naturally prone to gullying can be so eroded as a result of farming activities through field boundaries, foot paths, and lack of surface water disposal. Drainage water from cultivated fields courses down the slope and eventually leads to gully formation.

Even some of the best structured soils in the world, Andisols, for example, are eroded on steep slopes under cultivation, although the rate of soil loss may be less and farming can be attempted on steeper slopes than on other soils. For instance, it is impossible to visualize farming activities on steeper slopes than on St. Vincent. While soil erosion is important, the rate of soil loss is low enough that farming can be practiced on a permanent basis where slopes commonly exceed 58 percent. On such soils, surface erosion occurs through soil loosening during tillage. Some gullying also takes place in these porous soils. Farming activity on these soils is most likely responsible for any soil erosion that takes place because the soils are virtually uneroded if left undisturbed.

Farming Systems

Permanent Plantation Crops. A farming system on steepland that is well established in many parts of the world is the growing of the beverage crops tea and coffee. The farming practices during cultivation of these crops are now well established. They depend on high labor inputs because almost all of the operations must be manual to maintain the quality of the produce and because of the terrain. In this system, the soil is not disturbed, and ecological conditions approach those of the original forest. If well managed, the system is efficient and results in optimum use of plant nutrients and soil water.

Increasingly, rubber is being cultivated on steeplands in Malaysia and Indonesia with the use of leguminous cover crops such as *Calopogonium, Pueraria, Tephrosia*, and *Crotolaria*.

Shifting Cultivation. The most common farming system on steeplands is shifting cultivation. No inputs of fertilizers or other soil amendments are commonly used. Hillslope land is often state-owned, and landless farmers (squatters) occupy the land for farming. The vegetation is cleared and burned when dry to clean the land and to mineralize the available nutrients. The farmer then plants a range of crops, depending on his or her needs or what he or she can sell. Having cleared the original vegetation, he or she occupies the area of land for as long as some production can be obtained. When the area becomes unproductive, which is a variable length of time, depending on soil conditions, it is abandoned, and another piece of land is cleared and planted. Unfortunately, in many countries, such land has already been put through several cultivation cycles and is now no longer productive.

Multiple or Sequential Cropping. Multiple cropping can be highly productive and soil-conserving. Whether it is sequential or interrow cropping, it limits the extent of bare soil in the field. Throughout the world, there are many examples of multiple cropping—annual with perennial, annual with annual, and perennial with cover crops.

A farming system exists in some parts of the Caribbean that combines subsistence and commercial agriculture. In this system, the main crop is the commercial one, which is intended for sale. Other crops are sparsely interplanted for the farmer's household use. These crops are planted so they offer no competition to the main crop. Most are confined to ends of rows or along walkways within the cultivated fields. They are not given any fertilizer or soil amendments directly, but benefit from what is applied to the main crop.

In the case of the specialized farmer on steeplands, farming is usually intensive, with small holdings that tend to be permanent. Cropping is organized on an all-year basis. In the dry seasons, moisture conservation practices, such as mulching, are common. There may be one combination of crops for wet seasons and another for dry seasons.

Management of Steeplands in Agriculture

Tillage. Soil tillage practices vary greatly with tradition and the crops grown. In many Caribbean countries, hillside farmers cultivate root crops, the most important ones being sweet potato, aroids, yam, and white potato. The aim in land preparation for all of these crops is to loosen the soil for tuber development. Where the parent material is unconsolidated, as in volcanic agglomerate and tuff, land preparation involves the construction of ridges, which run across the slopes. The root crop is cultivated on these ridges. In Jamaica, as in parts of West Africa, surface soil is often heaped into mounds and the crops planted on these. In all of these cases, the land surface is completely disturbed; soil is loosened to a maximum degree; and the erosion hazard, as a result, is extreme.

In situations where cereals and grain legumes are grown, most often there is no general tillage of the land. Seeds are simply dibbled into the soil. Subsequent cultural operations involve hoeing to mound up the soil around the plants. There is some zonal tillage and soil loosening, but this is done gradually as the crop develops. This operation is usually done when the crop is still small and the soil surface mostly exposed, thereby posing a severe erosion hazard.

The specialized steepland farmer—growers of exotic fruits, vegetables, flowers, etc.—invariably practices thorough tillage and land layout to give his high-value crops the best conditions for maximum production. In aiming to achieve this goal, the soil is left exposed to erosion.

Ideally, agriculture on steeplands should be practiced with as little soil disturbance as possible. Any mechanical loosening of the soil will simply enhance the erosive effect of rainfall, leading to accelerated soil erosion. If tillage is necessary for crop establishment and production, surface protection in the form of mulches is clearly of great benefit.

The more practical and effective cultural measures are minimum tillage, high-density planting, use of mulches and other surface vegetative covers, and the practices of multiple cropping, reduced tillage, and intercropping. Maximum protection is necessary at both planting and harvest.

Soil Fertility Maintenance. Maintenance of soil fertility in steepland agriculture is conditioned by the farming system and the area's accessibility. Because fertilizers must be manually transported for at least part of the way to a field, most fertilizer is used only by the specialized, intensive farmer. Some of these farmers make manures from crop residues on-site and use them on the farm to reduce the need to transport fertilizers. Because of the value of the crops grown, these farmers make sure soil fertility maintenance is adequate either through manures or fertilizers, or a combination of both.

Some farmers in the more traditional systems achieve considerable recycling of nutrients and maintain their cultivations through this means. When fertility levels drop too low, the land is fallowed for varying lengths of time and then recultivated.

The shifting cultivator hardly practices soil fertility maintenance measures. The nutrients released by burning the cut vegetation is his main source. Should the rainy season begin abruptly and heavily, much of the ash produced by the burn is washed off the soil surface, and the soluble constituents are leached. In this system, the land is abandoned when productivity drops too low. With every cycle of cultivation, productivity declines progressively and the period of cropping becomes shorter. Finally, the land is abandoned. Inadequate maintenance of soil fertility on steeplands is hazardous because it leads to poor crop growth, inadequate ground cover, and accelerated soil loss.

In commercial tree-crop cultivation, soil fertility maintenance is usually adequate. Even in peasant agriculture, these crops are given preference. For example, in Ethiopia, the coffee crop is located concentrically closer to the household, and it receives household wastes. Food and other crops are farther away, and they usually receive no soil amendments.

Anti-Erosion Measures. Any farming on hillsides that is intended to be permanent or semi-permanent must incorporate measures for soil conservation. The experience of older civilizations in different parts of the tropics clearly have shown this to be so.

Anti-erosion measures can broadly be divided into two groups, mechanical and cultural (*4*):

Mechanical Measures. These measures basically consist of terraces of different sizes and shapes to suit the landscape and agriculture to be followed. Terraces are popular because they save labor and can be constructed quickly. Terracing inescapably involves movement of large quantities of soil material and complete disturbance and exposure of subsoil at the terrace base where the cultivated crops are to be grown.

In assessing whether terraces can be successfully constructed and maintained, it is most important to know the nature of the underlying soil parent materials. If this material is loose or only weakly consolidated, as in the case of most shales, clay sediments, volcanic tuff, or agglomerate, the chances of success with terraces are good. After construction, the exposed subsoil, which may consist essentially of soil parent material, can easily be turned into a productive soil by proper agronomic practices. If the subsoil has any chemical problems, such as salinity, high acidity, or petroleum impregnation, this should be taken into account, and terracing should be avoided.

If the underlying rock is indurated, as most igneous and metamorphic rocks and limestones are, mechanical construction of terraces should be attempted with great caution. This could lead to rock exposures or the creation of shallow soils over hard rock.

Terrace maintenance is of great importance. There are many examples in the tropics where maintenance has been inadequate and failures resulted. These failures often are associated with inadequate design for water disposal, without which terraces are likely to fail. Experience in the Caribbean has shown that if terraces are properly designed, constructed, and maintained on the right type of soil material, they can lead to a stable agriculture and an improvement of the environment. So far, though, in projects where terraces have been constructed and the land given to small subsistence farmers, the terraces have not been adequately maintained or even misused. The level of maintenance attempted varies with individual farmers.

Cultural Measures. The use of strips of grass or other vegetation established on the contour is possible. Certain grasses that tiller profusely establish extensive root systems and can provide a continuous vegetative barrier across the slope. An example is *Vetiver zizanioides*, which can retain soil that would otherwise wash away. The root system helps to prevent the soil from being dislodged and removed. The problem is that all farmers in any one area may not be equally diligent in establishing and maintaining the strips. This can greatly diminish the effectiveness of soil conservation on a watershed basis.

The farmer can also influence surface drainage by establishing grassed waterways in which runoff is safely removed. If this is not done, the land may become gullied. There is much opportunity for the farmer to use crop residues at all stages for soil protection.

Agroforestry is a concept now increasingly being emphasized that involves growing food crops and/or fruit trees in association with arable crops. In Caribbean agriculture, it is traditional to have a top storey of fruit or food-producing trees with other tiers of crops, ending with runners, such as sweet potato, or cucurbits. Alley cropping holds promise for erosion control and, at the same time, for providing useful forest products and nutritious livestock feed (5, 9). With the mulching materials produced by some species, even greater anti-erosion effects can be obtained. The combinations of trees, whether for timber, food, or fruit, provide some soil protection at all times. Also, the products from these trees may provide an additional source of income or useful materials for staking, firewood, etc. Much more emphasis must be given to this aspect of land use in the future.

Apart from the costs and work involved in constructing and maintaining anti-erosion measures, whether cultural or mechanical, the farmer faces a dilemma in the loss of land space that will inevitably result. Another problem is to get the farmer to appreciate the long-term effect of soil loss on the quality of his land and loss of production.

Hillside farmers should be encouraged to develop mixed farming systems, including livestock production. In such a system, the farmer can more easily be convinced to incorporate grasses in his cultivation because the cuttings can be used to feed his livestock. Likewise, alley cropping with traditional legumes, such as *Leucaena* and *Gliricidia*, make more sense to him because part of the cuttings can be used for livestock feed. If the farmer can obtain other uses from these soil protective plants, it will be easier to convince him to incorporate them into his farming system. However, many hillside farmers are highly specialized and may not be interested in mixed enterprises.

REFERENCES

1. Ahmad, N. 1975. *Erosion hazard and farming systems in the Caribbean countries.* In D. J. Greenland and R. Lal [editors] *Soil Conservation and Management in the Humid Tropics.* J. Wiley and Sons, Chichester, England. pp. 241-250.
2. Ahmad, N., and A. J. Roblin. 1971. *Crusting of River Estate soil and its effect on gaseous diffusion, percolation and seedling emergence.* Journal of Soil Science 22: 23-31.
3. Ahmad, N., and T. C. Sheng. 1988. *Land capability and land use of the steeplands of St. Lucia.* Organization of American States, St. Lucia.
4. El-Swaify, S. A., E. W. Dangler, and C. L. Armstrong. 1982. *Soil erosion by water in the tropics.* Research Extension Series 024. College of Agriculture, University of Hawaii, Manoa.
5. Kang, B. T., G. F. Wilson, and T. L. Lawson. 1984. *Alley cropping—a stable alternative to shifting cultivation.* Technical Bulletin No. 5. International Institute for Tropical Agriculture, Ibadan, Nigeria.
6. Lal, R. 1975. *Review of soil erosion research in Latin America.* In D. J. Greenland and R. Lal [editors] *Soil Conservation and Management in the Humid Tropics.* J. Wiley and Sons, Chichester, England. pp. 231-240.
7. Mohammed, A. 1982. *Erosion studies at two plant densities of maize on Maracas soil, Trinidad.* Masters thesis. University of the West Indies, St. Augustine, Trinidad.
8. Sheng, T. C. 1986. *Watershed conservation. A collection of papers for developing countries.* Chinese Soil and Water Conservation Society, Taipei, Taiwan, and Colorado State University, Fort Collins.
9. Wilson, C. F., and B. T. Kang. 1980. *Developing stable and productive biological cropping systems for the humid tropics.* In B. Stonehouse [editor] *Biological Husbandry.* Butterworths, London, England. pp. 193-204.

CONSERVATION DISTRICTS: A MODEL FOR CONSERVATION PLANNING AND IMPLEMENTATION IN DEVELOPING COUNTRIES

MAURICE G. COOK

T he reality of worldwide natural re-
source degradation is ever present. History has recorded the consequences
of ignoring such degradation. In a classic study, Lowdermilk (8) found that
neglect of the land was often a major factor in the fall of empires, and that
neglect accounts for the barren nature of much of today's world.

There has been an awakening to soil erosion and conservation problems
throughout the world. Although there is general awareness of the problems,
it appears that this awareness is not being translated into remedial action.
The remedy for soil erosion and its many related problems lies in the
development and implementation of a sound national soil conservation program (4). National soil conservation programs are needed to achieve the
broad objectives of increasing food production and enhancing the standard
of living.

The ultimate measure of success in any conservation program, however,
is the implementation of a conservation strategy at the farm level. Involvement of the land users themselves in planning and carrying out a conservation program is required if the program is to succeed (2, 3, 5, 6, 7).
In assessing the failure of conservation policies in developing countries,
Blaikie (2) cited a lack of participation by land users in government-
sponsored conservation. A lack of government efforts to involve local people
often contributes to projects that do not fit the practices of farmers. A Food
and Agriculture Organization consultant (6) states it more bluntly, "No
conservation project will work unless local people participate in developing and applying it."

The success of soil and water conservation programs in the United States can be attributed to several forces. A major agent in the development and implementation of a national program for soil and water conservation has been, and is, the local soil conservation district. The district is a special-purpose unit of government consisting of locally elected and appointed officials. Many of these officials are landowners and practicing farmers who have a vested interest in good soil and water management.

The soil conservation district might serve as a universal model to educate, encourage, and assist landowners in applying soil conservation practices to their land. Obviously, the model must undergo modification to be adaptable to a given country. Hudson (7) observed that the traditional North American style of conservation is often not appropriate in developing countries. Nevertheless, the basic precept of farmer-citizen involvement in promoting and executing soil conservation programs is applicable in many countries of the world. The U.S. experience with conservation districts is offered as a guide for tying together local implementation with a national program to achieve effective conservation.

Historical Background

The mid-1930s was a momentous time for soil conservation in the United States. The agriculturally productive section of the country was experiencing a serious drought. Wind-blown topsoil was carried more than 2,000 kilometers and deposited in the Atlantic Ocean. This event is often referred to as the Great Dust Bowl in the United States. No solution to the tremendous soil erosion problem was in sight. There was no national conservation program, and the United States was paralyzed economically.

Through the crusading efforts of one individual, Hugh Hammond Bennett, the U.S. Congress passed legislation in 1935 that became the basis for an extensive soil conservation program. The efficacy of this legislation is evident when one considers that no substantive amendments have been made since its passage more than 50 years ago. A federal agency, which became the Soil Conservation Service, was established and given the authority and responsibility for soil and water conservation.

Federal conservation officials soon recognized, though, that the federal government did not have the resources to single-handedly carry out a national conservation program. There was the thought that nationwide conservation would be accomplished more effectively, economically, and democratically if farmers and local governments were brought into the conservation operation. Thus, the idea of a conservation district was conceived.

The next step was to develop a proposal for the individual states, 48 at the time, making up the United States. In 1936, the federal government proposed the district concept to the states in a Standard State Soil Conservation Districts Enabling Law. This law, called the standard act, outlined district functions, powers, and organizational arrangements. In 1937, President Franklin Roosevelt sent the governors of the states a copy of the standard act and a letter encouraging them to organize soil conservation districts as governmental subdivisions. Within a week after President Roosevelt's letter reached the governors, states began to enact enabling legislation. The first soil conservation district in the world was chartered August 4, 1937, in the State of North Carolina. It was the Brown Creek District, which included Hugh Bennett's native home. Today, there are nearly 3,000 conservation districts representing almost all of the land in farms in the United States.

Organization and Structure

There has been disagreement on the governmental nature of the conservation district since its inception (9). Many have viewed the district as little more than the local appendage of a federal agency, namely, the Soil Conservation Service. Others contend that the district is an independent unit of local (county) government. The peculiar value of the district, perhaps, is that it is a hybrid in government. It merges the best values of local government with national programming in its operation. Nevertheless, soil conservation districts are, in their legal structure and authority, local governmental subdivisions of the state, completely independent of the federal government.

The establishment of a district is singularly dependent upon the wishes of the farmers of the area and upon the decision of a state soil conservation committee. According to the standard act, at least 25 land occupiers must first petition the state committee to establish a district. The committee is then required to hold a public hearing on the petition to define the boundaries of the proposed district and then to submit to all land occupiers living within the defined boundaries the question of whether the district should be created. A majority of the votes cast in the referendum must be favorable. District boundaries frequently coincide with county boundaries.

In developing their own legislation, the states adopted uniformly the language of the standard act proposed by the federal government. States have opted, though, to title their districts differently, for example, soil and water conservation districts, soil conservation districts, or conservation districts. The district officers are generally called supervisors. In some states they are called directors and, in others, commissioners.

The district board consists of five supervisors, three elected by the voters and two appointed by the state conservation commission. Names of candidates for the board positions appear on the general ballot for electing all local, state, and federal officials. This is a rather recent development and has enhanced public awareness of the role and function of the conservation district.

Supervisors serve without pay, although many districts reimburse supervisors for their travel expenses to and from meetings. Many districts appoint assistant supervisors to broaden the base of citizen involvement. Assistant supervisors do not have voting privileges, but they participate in all other aspects of district activities.

The last decade has seen a marked change in the character of conservation districts. Initially, the supervisors were farmers exclusively. Today, public-spirited citizens in business, industry, and the professions also serve on district boards. There is, however, a desire to maintain a strong representation of farmers, particularly in predominantly agricultural areas. In the early years of district operation, the conservation district consisted of supervisors, the technical support persons provided by the Soil Conservation Service, and perhaps a part-time secretary/bookkeeper. Many districts now have sizeable, full-time staffs of administrative and technical personnel. This has come about through recognition of local conservation needs, success in addressing those needs, and aggressive action in obtaining additional funding from local government.

As districts have evolved in their operation, four general responsibilities have emerged: (1) enlisting the technical skills and services of various federal, state, and local agencies that can contribute effectively to the advancement of their conservation programs; (2) bringing together local forces, including community leaders, civic organizations, business and educational institutions, and other individuals or groups who can directly assist the district; (3) promoting and selling conservation to farm operators within the district; and (4) governing the district (9).

In governing the district, supervisors perform specific administrative activities, such as reviewing and approving farm plans; procuring and distributing materials; collecting, handling, and using district funds; hiring and supervising district employees; and negotiating contracts.

Growth and Development

Conservation districts initially focused on one issue—soil erosion. But the perspective of conservation districts began to broaden in the 1950s and early 1960s. Prominent in the expanding conservation concept was a new emphasis on water. This was also an age of unprecedented technological advances, accelerating population growth, and rapid urbanization. The impacts of urbanization became a major conservation district concern. Suddenly, conservation districts found themselves working with a broader clientele. Prior to this time, they were primarily agriculturally oriented, and their clientele were mostly farmers and ranchers.

Concern for the environment exploded across America during the late 1960s and early 1970s. Many environmental battles were about land use, a subject of vital interest to conservation districts. The dynamism of conservation districts is seen in their involvement in a wide array of issues, many of which are a far cry from the original issue of soil erosion that brought the districts into being. As one conservation leader put it, "Today, conservationists are flying a new flag, the flag of the environment. Where do districts fit into this battle for the environment? The answer is— everywhere" (10).

The last 10 to 15 years have seen a broadly expanded agenda among districts. Many issues that arose during the 1970s had little to do with soil erosion. Their overriding characteristic was their natural resource orientation. Recreation, coastal zone management, urban conservation, farmland potential, and mined-land reclamation entered the picture. Some district leaders now feel that the new environmental and resource concerns have taken attention, dollars, and resources away from the fight against soil erosion. Others feel that these expanded concerns have kept the conservation movement in tune with the mood of the times and brought dollars and public visibility to districts.

Districts are no longer what they once were, let alone what they were originally conceived to be. Many districts today are viewed as local natural resource agencies that help pull together a broad array of public agencies and private resources to address the problems of natural resource management and conservation. Hudson (7) wisely noted that the development of technical solutions is only one part of solving the soil erosion problem. There are political aspects, social features, and economic constraints. The conservation district is uniquely equipped to apply this integrated approach to conservation.

What about the future of conservation districts? Conservation districts have filled a key role in building a bridge that can bring the technical knowledge of the scientist and the ethics of the conservationist into the mind of the landowner in a compelling way. As one conservation district leader expressed it, "Soil and water conservation does not start with planned treatment; it starts in the mind of the landowner" (10). Because districts are concerned with people and the land they live on, the districts will continue to find their places in the political and technical arena. Sampson (*10*) said it well, "Anyone who would seek to understand the political forces that move Americans to action on soil and water conservation issues would do well to understand the potential that lies in the dedication, commitment, and skill of those who love the land—the people of the soil conservation districts."

Establishing a Conservation District

The conservation district idea was conceived and developed in the United States. It was nurtured by the timely coincidence of a natural disaster—drought and wind erosion—and an articulate conservation crusader, Hugh Hammond Bennett. Although this is a possible scenario to conservation district development in new areas, it is unlikely that a similar conjunction of nature and man will repeat itself.

Worldwide soil conservation has very likely been advanced where the district concept has been transferred from the United States to developing countries. The case has been stated for an independent conservation authority whose responsibilities, powers, and scale of government are prescribed by law, but which are allowed to mobilize public and financial support (*5*). A conservation district fulfills these requirements. The value of 50 years of experience with conservation districts would be immeasurable in facilitating the establishment of a local conservation organization and the implementation of conservation policy. The transfer of information could occur in several ways and at different levels:

• *Farmer-farmer exchange.* Many successful practicing conservationists welcome the opportunity to share their expertise with their fellow farmers around the world. A group of progressive farmers from a developing country could visit various farmers in the United States to observe conservation practices on the land. The host U.S. farmers would reciprocate with on-site visits to a developing country to demonstrate the organization and function of a local district. Coordination would need to be made through the respective federal agencies in each country to ensure that appropriate technical personnel are present. Financial support for this exchange should be available through various international agencies, for example, the World Bank or The U.S. Agency for International Development.

• *Adopt-a-country program.* Local conservation districts are organized into state associations. Individual state associations have considerable financial and human resources. Individual state associations or groups of associations may promote the farmer-farmer exchange. They may serve as hosts for visiting farmers at district, state, and national meetings. Going a step further, they may sponsor conservation demonstrations in developing countries.

• *Affiliate status.* The National Association of Conservation Districts (NACD) in the United States is an aggregate of the nearly 3,000 conservation districts. It is a strong political force for influencing legislative policy. Individual officers of NACD have visited developing countries and shared their experience and expertise. However, the NACD has not extended its organizational function beyond the boundaries of the United States. NACD would have much to offer a conservation organization in a developing country regarding legislative processes, financial operations, and program development. This could be accomplished by establishing affiliates in selected countries. Affiliate status may be withdrawn when the organization becomes self-supporting. Or there may be a desire to form a coalition to promote and strengthen international conservation activities.

In Summary

The 50-year conservation district movement in the United States has experienced unparalleled success. The pathway to success has not always been upward because, as an entity of government, districts have experienced temporary setbacks through political decisions and actions. Nevertheless, the success is evident by their growth to nearly 3,000 in number in less than 50 years; an increase in the human and financial resources of local districts, state associations, and a national association; and broadening and expansion of district programs and increased involvement of districts in environmental issues. The most important evidence, though, is seen on the land and in the lives of people. The application of conservation technology is having a dramatic impact on the quality of land and, perhaps more importantly, on the quality of life of those who depend on the land for their livelihood.

The important role of conservation districts cannot be overstated. Hugh Bennett, affectionately known as the "father of soil conservation," was the foremost personality in the district movement. In his later years, he remarked many times: "I consider the soil conservation district movement one of the most important developments in the whole history of agriculture. It has proved even more effective, I am convinced, than we had dared to expect" (*1*).

The success story of conservation districts in the United States needs to be told to developing countries experiencing serious conservation problems. True, the concept must be adapted to the cultural, political, and social setting of the local people. Nevertheless, the conservation district idea can provide the institutional and organizational framework to allow the provision of the necessary technical services. Perhaps it is an idea whose time has come in the international dialogue on soil conservation.

REFERENCES

1. Agricultural Foundation, Inc. 1959. *The Hugh Bennett lectures.* Raleigh, North Carolina.
2. Blaikie, Piers. 1985. *The political economy of soil erosion in developing countries.* Longman Inc., New York, New York.
3. Dudal, R. 1982. *Land degradation in a world perspective.* Journal of Soil and Water Conservation 37(5): 245-249.
4. Food and Agriculture Organization, United Nations. 1976. *Soil conservation for developing countries.* Soils Bulletin 30. Rome, Italy.
5. Food and Agriculture Organization, United Nations. 1983. *Guidelines for the control of soil degradation.* Rome, Italy.
6. Food and Agriculture Organization, United Nations. 1983. *Keeping the land alive.* Soils Bulletin 50. Rome, Italy.
7. Hudson, Norman. 1981. *Soil conservation.* Batsford, London, England.
8. Lowdermilk, Walter C. 1953. *Conquest of the land through 7000 years.* Information Bulletin 99. Soil Conservation Service, U.S. Department of Agriculture, Washington, D.C.
9. Parks, W. Robert. 1952. *Soil conservation districts in action.* Iowa State College Press, Ames.
10. Sampson, R. Neil. 1985. *For love of the land.* National Association of Conservation Districts, League City, Texas.

LAND USE PLANNING
FOR HILLSLOPES
IN NORTHEASTERN INDIA

J. P. JAISWAL

Indian's northeastern states, Arunachal Pradesh, Assam, Manipur, Meghalaya, Mizoram, Nagaland, and Tripura, lie between 21.5° and 29.5° north latitudes and 85.5° and 97.5° east longitudes. Difficult, hilly terrain is common in the region. Elevation ranges from a few hundred meters to about 8,500 meters above sea level. Climate in the region varies from tropical and subtropical to temperate. Rainfall and temperature patterns also vary greatly. Annual rainfall in the Cherrapunji-Mawphlang-Pynursla belt in Meghalaya is the highest in the world, totaling about 12,500 millimeters. In contrast, total annual rainfall in the Lanka area of Assam is only 1,100 millimeters. Similarly, a difference of about 10°C in mean maximum temperature and about 8°C in mean minimum temperature occurs at high and low altitudes during winter and summer seasons. Soils on hillslopes are mostly sandy loams, but clay loams and silty clay loams also are found. Soils are generally acidic; pH ranges from 4.5 to 5.9.

The Current Setting

Current land use on hillslopes in the northeastern hill region of India must be seriously reviewed, and a change in land use pattern is essential to achieve the ultimate goal of conserving soil on cultivated hillslopes and checking the degradation of soil on hillslopes. Of 25.5 million hectares in the region, a net area of 3 million hectares is under settled agriculture. An estimated 1.5 million hectares is under shifting cultivation. At any specific time, however, an area of only 390,000 hectares is affected by shifting cultiva-

Table 1. Losses resulting from the degradation of land in shifting cultivation.*

Item	Losses
Soil (t/ha)	40.90
Organic carbon (kg/ha)	698.00
Available P_2O_5 (kg/ha)	0.15
Available K_2O (kg/ha)	7.10

*Adapted from the proceedings of a workshop on agricultural research in the northeastern hill region, 1980.

Table 2. Classification of hillslopes.

Nature of Slope	Length of Hillslope	Depth of Soil
Less than 15° (27%)	Less than 40 m	Less than 60 cm
(S_1)	(L_1)	(D_1)
15°-45° (27%-100%)	40-80 m	60-90 cm
(S_2)	(L_2)	(D_2)
More than 45° (100%)	More than 80 m	More than 90 cm
(S_3)	(L_3)	(D_3)

tion, which constitutes about 38 percent of the total area under this practice. About 440,000 tribal families are involved in this practice. The magnitude of shifting cultivation in the region can easily be understood by the fact that in Nagaland the ratio of the area of settled agriculture to that of shifting cultivation is 1:1; in Mizoram, the ratio is 1:3; in Meghalaya, 1:1.5; in Tripura, 1:0.5; in Arunachal Pradesh, 1:2; and in Manipur, 1:2.5. This inappropriate land use has caused a tremendous amount of land degradation (Table 1).

Classification of Hillslopes

For the purpose of classifying hillslopes, three physical and topographical factors, which are of prime importance, have been chosen. They are nature of slope, depth of soil, and length of hillslope. The classification matrix proposed herein (Table 2) is based on the author's experiences in the region.

Proposed Land Use Planning for Hillslopes

Various limitations occur on hillslopes that are normally not present on plains. The major ones are landslope and depth of soil. Because of these limitations, converting every hillslope into bench terraces is neither practical nor advisable. Even where it is possible to convert an entire slope length into bench terraces, it may not be advisable to do so because of the huge amounts of labor and money requirements. Dividing a hillslope

Table 3. Extent of shifting cultivation in northeastern India.

State	Area	Net Area Sown	Annual Area Under Shifting Cultivation	Total Area Affected by Shifting Cultivation	No. of Families Involved in Shifting Cultivation
			1,000 hectares		
Arunachal Pradesh	8,374	112	70	210	54,000
Assam	7,852	2,696	69.6	139.2	58,000
Manipur	2,230	140	90	360	70,000
Meghalaya	2,249	193	53	265	52,290
Mizoram	2,108	65	63	189	50,000
Nagaland	1,658	153	19	191.3	116,046
Tripura	1,049	246	22.3	111.5	43,000
Total	25,520	3,605	386.9	1,466	443,336

Source: Directorate of Economics and Statistics, Ministry of Agriculture, Government of India.

Table 4. Proposed land use planning for hillslopes.

Nature of Slope and Length of Hillslope	Depth of Soil		
	D_1	D_2	D_3
S_1L_1	BT* or H on entire slope	BT only	BT only
S_1L_2	BT or H, on entire slope	BT only	BT only
S_1L_3	a. BT or H, on entire slope, or b. BT in lower section + H in upper	BT in lower section + H in upper	BT in lower section + H in upper
S_2L_1	H only	BT or H, on entire slope	BT or H, on entire slope
S_2L_2	H only	a. BT in lower section + H in upper, or b. BT or H, on entire slope	BT in lower section + H in upper
S_2L_3	H only	BT in lower section + H in upper	BT in lower section + H in middle + F in upper
S_3L_1	To be kept under natural cover/ forestry	H or F on entire slope	H or F on entire slope
S_3L_2	-do-	H in lower section + F in upper	H in lower section + F in upper
S_3L_3	-do-	H in lower section + F in upper	-do-

*BT, bench terracing; H, horticulture; F, forestry.

into two or three sections is more pragmatic. Different land uses can then be assigned to different sections.

Over-exploitation of hillslopes in the region is due mainly to shifting cultivation (Table 3). Keeping in mind the objective of replacing this damaging practice, the different land uses are given: (a) agronomic crops (bench terracing recommended); (b) horticultural crops, including fruit crops, vegetable crops, and plantation crops; and (c) forestry.

Table 4 provides the details of the land use planning that has been proposed for different combinations of nature of slope, length of slope, and depth of soil.

Conclusion

Because the classification of hillslopes cannot be done as precisely as one might hope, overlapping may occur in borderline cases. It is, therefore, necessary to exercise a judicious and cautious approach. Table 4 should serve as a general guide for land use planning on hillslopes. There can be no single prescription for all situations.

USE OF BASIC EROSION PRINCIPLES TO IDENTIFY EFFECTIVE EROSION CONTROL PRACTICES

L. DONALD MEYER, CHIA-CHUN WU, and EARL H. GRISSINGER

Soil conservation is essential for continued productivity on agricultural cropland, particularly hillslope fields. Without conservation practices, serious soil erosion can occur, resulting in land degradation, severely reduced productivity, increased runoff, and off-site sedimentation problems. To cultivate sloping cropland safely, effective erosion control practices and techniques must be developed and used widely by farmers. Although many effective erosion control practices have evolved from farm experience plus limited research, the methodology employed for erosion control has seldom fully used available knowledge of the principles and processes involved in soil erosion by water.

Persons who understand basic runoff and erosion principles and processes are more likely to be better soil conservation farmers, erosion control advisers, and researchers. If one understands the basic principles and recent concepts of soil erosion processes relative to the techniques that effectively reduce soil erosion by water, this knowledge can then be applied to help identify appropriate erosion control methods and practices for specific problems encountered when developing soil conservation plans for hillslope farms.

Erosive Agents

Soil erosion is caused by various erosive agents, including rainfall and the resulting runoff, wind, and gravity. Cropland erosion on hillslopes is primarily due to rainfall and runoff, although other erosive agents may be important for some conditions.

Much of the hillslope land that is farmed throughout the world receives a meter or more of rainfall each year. One meter of rain falling on 1 hectare of land has a volume of 10,000 cubic meters, a mass of about 10 million kilograms, and falls with an impact energy of 200 to 300 megajoules. Raindrops vary in size from mist to about 7 millimeters in diameter, with an average diameter between 1 and 3 millimeters for the more intense storms. Trillions of these raindrops annually bombard each hectare of land in the humid regions of the world at impact velocities up to 9 meters per second. Runoff from hillslope fields totals several hundred millimeters annually in many parts of the world, yet only 100 millimeters of runoff amounts to 100 million liters per square kilometer. These great quantities of rainfall and runoff can erode large amounts of soil from unprotected areas of erodible land.

Soil Erosion and Sediment Transport Processes

The companion processes of soil erosion and sedimentation by water involve the detachment, transportation, and deposition of soil material. These processes often recur intermittently as rainstorms progress. Soil detachment is the separation and movement of soil material from the position where it rests. During rainstorms, raindrops strike exposed soil as tiny bombs, detaching soil material as the near-spherical drops flatten outward from the point of impact. Detachment by raindrops is relatively uniform over an entire area of exposed soil and does not change greatly as the land surface steepens. When rainfall exceeds infiltration and runoff occurs, the runoff detaches soil by its scour forces. Detachment by runoff occurs primarily where flow concentrates on a rather small portion of the area, and it increases rapidly with the steepness of the flow route. Any precipitation that falls as snow may melt and cause detachment by runoff long after the precipitation has occurred, or it may add major amounts of runoff to subsequent rainstorms.

Transportation of detached soil results from both raindrop splash and flowing runoff. Most soil moved by water for major distances is transported by surface runoff, although considerable soil may be moved short distances by raindrop splash to flow concentrations. The quantity and size of material that can be transported are functions of runoff characteristics, such as flow velocity and turbulence, which generally increase as the slope steepens and as runoff increases. The transport capacity of runoff on steep slopes is often much greater than the available sediment detached by rainfall and runoff from cohesive soils, so all or most of the detached material will be transported to or beyond the end of the slope. On much flatter slopes, runoff may not be capable of transporting all available sediment; so some may deposit along the flow route.

Deposition of transported soil due to the insufficient transport capability of surface runoff is a selective process. Larger and more dense materials settle first, while finer materials are transported for longer distances. Therefore, the size distribution of sediment leaving an eroding area may not be representative of the material detached within that area if major deposition has occurred upstream of the point of measurement.

Sediment Sources

Sediment that is eroded from hillslopes comes from three sources: (1) interrill areas, the areas between locations where runoff has concentrated; (2) rills, relatively small, easily obliterated channels eroded by relatively small concentrations of runoff; and (3) gullies, larger, more persistent channels eroded by major concentrations of runoff.

Interrill erosion results from soil detachment by raindrop impact plus transport of detached soil by splash and thin-film runoff. Because rainfall is relatively uniform over a hillslope, interrill erosion varies little unless soil or cover change. Great amounts of soil may be eroded by interrill erosion, but this form of erosion is usually relatively inconspicuous compared with the more obvious rill and gully erosion.

Rill erosion results primarily from locally concentrated runoff. It occurs on only a small portion of the land surface. Rills often develop where runoff concentrates because of minor topographic variations, tillage marks, or random irregularities in the land surface. Rill erosion does not begin until the flow's erosiveness exceeds the soil's ability to resist detachment. As a result, runoff may flow for a considerable distance downslope before rilling occurs. Rilling, once it begins, increases rapidly as the flow accumulates. It also increases with slope steepness. On steeper slopes, rills often progress upslope by a series of intensively eroding headcuts or nickpoints, where gravity may be a major contributing cause of soil detachment.

Gully erosion also results from concentrated runoff, but it is larger in scale and affects the landscape more than does the relatively transient rill erosion. Both ephemeral gullies and major permanent gullies develop and persist because of dominant features of land topography, whereas rills may change locations from time to time because of farming and other land use operations. Slumping of gully sidewalls, induced by gravitational forces, often provides much of the soil debris that is removed by subsequent runoff. The presence of gullies is evidence of serious soil erosion and poor land management.

The relative contributions of interrill, rill, and gully erosion to total erosion vary depending on topography, climate, cropping system, and soil characteristics. Interrill erosion changes relatively little over a hillslope field. Rill erosion varies from none near the top of a slope to major amounts downslope. Severe gully erosion generally does not begin until major quantities of runoff have accumulated. For sloping land with much exposed soil, interrill erosion generally dominates at the shorter distances, rill erosion is greatest at moderate slope lengths, and gully erosion may exceed that from other sources on long or steep slopes. The proportion of sediment originating from rill and gully erosion relative to that from interrill erosion generally increases with steeper slopes, more intense rain, greater soil cover, and less permeable soils.

Sediment Characteristics

Sediment characteristics, especially size and density, affect the transportability of sediment by runoff and the likelihood of its subsequent deposition. Sediment eroded from cohesive cropland soils consists of both primary and aggregated soil particles. The size distribution of sediment from hillslope fields depends on soil texture, extent of soil aggregation, and stability of the aggregated portion. Aggregation and stability are affected by various soil properties, including the amount and type of clay, organic matter content, and amount of iron. For well-aggregated soils, the sediment may be much coarser than the texture of the soil from which it eroded.

Sediment that erodes as primary particles has a density of about 2.65 megagrams per cubic meter, whereas the density of eroding aggregates is considerable less. Aggregate density depends on soil mineralogy and aggregate size. Even though aggregates are less dense, they are generally more difficult to transport in runoff than the primary particles of which they are composed because the aggregates are so much larger.

Erosion Control Principles

The control of soil erosion by water involves avoiding, reducing, or counteracting the erosive forces of rainfall and runoff to reduce soil detachment and sediment transport and/or to increase sediment deposition. Principles of erosion control include dissipating raindrop impact energy and runoff scour forces on nonerodible materials rather than on erodible soil, reducing the amount of runoff, slowing runoff flow velocities, improving soil characteristics that resist erosive forces, and preventing massive soil movement.

Because soil erosion by water begins when falling raindrops strike exposed soil, any nonerodible material that intercepts the raindrops and dissipates their energy will reduce soil detachment. Such soil protection is afforded by standing vegetation, plant residues, nonvegetative mulches, and even thick films of surface water. Soil cover also may reduce soil surface sealing, thus promoting infiltration and reducing runoff.

Exposed soil also may be detached by runoff scour forces, so soil protection that dissipates scour forces on nonerodible surfaces will help control erosion. Dense vegetation is very effective in protecting the soil surface from scour and in dissipating the erosive forces of runoff. Surface mulches also are effective unless they are floated away by the runoff. Plant canopy cover above the depth of runoff does not prevent scour erosion.

Because the amount of sediment that runoff can carry depends on the amount of runoff, transport of eroded soil can be reduced by reducing runoff. Less runoff results from increased infiltration when soil surface sealing is prevented and when the soil surface is kept rough enough that it ponds major quantities of potential runoff.

The erosiveness of runoff depends greatly on its flow velocity. Runoff is incapable of detaching soil until its shear stress is greater than the soil's critical shear stress. Furthermore, the size of sediment that can be carried and the flow's capacity to transport sediment increase as flow velocity increases. Therefore, erosion can be controlled if runoff is slowed by vegetation or by routing runoff around the field slope at small gradients rather than allowing it to flow directly downslope. Whenever runoff velocity is reduced, runoff loses sediment transport capability, and some of its sediment load may deposit.

Soil erosion occurs when the soil can no longer resist the erosive forces of rainfall and runoff. Anything that helps the soil withstand these erosive forces has the potential to reduce erosion. For instance, vegetation and vegetative residues tend to improve soil structure and strengthen aggregation. The influence of vegetation is greatest during its period of growth and decreases for several years thereafter. Intensive cultivation of land generally degrades soil structure and reduces aggregation, with some crops doing more harm than others. In addition to the benefit or harm that different cropping and tillage systems have on soil properties, they also may affect sediment size. Improved soil structure and better aggregation not only retard erosion but also generally result in coarser, less transportable sediment.

Land experiencing massive soil erosion generally loses its productivity rapidly. Farming methods must be designed to eliminate uncontrolled rilling and gullying because, once these begin, land degradation proceeds rapidly. Often, such land becomes so dissected with deep channels that farming is almost impossible. Prevention of severe soil movement by vegetative cover, runoff routing, and conservation structures before serious problems develop is important because thereafter cropland is less valuable and control measures are much more difficult and expensive.

Selecting Erosion Control Practices

Effective erosion control is the ultimate goal of most efforts to better understand the complex processes involved in soil erosion and sediment transport. The increasing body of knowledge needs to be used more in selecting control practices that are both effective and practicable. Certainly, many control practices have been developed and improved by trial and error. Even these may be improved further by considering the principles and processes that are important in specific situations. For each application, the individual processes critical for control need to be identified as a basis for selecting appropriate control measures. Furthermore, conservationists must recognize that control often involves a system of conservation practices, not just individual practices. Often, selected combinations of conservation practices enhance each other toward effective erosion control.

When selecting practices for soils and climatic conditions where serious interrill erosion due to raindrop impact is a problem, protection of the soil surface by vegetation or mulches can be very effective. Maintenance of soil surface cover throughout the year is especially important, so minimizing tillage and use of cropping systems that require land disturbance only during those times of the year when major rainstorms are uncommon should be emphasized. Close-growing vegetation may be very important, along with or instead of wide-row crops.

For land where the topography and cropping system are susceptible to serious rilling and gullying, runoff reduction and management must be given high priority. Practices that increase infiltration and thereby reduce runoff will be very helpful. Such practices may include vegetation or plant residues to reduce surface sealing and maintain good soil structure and tillage practices that minimize soil compaction. Control of the remaining runoff can be achieved by routing collected runoff around the slope at nonerosive velocities using such practices as terraces and controlled row grades. If runoff is so great that it cannot be controlled in this way, detention structures and/or vegetated waterways may be required.

High-silt soils or poorly structured clay soils produce fine sediment that is easily transported. Deposition of sediment from such soils is unlikely once it has been detached, so practices that provide good soil cover and

Table 1. Effective approaches and control practices for erosion problems on hillslopes.

Erosion Problem	Effective Approaches	Control Practices
Interrill erosion by raindrop impact and/or	Improve ground cover	Vegetation or mulches to protect soil surface during seasons of major rainstorms.
Rill/gully erosion by runoff scour	Increase infiltration	Soil cover to prevent surface sealing. Rough soil surface to increase ponding.
	Control runoff	Runoff routing to reduce flow velocities. Vegetation to dissipate scour forces. Structures to detain and control flow.
Fine sediment and/or	Prevent soil detachment	Vegetation or mulches to protect soil.
Coarse sediment	Prevent soil detachment Trap detached sediment	Vegetation or mulches to protect soil. Dense vegetation to slow runoff. Runoff routing to slow runoff. Structures to detain and control flow.
Steep, long slopes or	Prevent soil detachment Control runoff	Vegetation or mulches to protect soil. Runoff routing to reduce flow velocities. Vegetation to dissipate scour forces. Structures to detain and control flow.
Flatland fields	Prevent soil detachment Reduce sediment transport capability	Vegetation or mulches to protect soil. Vegetation to slow flow velocities.
Intense rainstorms or	Prevent soil detachment Control runoff	Vegetation and mulches to protect soil. Runoff routing to reduce flow velocities. Vegetation to dissipate scour forces. Structures to detain and control flow.
Low-intensity storms and snow	Increase infiltration	Soil cover to prevent surface sealing. Rough soil surface to increase ponding.
	Control runoff	Runoff routing to reduce flow velocities. Vegetation to dissipate scour forces. Structures to detain and control flow.

thereby prevent soil detachment are important. In contrast, much of the sediment detached from coarse-textured or well-aggregated soils will be relatively coarse. Such sediment can be trapped more easily in vegetation, furrows or terraces of controlled grades, or detention structures. For the latter soils, preventing detachment at the source is still the most desirable practice, but other means that reduce runoff and cause local deposition of eroded material also will prevent major sediment losses.

During intense rainstorms, land with steep or long slopes that lacks runoff control practices will have runoff with high transport capability. Soil losses for such conditions will seldom be limited by the runoff's capacity to move sediment, so prevention of initial detachment of sediment is important. In contrast, runoff on land with nearly flat slopes usually will have low velocities with limited transport capability. Soil losses can be reduced on such land by practices that further slow runoff velocities.

Hill land that is subject to large, intense rainstorms especially needs good soil cover to prevent both detachment by raindrops and scour by runoff. Other hillslopes that are subject mostly to low-intensity rainstorms and/or frozen precipitation need protection from concentrated runoff much more than protection from raindrop impact. For such land, increasing infiltration of precipitation and use of practices to properly manage runoff will be effective erosion control methods.

Obviously, these illustrations, summarized in table 1, are not an exhaustive list of approaches to the wide range of erosion problems that are encountered worldwide. They are simply examples of approaches that should be considered. Hopefully, they will help conservationists realize the merits of assessing the specific problems of each site and then using their knowledge of soil erosion and sediment transport principles and processes to select effective and farmer-acceptable practices.

Summary

Soil erosion and sediment transport by water involve complex interrelationships of many principles and processes. Control of soil erosion involves identifying effective control practices that successfully combat the forces of rainfall and runoff occurring on a specific site. Practices control erosive processes by dissipating raindrop-impact and runoff-scour energy, reducing runoff amount and velocity, and/or improving soil conditions to resist erosion. Some practices are more effective than others in dealing with specific problems, but even the effective ones from a scientific standpoint also should be assessed for practicability from the farming viewpoint. Persons who understand basic runoff and erosion principles and processes are better equipped to be farmers, conservationists, and researchers. Understanding major control principles and processes will also allow their use in selecting or developing effective practices, rather than arbitrarily applying standard methods to conditions for which they are not the most appropriate.

CONSERVATION FARMING 4

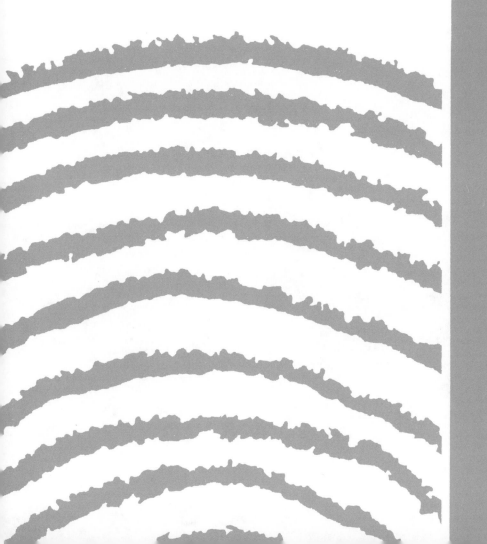

CONSERVATION FARMING:
A CHALLENGE TO ALL

TED C. SHENG

Conservation farming is a new term that has been used extensively in recent years but which has not yet been clearly defined. It is by no means synonymous with "conservation tillage," which is a kind of practice "that reduces loss of soil and water relative to conventional tillage" (5). Nor does conservation farming simply mean farming on land treated with some conservation measures.

One definition could be: "Farming according to conservation principles." But conservation farming implies more than that. A tentative definition follows: "Conservation farming is a type of farming system that reduces soil erosion and maintains or improves land productivity at the same time for the purpose of benefiting farmers' and nations' soil and water resources."

If this definition is agreeable, let's look further into several key elements of conservation farming. First, it should be a farming system. Experience indicates that unless soil conservation is integrated into a farming system as one package, or unless it emerges as a new system, it will not be accepted easily by farmers. Second, conservation farming stresses "sustainability," not only the sustainability of land productivity, but also the sustainability of the whole system of production, including maintenance of conservation practices. Third, the system should be beneficial to a nation or society; more importantly, it should benefit the farmers who practice it. This is probably most crucial and certainly the most essential element.

Scope of Conservation Farming

Existing Examples. There should be no lack of examples of conservation farming in the world. The problem is that until recently we have

135

not studied or investigated this area. We are not talking about farming systems in general; we are talking about farming systems that apply conservation principles and benefit both the land and the people. Except for the wet rice paddy system, which has sustained Asia's population for a thousand years, what do we know about other conservation farming systems? Should we study the multicultural systems in the hills of Central America and examine their protection functions? What about tea and rubber plantations in Asia where conservation principles have been observed, or coffee plantations in Latin America where agroforestry is practiced? In Taiwan, for instance, vegetables, fruits, cut flowers, and other horticultural crops are grown on terraces. Does this form of intensive cultivation and cash crops induce or promote conservation work? What about hill farms around the cities or towns of the world where water is available and vegetables are grown? Have these farmers easily accepted soil conservation as a necessary measure? No doubt we could learn much from these and other existing examples.

Scope of Work. Because knowledge of conservation farming is limited, only a temporary list of the work encompassed by conservation farming can be constructed. Included are the following categories:
   • Cropping practices that provide protective cover to the ground, temporally or spatially, for the purpose of minimizing soil detachment and/or increasing production.
   • Land treatments that control or slow down runoff and soil transportation and, at the same time, facilitate irrigation, drainage, or farming practices on hillslopes.
   • Farming activities that improve soil fertility, structure, infiltration capacity, and other soil properties and that increase water supplies or conserve soil moisture.
   • Other farm work that conserves energy, increases biomass, or recycles organic matters and farm waste.

Research and Development

Trends of Farming System Research and Development. A brief introduction to trends in farming system research and development is essential to understanding and discussing conservation farming systems. Farming system research and development is a new activity stemming from the small farmers in the Third World being unreceptive to research results delivered by government stations or extension agents. A close study of the problem, therefore, is needed, with emphasis on viewing the whole farm as a system (7).
   In the past, most studies concentrated on cropping systems or farming

practices. The new approach stresses reaching an overall understanding of farming systems from both micro and macro standpoints and thereby developing technologies to fit farmers' needs (*1*). This kind of client-oriented research and development is based on the farmers' perspective rather than "push out" from government researchers (*2*). To develop or improve any farming system, farmers' active participation is necessary (*3*).

What Can We Learn from Farming System Research and Development?
Three things can be learned from farming system research and development. First, from a broader perspective, conservation farming is a farming system (or systems) that is very necessary on hillslopes. Such systems are not yet recognized by many, not to mention receiving profound research and study. Farming system research and development approaches must be learned, and cooperation with experts in this field must be made to study various systems of conservation farming in the world. As farming system research and development people point out, any farming system is not a closed system. It actually interacts within a milieu of other systems (*1*).

Second, soil conservationists in developing countries face much more difficulty in selling their technology than agricultural researchers or extension people simply because small farmers traditionally exploit their land to maximize returns. From a farmer's view, soil conservation may do just the opposite—benefiting distant future with an additional cost for land treatment. Soil conservation is thus less receptive to them than other agricultural improvement activities. For this reason alone, conservationists should work harder than researchers and people in extension to understand the constraints and problems of the small farmers and their overall farming systems in order to get the message across. More techniques must be learned from farming system research and development.

Third, soil conservation is a science and an art. It is also field-specific. No one predetermined technology or practice, such as bench terracing, can be applied on every farm. Conservationists should devise a host of techniques for a farmer to choose from according to his or her interest, resources, and cropping plans. The real challenge is how to fit farmers' needs and keep the work cost-effective because farmers tend to invest as little as possible in soil conservation. Something may be learned from farming system research and development.

The Challenge

For any farming system to succeed, it must be productive, profitable, acceptable, and sustainable (*4*). Although sustainability is the conservationist's chief skill and goal, to achieve it still requires proper technology to fit each farm. After farmers adopt recommended conservation measures, maintenance may still pose a problem.

Acceptability is always a problem confronting most soil conservation projects. It is related to problems of tradition, culture, and socioeconomic conditions of the farmers. Because soil conservation means extra cost or labor and its benefits may be distant, it contradicts the farmers' immediate goal of maximizing returns. Taking away productive land for conservation installations makes conservation projects even more unpopular. Here, in addition to persuasion, compensation or other incentives may be required. However, these measures could become a burden to many developing countries.

Productivity cannot be easily attained by simply building terraces and putting compost and fertilizers into the soils. Increasing productivity may involve the entire cropping system and a series of farming activities, including better seeds, weed control, tillage techniques, and insect and pest controls. Sometimes, irrigation, water-harvesting, and moisture retention techniques are also required. Does all this expertise exist?

Probably the most crucial criterion is profitability. Increasing crop production does not necessarily mean higher profits for farmers if the products cannot reach the proper markets or prices are low. On the other hand, all conservation and cropping improvements mean more inputs. Farmers' risks are high unless an interdisciplinary approach, including better access to market and price support, is provided.

All these constitute a serious challenge. The task cannot be done single-handedly; a team approach is a must. Most soil conservationists are physical scientists, such as agronomists, foresters, engineers, or soil scientists. To search for or develop proper conservation farming systems, close support is needed from experts in farming systems and from economists, sociologists, and people in other disciplines.

In developing countries, where human resources and institutional capacity are limited and erosion and land degradation hazards are serious, the challenge is enormous.

Some Recommended Strategies

To deal with this challenge, strategies must be devised carefully to alleviate the problems involved. A farming systems approach will have a better chance to succeed than a narrow-minded or over-specialized one.

Study of Existing Systems. As mentioned, local farming systems must first be studied, whether they are conservation-oriented or not, to comprehend the problems, constraints, and improvement possibilities. Only after such studies are completed can a practical system that is integrated with conservation principles be devised or modified for the farmers in a particular area.

Interdisciplinary Approach. An interdisciplinary approach is needed for studying or introducing conservation farming systems. In the past, over-specialized approaches resulted in providing fragmentary or even conflicting information to farmers. For any conservation program or project, interdisciplinary teams should be organized at the field level to assist farmers who are interested in conservation farming. Governments in developing countries should try their best to place such teams in project or watershed areas.

Bottom-Up Planning. For planning an individual farm or a cluster of farms in a conservation program, farmers should be actively involved in the planning process and decision-making (8). Many conservation projects fail because farmers are not involved at all in such processes. Meanwhile, the emphasis of conservation farm planning is best placed on viewing the whole farm as a system. A farmer's ability, resources, interest, and constraints all must be considered. In addition, the macro settings of the farming enterprise, such as government policy, incentive schemes, credit availability, and marketing, should also be taken into consideration. After explanation and advice from government technicians, the final decision should be made by the farmers.

There is no lack of theories regarding bottom-up planning. The real problems are putting these theories into practice with hundreds or thousands of small farmers in a project area and whether governments have the will, patience, and resources to do so. Soil conservationists must insist on bottom-up planning. In the meantime, they need to develop practical ways and means to do such planning, for example, using a subwatershed or neighboring area as a unit, applying stratification techniques (6), and employing computer-expert systems and geographic information systems mapping.

Policy Support. The need for government policy support for conservation farming cannot be overemphasized. In many developing countries, inconsistent policy sometimes encourages soil depletion rather than conservation. For instance, subsidies are given to farmers to open and cultivate new hillslopes, regardless of conservation necessity. Government land settlement or crop expansion schemes on hillslopes omit soil conservation inputs. Farmers are confused, and many of them practice conservation farming and slash-and-burn agriculture at the same time. Government should, therefore, hold a steady policy everywhere in the nation. For instance, farmers who practice conservation farming could be given priorities for government technical and financial assistance. On the other hand, government itself should set good examples and include soil conservation in its own land development schemes.

System and Management Research. Most research in soil conservation today centers on erosion rates and conservation techniques. Seldom have research activities been channeled, for instance, to study whole systems of conservation farming, farmers' attitudes toward conservation, or constraints and risks in applying soil conservation. More studies need to be done in this respect. In addition, management research on policy issues, on incentives, on cost-sharing, and on other socioeconomic elements of conservation should be emphasized. This kind of system and managerial research is much needed in the Third World.

REFERENCES

1. Axinn, G. H., and N. W. Axinn. 1987. *Farming system research in its macropolicy dimensions.* In *How Systems Work. Proceedings, Farming Systems Research Symposium.* University of Arkansas and Winrock International, Little Rock.
2. Collinson, M. 1988. *FSR (farming systems research) in evolution: Past and future.* In *Proceedings, Farming Systems Research Symposium.* University of Arkansas, Fayetteville.
3. Friedrich, K. H. 1986. *Farming systems development: An approach to small farmer development in developing countries.* Food and Agriculture Organization, United Nations, Rome, Italy.
4. Herdt, R. W. 1987. *Whither farming systems.* In *How Systems Work. Proceedings, Farming Systems Research Sympoisum.* University of Arkansas and Winrock International, Little Rock.
5. Mannering, J. V., and R. F. Charles. 1983. *What is conservation tillage?* Journal of Soil and Water Conservation 38(3): 140-143.
6. Shaner, W. W. 1984. *Stratification: An approach to cost-effectiveness for farming systems research and development.* Agricultural Systems 15. Elsevier Applied Science Publishers Ltd., London, England.
7. Shaner, W. W., P. F. Phillip, and W. R. Schmehl. 1982. *Farming systems research and development.* Westview Press, Boulder, Colorado.
8. Sheng, T. C. 1978. *Programming conservation farming: Some essential steps in assisting small farmers.* In *Watershed Conservation.* Chinese Soil and Water Conservation Society, Taipei, Taiwan, and Colorado State University, Fort Collins.

CONSERVATION FARMING: THE BALANCED FARMING WAY

ALBERT R. HAGAN

Conservation farming, in principle, is widely acclaimed throughout the world as a system of farming essential for the well-being of individual farm families and an enduring agriculture. Helping farm families achieve such systems has been an ongoing challenge for agricultural leaders in every country in which soil erosion and depletion have taken a heavy toll.

Several decades ago in Missouri, a unique approach to achieving conservation farming was conceived. It evolved into a statewide program called "Balanced Farming for Better Living." For the thousands of farm families who participated, it became a system of farming that eliminated soil erosion, generated higher productivity and income, and enhanced family living.

Balanced farming is based on the premises that farm families want to do better, that their long-range goals can be specified, and that problems that hinder their achievement can be identified and minimized. With this background and a realistic inventory of all available resources, each family can plan, evaluate, and compare various systems to determine the one most suitable for achieving family goals.

The basis for the new conservation system for the farm and family is a long-range balanced farming plan that serves as a guide or blueprint for year-by-year development. Planning is simplified by separating the overall system into three major components—family living, land use, and livestock (where applicable)—all of which are closely interrelated and competitive for family resources.

The planning procedure involves a logical step-by-step process for evaluating and comparing the economic consequences of various systems under consideration before any changes are actually made. It has proved successful on thousands of Missouri farms for almost 50 years and has been adapted for teaching and experimental use in developing countries around the world, such as Tunisia, Libya, Tanzania, Kenya, Nepal, India, Barbados, Taiwan, Philippines, and Central America.

Balanced farming is a true farming systems approach in contrast to the piecemeal efforts that have been attempted in many development projects in recent years. It is in accord with the way farm families naturally think of their farming operations—as integrated, overall systems of farming and family living, rather than as separate, isolated technologies and enterprises. The latter is too often the case in conservation efforts in the United States and aid agencies worldwide.

Why the Balanced Farming Approach?

The need to develop a coordinated farming approach has been expressed by numerous conservation writers in recent years. For example, Norman Hudson, past president of the World Association of Soil and Water Conservation, has stated: "Although the objective of conservation farming is quite clear, there is often a shortage of information on how to do this. There is need for adaptive on-farm research on conservation farming systems—not looking for new crops or breeding new varieties—but putting together existing knowledge into farming systems that meet local needs" (5).

The balanced farming approach is unique in a number of ways when compared with other widely used approaches. It differs in basic concepts and premises, in planning procedures, in economic evaluations of alternative farming systems, and in program methodology.

Planning Procedures for Balanced Farming

The Systems Concept. The key feature of the balanced farming approach is a long-range plan for the whole farm and family unit. It embraces all of the resources available to the family: the land, crop and livestock enterprises, family labor, and the equipment and other forms of capital.

Some argue that the systems idea is far too complex for farmers to understand, especially for small-farm operators who often have very little formal education. Even highly trained scientists, they contend, have difficulty in comprehending and evaluating overall farming systems.

But for farmers such comprehension is not difficult. They already have a farming system, whether in Missouri, Taiwan, or any other country throughout the world. It may be an unsophisticated, traditional system handed down from generation to generation, but they understand how it works and how it performs. Furthermore, they will be reluctant to adopt any new system, with associated individual technologies, unless its future performance is clearly understood and assured.

Farming System Components. Planning the farming/family-living system and comparing the economic consequences of alternative plans is simplified by coordinating three major components of the complete system. These components and some of their interrelationships are illustrated in figure 1 as one working model of the overall system.

• *Component 1—family living component.* The family living component is the decision-making unit responsible for all managerial decisions, those affecting the organization and use of all resources available to the farm and family.

• *Component 2—land use component.* The land use component is the primary income source. It includes all production from the land, including that for sale, for family consumption, and for livestock feed. This component is of primary concern in conservation farming. It concerns the crops produced and the support technologies to enhance productivity and save the soil. The combination of all these constitutes the cropping system.

• *Component 3—livestock component.* The livestock component includes all livestock included in the farming system, including production for sale and for family consumption. The combination of all livestock enterprises and supporting technologies constitutes the livestock system.

As will be illustrated later, this breakdown of the farming system simplifies and expedites planning alternative systems, and evaluating and comparing the potential performance of each plan before any changes are made.

The Planning Process. Every proposed change in a farm family's system of farming and family living, whether it be adopting a single conservation practice, or changing crop and livestock enterprises, is a major undertaking. Before accepting such an undertaking, some very logical and pertinent questions often are asked:

• Will it work on my farm?

• What is required? How much additional labor and capital will be needed?

• Can I afford to do it? Will it pay in the long run and how will it effect cash flow year by year?

• Is it feasible from the standpoint of government programs and policies, market accessibility, facilities for implementing, cultural and religious constraints, etc.?

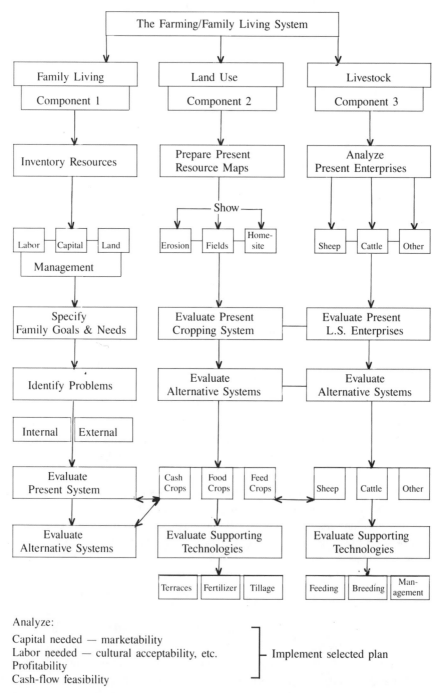

Figure 1. The Farming Systems Approach—Components & Relationships.

• Will it enhance the long-range welfare, security, and survival of my family?

Answers to these and similar questions must be obvious before most farm families will adopt new technologies and farming systems. Finding answers is not easy, especially since they want to know before changes are made. Providing some assurance requires procedures for evaluating proposals, from the physical and economic standpoint, before adjustments are made.

Economic Evaluations of Alternative Systems. A logical, step-by-step procedure was developed long ago for bringing together the various components, and evaluating the economic consequences of combining them in various kinds of overall systems for farming and family living.

Measuring and evaluating future performance is always a challenging task. For specific technologies and farming practices, the job is comparatively simple and straightforward. For example, field trials, either at the experiment station or on the farm, used to compare various crop varieties and soil treatments can be evaluated in physical terms by the relative yields from each variety, as well as other characteristics. This has been done by agronomists for many years.

Economic evaluations and comparisons also can be made by pricing the outputs and costing the inputs used in the production processes. These, too, are long-standing research procedures.

Evaluating economic performance of a complete system for the farm and family unit is somewhat more involved and, unfortunately, often is not done in most conservation planning. It requires a different kind of analytical procedure. The procedure developed in Missouri and a few other states several decades ago was a process of comparative budgeting, sometimes called "block budgeting." This procedure, with accompanying worksheets and reference data, was simple enough for use in the field by extension workers and farm families who had no special training in economics. It required no special calculating equipment although small hand calculators, which became available later, contributed to the speed and accuracy of calculations.

This procedure was designed to help farm families evaluate and compare the requirements and returns from various acceptable long-range plans before any changes are made. Comparative measures included the requirements for labor and capital, and the potential profitability, cash-flow feasibility, marketability of products, cultural acceptability, etc., as illustrated in figure 1.

Enterprise Budgets. To expedite calculations, the cropping system in component 2 and the livestock system in component 3 are separated further into smaller units or blocks. Each block is one unit of either a crop or livestock enterprise budget. It is called either a "gross-margin" or an "income-over-variable-cost" budget for each unit.

Because long-range plans for the whole farming/family-living system are designed to estimate the anticipated performance over a period of years, evaluation of each plan is based upon the expectations for a typical year after the plan is fully implemented. For the same reason, the yields, prices of products, costs of inputs, etc., for the enterprise budgets are based upon long-range estimates rather than current data.

Each enterprise budget consists of four major parts:

1. The yield or output from one unit (hectare, cow, etc.) of the enterprise, the price per unit of output, and the gross income per unit.

2. Itemized and total variable costs for inputs required per unit of the enterprise.

3. The income over variable costs (gross margin) per unit.

4. The hours of labor required per unit. Total investment capital needed for the enterprise unit sometimes is an added item.

The calculations, as noted, provide four measures of requirements and returns from one unit of each enterprise, which is the basis for an economic evaluation of the enterprise itself. In addition, these unitary budgets then become essential building blocks for economic evaluations of the entire farming system.

Preparation of enterprise budgets is an interdisciplinary activity in which cooperative efforts of both extension and research personnel are essential. The advice and help from local extension workers and farmers themselves often are needed in developing realistic and usable budgets. Such interactions are quite challenging and useful as they focus attention on the economic significance of each enterprise and technology recommended, not only within themselves, but also as integral parts of the overall farming system in which they are included.

Steps in Farm Planning. After preparing adapted enterprise budgets (or blocks) as indicated above and assembling other reference data pertinent to an area, preparing and evaluating plans for alternative farming systems with individual farm families can begin. A logical, systematic procedure for assembling and analyzing the various parts of the overall system is needed.

This procedure has been adapted for use in countries other than the United States. One example of this is the "Farming Systems Planning Book," which was prepared for a special farm planning shortcourse conducted in 1981 in Bulacan Province in the Philippines for the Farming Systems Development Corporation.

Following is a brief description of each step in the planning procedure. Worksheets for each step simplify calculations.

Step 1—inventory resources. The starting point for all long-time plans is to summarize the present situation for the farm and family. A simple, classified inventory will provide an overall picture of available resources. By adding monetary values, a financial statement can be prepared quickly, as well as a brief summary of investment-type capital needed for further calculations.

A map of the complete farm unit, showing all tracts, fields, physical resources, etc., also is essential for well-designed plans. A more detailed map of the homesite (often separate from field tracts) will help identify small areas where fruit and vegetable crops, and small-scale livestock enterprises may be added to enhance the family food supply and salable products.

Step 2—specify family goals. Specific family goals are unique for each farm family and form the basis for realistic farm plans that can be evaluated over time. Saving the soil, increasing production, and stepping up family income are common goals, but others may have higher priority, such as family security and survival on many small-farm family units.

Step 3—identify problems. Every farm family has problems that hinder goal achievement, and each can quickly list them in order of severity from ongoing experience. Some problems may relate directly to the farm and family, such as soil erosion, low yields, lack of equipment, shortage of family labor, lack of water for the household, not enough family food, etc. Other external problems often are outside the family's control, such as bad roads, lack of rain when needed, low prices, inaccessible markets, restrictive governmental policies, and cultural constraints.

Long-range planning should be a problem-solving procedure. Unless designed for the unique goals and problems of the individual family, such plans have little realism and usefulness. Most often, they will be ignored.

Step 4—evaluate alternative plans. The first step is to evaluate the present system, using the family resource and investment data, and the crop and livestock enterprise budgets to be used in evaluating alternative systems. By using the appropriate worksheets, the income over variable costs for the overall cropping and livestock systems (including any additional family food produced), and the labor requirements can be calculated.

Summary data for these calculations can then be transferred easily to worksheets for computing several profitability and cash-flow feasibility measures, such as: (1) total capital and labor requirements, (2) total income over variable costs, (3) net cash farm income, (4) net farm profit, (5) return to family labor, (6) return to capital, (7) total cash family income, and (8) net cash available for the family.

Various alternative systems, including various combinations of crop and livestock enterprises, new technologies and farming practices, off-farm employment opportunities, etc., can then be evaluated using the same procedures and standards as outlined above. Only systems considered to be workable and acceptable to the family should be evaluated with them.

Step 5—choose a plan. By comparing the various measures of performance calculated for each alternative system, the family can choose a plan best suited to meet the goals and needs specified earlier.

Step 6—implement the plan. No improved plan has value to the family until implemented, usually a step at a time over a period of several years. Getting started quickly with a major improvement or two that have the greatest impact on family income and welfare is a strong motivating force for further adjustments. Outside help from extension/research personnel, government agencies, business firms, contractors, etc., often will expedite implementation.

Step 7—evaluate progress. Physical improvements made in a well-designed plan soon become obvious. Less visible, but perhaps more important, are the improvements in farm profits, net cash family income, labor requirements, and other such performance measures as calculated in the earlier farm planning.

To check performance year by year, some record-keeping system is needed. For small-farm families, a rather simple, easy-to-keep cash record may be sufficient. One designed for this purpose is available from the University of Missouri, Agricultural Economics Department, Columbia, Missouri 65211, on request.

Several kinds of record-keeping systems are available to Missouri farmers, ranging from simple cash record books to a computerized, mail-in record system conducted by the Agricultural Economics Department of the University of Missouri on a fee basis. Some balanced farming cooperators have participated in this for more than 25 years. Analysis of such records each year from several hundred Missouri farmers, with various types of farming and crop and livestock enterprises, provides valuable information for updating reference data, such as that included in enterprise budgets.

Step 8—control and adjust. All long-range plans need some adjustment over time as conditions change and new technologies emerge. Evaluating the economic impact of such changes before they are made may enhance further progress and forestall the financial difficulties that sometimes occur.

This kind of planning procedure is workable and teachable for use by extension/research personnel in planning activities with individual farm families and small neighborhood groups. No expensive calculating equipment is needed. Hand calculators can provide greater speed and accuracy in computations, however. Still greater speed and accuracy in budgeting alternative farming systems can now be performed with computer budgeting programs where available.

Philippines Shortcourse. This step-by-step planning procedure has been adapted for use in several countries. One example was its use in a farm planning shortcourse in the Philippines in 1981. It was sponsored by U.S. Agency for International Development (USAID) offices in Manila and Washington and conducted in cooperation with the Farming Systems Development Corporation (FSDC). The shortcourse training included 40 FSDC staff members, 10 from the national office in Manila and five from each of the six administrative areas throughout the country. It was conducted at the Area II Training Center in Bulacan Province, 72 kilometers north of Manila.

In addition to general instruction in farm planning principles and procedures, all participants enjoyed first-hand experience in planning and evaluating alternative systems for the two-hectare farm unit of the Danilo Hizon farm family not far from the training center. Although the Hizon family members had no previous contact with either FSDC or the Extension Service, they were very cooperative in providing all the data needed for the farm planning problem and participated in a final class session in which all plans were explained and discussed.

All shortcourse members were divided into two-person work teams for the planning project, providing 18 teams in all. Each team first evaluated the present system for the Hizon farm based upon data the family provided. Calculations were continued until all teams agreed on all computed measures. Then, each team was assigned an alternative system to evaluate for the farm unit, after visiting the farm and family personally to get a first-hand view of the farm and the family goals and problems. Table 1 shows an evaluation of the performance of the Hizon present system in comparison with an alternative evaluated by one planning team. Actually, the 18 alternative plans varied widely in potential performance. The projected net cash available ranged from a 10,000-peso loss for one plan to almost a 12,000-peso gain for another (1 peso equals 0.05 US$).

Other Country Examples. Small hillside and mountainside farms in most developing countries have many common problems, such as severe soil erosion, low crop yields, low cash income, burdensome debts, bad roads, poor markets, and lack of know-how for planning and evaluating farming systems. Others are far more troublesome. Farms are small and often fragmented through intergeneration transfers. Large families place heavy burdens on limited land resources. Governmental policies on pricing and allocation of resources often are restrictive, and social and cultural conditions sometimes hinder adjustments.

Despite major constraints, however, notable progress has been made in developing and applying various aspects of the farming systems approach to help achieve soil conservation and other family goals. Some examples with which I have been involved personally indicate a variety of approaches.

Nepal. Early assignments in Nepal (1971-1974) included travel throughout the country to visit most of the 13 research stations and research farms

Table 1. Comparison of alternative farming systems for the Danilo Hizon farm, Bulacan, Philippines.

Planning Team No. 10—Fe Corazon V. Dantis and Harley Amaranto

Farm profile: Farmer—Rice and vegetable grower.

0.5 hectares owned; 1.5 hectares leased, rainfed lowland; supplemental deep well.

Assumption: Present system: Rice and vegetable production.

Plan No. 10:   Rice—2 hectares—June-September
Ampalaya—2 hectares—October-January
Corn—2 hectares—February-June

Wage rates: 12 pesos per man-day (MD)
13 pesos per man-day (AD)

Analysis Factors	Present System	Alternative No. 10
Investment capital	54,910*	54,910
Labor requirement (MD)	378	428
Income over variable costs	13,325	28,428
Unallocated variable costs	3,416	3,857
Net cash income	9,609	24,571
Farm business profit	7,138	22,100
VFP (value of family food produced)	3,483	34,883
Total farm profit	10,620	25,583
Return to capital	8,020	22,983
Percent return to capital	14	42.0
Return to labor and management	4,031	18,994
Return to labor per month	155	730
Return to management	1,431	16,394
Net cash available	(5,041)	9,921

Source: Hagan, Albert R. Farm Systems Analysis (Management), Planning and Budgeting. A Shortcourse conducted by FSDC Area II Training Center, Bulacan Province, Philippines. January-February 1981. University of Missouri-Columbia, p. 33.
*1 peso = 0.05 US$.

established at that time. A map showing locations of these research units is included in the introduction of a publication resulting from these assignments (*3*). Just as in early work in Missouri, these branch stations provided an excellent opportunity to explore and adapt research findings to local conditions. Consultation with staff members at those stations, along with personal visits to numerous small-farm family units in nearby areas, provided a basis for publications such as the one mentioned above. Establishing such a network of branch research stations, when closely allied with extension programs in the areas, seems to be a fundamental step for undergirding future programs in conservation farming and other farming systems efforts.

One young man, Bekha L. Maharajan, who accompanied me during in-country travel, later came to the University of Missouri for graduate study. For his doctoral thesis research, he returned to Nepal for a few months to interview almost 200 small-farm families in the Terai, the Inner Terai, and the Far West Development Region, areas familiar to me as well. His 500-page dissertation provided valuable insights into the unique problems confronting small-farm families in these mountainous areas and into the kinds of improved farming systems that are feasible and workable. By adapting planning procedures studied at Missouri, he evaluated the economic consequences of alternative systems for representative farm units in the selected villages.

In a 1984 follow-up study of the Jumla district in the rugged northwestern area of Nepal, Dr. Maharajan made incisive evaluations of problems confronting the hill farmers and suggested policies and strategies for helping improve their productivity and income. His study results contain valuable suggestions for alternative systems and associated adjustments that are more feasible and workable for the subsistence-type family units (*6*).

Orissa, India. Another graduate student, Arun K. Misra, returned to his home in Orissa, India, to conduct an intensive study of small, village-type, farm-family units in selected areas for his doctoral dissertation research. I served as his thesis supervisor and had visited some of the village farms during earlier work in the country to observe some of the unique problems of the areas studied.

The balanced farming procedures described earlier were adapted to Orissa conditions and used to plan, evaluate, and compare alternative systems for selected pilot-study units to represent the village farms that were selected. The model units included in Dr. Misra's dissertation were designed as working guides for extension/research staff members of the College of Agriculture in that country.

Tunisia. In early 1978, a team of four staff members from the University of Missouri spent several weeks in the semiarid highlands of Central Tunisia to assess problems and recommend alternative solutions to those unique to the area. In a report of the study (2), sponsored by USAID and the Tunisian government, specific innovations for improved farming systems in the area were suggested. In addition, with the help of personnel from the USAID office and government research and extension divisions, gross-margin budgets were prepared for most of the crop and livestock enterprises feasible under the dryland conditions and limited irrigation possibilities. Then, planning procedures were adapted for analyzing overall farming systems that might be initiated in the area as pilot studies.

In a follow-up study later in the year, specific recommendations were made for irrigation, erosion control, and dryland farming interventions in the Central Tunisia area. These were summarized in a publication prepared for the sponsors and translated into French (4).

Indonesia. Consultations, staff seminars, and farm visits in Indonesia in 1983 revealed impressive progress in developing aspects of the farming systems approach, especially in conceiving and demonstrating the value of the major components of overall systems. Especially notable were the interdisciplinary workgroups at Bogor, Indranayu, and Lampung, which combined forces to develop overall cropping systems to increase productivity and profits from land use. The close working relationships among research scientists in different disciplines and the cooperative efforts with field extension workers in extending the new systems to farmers are described in a recent publication (1). As associated publication by Siwi and associates (7) describes an interdisciplinary case study of the impact of cropping-systems research in Indonesia.

Another impressive feature was observed in connection with seminars and discussions with extension and research staff members at Semarang in Central Java, Surabaya in East Java, and the island of Madura. Detailed planning for intensive use of homesite areas of the village farm families was evident through visits arranged by local staff members and leaders. A wide variety of fruit and vegetable crops were included through sequential planting to enhance family diets and yield a salable surplus. Small-scale livestock enterprises, including goats, chickens, rabbits, milk cows, etc., also were added for the same purposes.

Thailand and Taiwan. Progress toward the overall systems approach was evident in connection with assignments with the Asian Vegetable Research and Development Center in 1982-1983. Garden systems used to enhance family nutrition throughout the year were designed to add to family income as well. They form excellent components of overall systems and, with careful planning, require only limited areas around the homesite.

Part of the responsibilities for these assignments was to help design more workable procedures for planning and evaluating gardens, and the overall farming systems of which they are a part.

In Summary

Experiences in these and other countries, as well as the many years of development in Missouri, strengthen the view that the balanced farming approach is a sound way to achieve true conservation farming, as well as more productive and profitable systems of farming and family living.

These experiences and observations reveal a number of features that seem essential for a successful program over time. They include:

• Strong and continuous administrative support from the sponsoring institution or agency.

• A well-trained and dedicated field staff to maintain frequent, on-farm contact with cooperating farm families.

• Close coordination among research and extension specialists in numerous multidisciplinary efforts.

• Ongoing technology research to update performance data needed for crop and livestock enterprise budgets essential for farm planning.

• Well-designed pilot studies with representative farm families in new areas to show the results of applying new technologies in well-planned farming systems ("seeing is believing," and farm families accept and adopt what is working well on neighboring farms).

• An ongoing program to inform and motivate farm families through field days, tours, meetings, demonstrations, news stories, workshops, etc.

• Close cooperation with related agencies and institutions, especially during implementation stages of developing programs.

Finally, the long-range nature of developing a program of this kind to revolutionize farming systems in an area must be recognized. Major changes in farming systems come slowly over a period of years. Continuous efforts are required. But the results often prove to be dramatic.

REFERENCES

1. Agency for Agricultural Research and Development. 1986. *Indonesian farming systems research and development, the food crop system.* Central Research Institute for Food Crops, 99 Bogor, Indonesia.
2. Cromwell, C. F., Jr., A. R. Hagan, E. M. Kroth, and M. F. Nolan. 1978. *An assessment of the agricultural potential of central Tunisia: Evaluations and recommendations.* USAID Work Order No. 5. AID/Aft-C-1139. Agricultural Experiment Station, University of Missouri, Columbia.
3. Hagan, Albert R. 1976. *The agricultural development of Nepal: Analysis of the agricultural sector.* Special Report 189. International Series II. Agricultural Experiment Station,

University of Missouri, Columbia.
4. Hagan, A. R., I. E. Asmon, F. E. Bolton, and C. F. Cromwell, Jr. 1978. *Agricultural development in Central Tunisia: Recommendations for irrigation, erosion control and dryland farming interventions.* USAID Work Order No. 6. AID-Afr-C-1139. Agricultural Experiment Station, University of Missouri, Columbia.
5. Hudson, Norman. 1988. *Soil conservation strategies for the future.* In S. Rimwanich [editor] *Land Conservation for Future Generations.* Volume 1. Department of Land Development, Ministry of Agriculture and Cooperatives, Bangkok, Thailand. pp. 117-130.
6. Maharajan, Bekha L. 1984. *Small farm development problems and strategies.* Royal Printing Service, Ombahal, Kathmandu. 114 pp.
7. Siwi, B. H., et al. 1986. *A case study of the impact of cropping systems research in Indonesia.* Central Research Institute for Food Crops, Indonesia, and International Development Research Center, Canada.

TECHNICAL AND ECONOMIC INTERVENTIONS FOR SOIL CONSERVATION IN JAVA'S UPLANDS

SOLEH SUKMANA and PERVAIZ AMIR

Indonesia is richly endowed with abundant land, rivers, minerals, and, above all, a population of more than 180 million people to harness this wealth of natural resources. However, it confronts a major regional development problem because of the imbalances in population distribution on its islands. More than 65 percent of the population lives on Java, which has only 7 percent of the total land area. A related problem concerns unequal incomes between rural and urban populations. Within the agricultural sector, there is an unbalanced investment between uplands and lowlands. These issues pose challenges for regional development planners, policymakers, and politicians.

In recent years, few proposals have been made to reduce the disparity in the allocation of resources for upland versus lowland development. Aside from productivity and environmental issues, induced changes in the uplands may also help reduce out-migration, which is a concern in policy debates.

This paper is concerned with two watersheds: Jratunseluna (Central Java) and Brantas (East Java). These watersheds cover approximately 1.87 million hectares, with a human population of 16.25 million. Addressed here are new-technology interventions being explored by the Upland Agriculture and Conservation Project (UACP) that may improve farmer income and reduce soil erosion over the next 10 years. Factors influencing a farmer's decision to invest in soil conservation practices and government options to increase this investment also are considered.

The failure among farmers to allocate resources efficiently is due to capital and labor constraints, inadequate information, tradition, lack of motivation, and the risk posed by climate, price, and disease. Adoption of soil conservation practices can, therefore, be looked at in the much broader perspectives of farmer investment opportunities and hierarchial decision patterns.

Upland Erosion

Several studies provide estimates of erosion in Java, but there is little consensus among technical scientists as to the actual rate. Most estimates are, at best, intelligent guesses. The Food and Agriculture Organization reported that soil eroded at a rate of approximately 384 tons per hectare (4). Based on field studies conducted at UACP sites in Sri Mulyo (East Java) and Klari (Central Java), erosion is estimated to be about 30 tons per hectare. Carson and Utomo (2) estimated that erosion in parts of the Java uplands with volcanic soils is about 20 tons per hectare (Table 1). However, this estimate is based on visual observation and is not supported by quantitative data. A review of methods and the difficulties in measuring erosion in the Java uplands was provided by Schoemaker (7). All studies, despite differences in estimates, highlight that erosion rates are many times higher than permissible limits.

Information on factors that significantly contribute to erosion is also lacking. How much erosion should be attributed to agriculture-related activities compared to poor forest management? It is difficult from the information at hand to assess the impact of changes in farm technology in the uplands on sedimentation reduction in the lowlands.

Table 1. Estimated soil and nutrient losses by rainfall erosion associated with different land uses (2).*

	Bench Terraces with Maize	Sloping Terraces with Maize and Cassava	Sloping Land with Potatoes
Soil loss depth (mm/year)	0.4	1.6	8.0
Soil loss (ton/ha/yr)	5	20	100
Organic matter loss (ton/ha/yr)	0.15	0.6	3
Nitrogen loss (kg/ha/yr)	7.5	30	150
Phosphorus loss (kg/ha/yr)	5.0	20	100
Potassium loss (kg/ha/yr)	10	40	200

*Based on a soil developed over limestone.

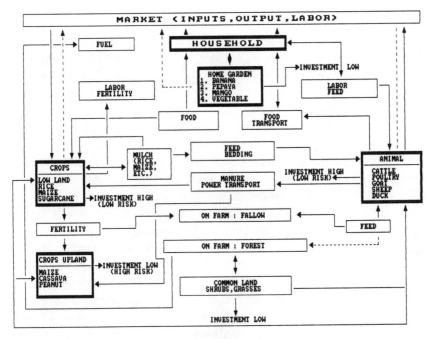

Figure 1. Upland mixed farm systems of Java.

Interactions Among System Components

Any strategy aimed at small-farm development in the uplands must recognize the important interactions among various farm components: crops, livestock, horticulture, agroforestry, and off-farm employment (Figure 1). The flow of inputs and outputs from one component to the other determines the productivity and limitations of the system. Change in each component should be evaluated for its impact on the total farm system. It is important that principal interactions as observed and communicated by the farmer be documented.

Technical Interventions

The goal of the applied research component of the UACP is to help develop sustainable upland farming systems. The focus is on technology that will improve small farm income and stabilize production by reducing soil erosion.

Crop Interventions. From the inception of the project, emphasis was given to testing new and improved cropping systems on various levels of slope. These cropping patterns were tested under field conditions with guidance from researchers. They included various crops, varieties, agroforestry species, agronomic practices, and intercrop options. Crops included maize, cassava, peanut, soybean, cowpea, and upland rice (*3*). Two grasses introduced at the project sites, *Setaria* and elephant grass (*Pennisetum purpureum*), have not only helped to control soil erosion but are popular among farmers as a source of feed.

In addition to promoting grasses for stabilization, bench terracing is a general recommendation of project officials. Ridge terraces have been promoted in areas with sedimentary soils. Also, there is interest in the use of multipurpose species for erosion control, but little work has been started at the farm level. *Leucaena leucocephela* was introduced in some areas, but problems with jumping lice have discouraged its widespread use.

Some crop interventions have been in place for almost 3 years. A recent adoption study conducted at UACP research sites and in nearby villages provides insight into the acceptance of project technology. Except for *Setaria* and elephant grass, farmers have not found proposed cropping systems technically or economically acceptable. Sometimes peer pressure discourages adoption. Most systems promoted by the project are complex and difficult to carry out under farm conditions. Also, there are high input requirements and problems with marketing certain produce. Farmers' and researchers' perceptions differ as to the ability of these cropping systems to bring about an income increase that is stable and sustainable. An area of research that needs more attention is the measurement of output and input on upland farms with high inter-farm variability. Perhaps with improved methods of measurement, results obtained through joint researcher-farmer evaluation will be more acceptable.

Our staff found that methods suitable for lowlands and promoted by several international centers are difficult to use in uplands without significant modification. This is because of high inter-farm variability, problems of transportation and access, fragmented land holdings, and high soil and slope variability within experimental fields, etc. An optimistic assumption of the farming systems research approach is that components of a technological package already exist. Therefore, efforts are focused on the description and diagnosis of the problem. When the time comes to design and test potential solutions, research centers often do not have technology suitable for uplands. Likewise, it is mistakenly assumed that what is suitable for lowlands is equally applicable to uplands.

Technology developed for lowlands is less suitable for uplands for two reasons:

1. Land holdings of upland farmers are often small in Java, averaging 0.70

hectare per farm. Because of unstable climatic conditions and low soil fertility, farmers are slow to make changes that are risky or of uncertain consequences.

2. Economically, the allocation strategy in lowlands is rather straightforward. Farmers allocate scare resources, such as land and capital, among enterprises and inputs that yield high returns. On uplands, because of low farm incomes, much attention is given to a "safety first" principle in which the farmer ensures his subsistence needs first. Unused resources are then allocated among many competing needs and desires, such as social obligations, child education, capital investment, etc. Because most small farmers own both upland (tegalan) and rainfed paddy (sawah) fields, their first choice for investment is rainfed paddy (lowlands), where the marginal returns are high. Additional savings are invested in livestock and home garden development, which bring high, safe returns. Livestock also serves as a source of saving.

Most lowland technologies, such as varieties, fertilizers, and pesticides, are considered scale neutral, implying that additional inputs applied to fixed resources, such as land, yield the same benefit. However, major limitations are imposed by water availability and rainfall variability. Given the great diversity in soil type and slope, such technology must be tested extensively before it is promoted among farmers. Thus, promoting lowland maize, rice, and cassava technology on uplands can be counterproductive.

Horticulture and Agroforestry Technologies. Farmers in the uplands show keen interest in horticultural development. While productivity falls significantly below potential levels, there is ample room for improvement through introduction of improved species and new horticulture practices. Lack of nursery material appears to be the major constraint (5). A successful recommendation made by the project and adopted on a wide scale is banana cultivation on terraces. Besides serving as a useful, multipurpose species, banana leaves can be used for feed during the dry season.

The project staff is paying special attention to mango, papaya, coconut, and banana. Trials to show the use of pruning practices, fertilization, pest control, plant spacing, and adoption of good marketing strategy are underway in the project villages under actual farm conditions.

Livestock Interventions. Livestock contributes 25 to 40 percent to upland farm income. It is the preferred source of saving and investment, readily disposable to meet urgent family needs. As stated earlier, it is the second choice of farmers. The main problem with livestock is feed shortages during the dry season. There may also be a conflict between the objectives of erosion control and livestock development, especially since the former promotes maximum crop cover. This can be resolved by developing a broad feed resource base.

The project is particularly interested in the development of livestock for three reasons:

1. Livestock provides a cheap source of organic matter, of which an adequate supply can support other soil conservation practices, such as terracing and alley cropping. Most soil conservation specialists view the development of livestock favorably so long as the carrying capacity does not significantly reduce biomass cover.

2. Livestock contributes significantly to farm income. For farmers to invest in long-term soil conservation efforts, they must have spare capital, which livestock can provide. Uplands have a carrying capacity of 2.6 to 4.0 animal units per hectare. The first investment priority is to achieve the upper limits of this herd size. Because farmers have limited opportunity to invest on lowlands, because of small holdings, there is potential for using leftover investment capital for the uplands. Thus, integrated crop-livestock development can increase investment in upland conservation practices.

3. Livestock is the prime source of draft power in the uplands. To ensure that land is well maintained with crop cover, it is essential that draft-power availability on small farms be increased. Expansion of animal numbers and improved nutrition can increase this draft power.

It is important to note that, while crop technology is site-specific and sensitive to agroclimatic changes, livestock technology has wider applicability. It is easy to transfer a set of established livestock husbandry practices and new multiple tree species to upland areas for the benefit of farmers.

The project is testing several animal husbandry components, such as feed choppers, mineral mixes, drenches, feeding method, housing, and stock upgrading, by placing bulls at the village level. Improved techniques for feed preservation are planned. Most work is now concentrated on large ruminants. Introduction of new crops, such as sorghum, will improve the feed base.

Impact on Soil and the Natural Environment

At this stage of the project it is difficult to ascertain the impact of the applied research component on the soil or the natural environment. There is preliminary evidence that agronomy practices promoted by the project contribute to soil stability. How much reduction in soil erosion should be attributed to modifications in farm systems remains to be answered.

Project staff attempts to ensure that technology tested and promoted among farmers is stable and sustainable. In no way should it disturb the existing system and further aggravate the erosion problem.

Direction of Research

Research in the UACP is now moving away from a narrow researcher-managed experimentation program to direct farmer participation in a broad, focused technology testing program. Some of the earlier research was useful in identifying improved varieties and fertilizer rates appropriate under upland conditions. Now, the focus is to increase the direct application of several promising technologies under farmer management. This screening process allows evaluation of the technology beyond a controlled and artificial environment. The research component must strive to provide policymakers with factual and meaningful information on performance and adoptability. Policy instruments needed to support broader adoption is a separate question beyond the realm of farming systems research.

Economic Interventions

Micro-portfolio Under Risky Environment. The assets of small farmers in tropical uplands consists primarily of a small wooden house, a few furnishings, a small home garden where fruit trees and vegetables are grown, and livestock (draft cattle, primarily Ongole/Brahmin; sheep or goats; and a few chickens). As stated earlier, landholdings are variable, ranging between .05 to 1.8 hectares. Investment alternatives with farmer-preferred choices are shown in table 2. When farmers were asked where they preferred to invest if they had a certain amount of cash, most chose beef cattle. Because farmers normally do not borrow from formal sources, demand for cash is high and credit exchange normally occurs only between close relatives and friends (8). Assets that can easily be converted into cash and offer an attractive and low-risk return are preferred.

Annual interest rates offered by banks in Indonesia are between 14 and 21 percent. At such a high opportunity cost of capital, farmers weigh their options carefully before deciding to invest in long-term capital.

Analysis of portfolio choice is critical to determine whether any independent investment in particular assets will take place. We can construct a simple model to explain choice of investment alternatives for upland farmers:

$$Y = Ic + Ia + Ih + Iof + Io - T$$

Table 2. Farmers Investment preference in Gunungsari DAS Jratunseluna, Central Java, 1988.

Capital Available to Farmers* (000 Rp)†	Preference Rank	Option							
		Buying Cattle	Buying Goat/ Chickens	Repair/ Construct House	Buying Fertilizer	Buying Land	Terrace Maintenance	Consumption Expenditure	Other‡
		%							
250	I	23.3	33.3	13.3	26.7	-	3.3	0	-
	II	6.7	30.0	16.7	3.3	-	3.3	20.0	-
	III	0	3.3	6.7	3.3	-	3.3	3.3	-
	IV	0	0	3.3	0	-	0	0	-
500	I	63.3	3.3	23.3	0	3.3	3.3	0	3.3
	II	13.3	33.3	6.7	3.3	0	6.7	3.3	6.7
	III	0	6.6	3.3	20.0	0	0	3.3	0
	IV	0	0	6.7	0	0	0	6.7	0
750	I	53.3	0	30.0	3.3	0	0	0	0
	II	3.3	30.0	26.7	0	6.7	3.3	0	3.3
	III	3.3	0	10.0	26.7	3.3	0	0	3.3
	IV	0	3.3	10.0	0	0	0	3.3	0
1.000	I	60.0	0	20.0	3.3	10.0	0	0	3.3
	II	10.0	33.3	16.7	3.3	3.3	3.3	3.3	0
	III	3.3	10.0	10.0	0	0	3.3	0	3.3
	IV	3.3	3.3	10.0	0	0	0	0	0

*Farmers were asked, if they were provided an amount of money, how would they prioritize their investment.
†100 rupiah=0.6 US$.
‡Other: (a) buying motorcycle; (b) buying sewing machine; (c) capital for trading; (d) give to the son; and (e) buying rice mill.

where Y is gross family income after taxation; Ic is income from the crop component; Ia is income from the animal component; Ih is income from the horticultural and agroforestry component; Iof is income from off-farm and nonagricultural activities; To is income from other assets, savings, rental, etc.; and T is taxation.

Short-term investment is based on expected periodic returns for each rupiah invested. Rational farmers in risky environments will invest in those inputs with proven returns.

Thus,

$$IS=Y-C- z(Sa)$$

where IS is short-term investment; Y is after-tax income; C is family consumption (food, shelter, clothing, and education); and Sa is security allowance, dependent on risk parameter z where $0<Z<1$.

$$IL=S-k(IS_i)$$

where IL is long-term investment; S is saving; IS_i is short-term investment in all possible options; i is 1...n; k is the investment parameter for each farmer and ranges between $o<k\leq1$ (for k=1, S=IS; thus, IL=0. Hence, all savings is used for short-term investment).

The main parameters of interest in the above equations are k and z, which can be statistically estimated. Sensitivity analysis can be performed to account for different levels of risk.

The determinants of long-term investment are the expected discounted net benefits:

$$E(DNB)=r_j(Bt_i)/(1 + ie)^t$$

where E(DNB) is the expected discounted net benefits for the portfolio; Bt_i is the net benefit for time period t for i=1...; e is the expected rate of return; r_j is the associated risk factor for each investment option where j=1...n (i.e., terracing, horticulture trees, livestock, small-scale industry, and child education).

The above theoretical model illustrates that investment in erosion control is only one option available to farmers. Given high uncertainty about rainfall, prices, labor requirements for maintenance, distance from homestead that increases security costs, and delayed stream of benefits, farmers find investment in soil conservation of low priority. However, rapid expansion and popularity of grasses, such as *Setaria*, which improve crop cover and stabilize soil around bunds, suggests that technologies that require lower cash inputs and generate short-term benefits through an associated component, such as livestock, are preferred over those with delayed benefits.

In summary, regional development efforts aimed at encouraging soil conservation on small farms must be based on careful analysis of farmers' portfolio composition. Risky investment in terracing that requires high initial capital must be attractive enough or supported by income transfer payments that encourage farmers to adopt capital-intensive terracing. A look at terraced versus nonterraced land and terraced versus lowland terraced land (sawah) reveals a difference (Table 3). Because values of terraced land reflect accumulated improvements over time, it is important that new technology show significant improvements in crop productivity for farmers to allocate additional resources to soil conservation. As price relationships change in favor of lowland crops, such as rice and sugarcane, that attract heavy government support, farmers will be further discouraged from investing in conservation measures and maintenance of terraces on uplands where comparatively lower-valued crops, such as cassava and corn, are grown. In the future, increasing farmers' enterprise mix, particularly crop choice, seems an appropriate strategy to achieve balanced growth in the farm sector.

Policy Interventions. Several policy instruments are available to encourage upland development. Some can be targeted directly at all or selective segments of the upland population. Some general guidelines for formulating policy options for soil conservation are well stated by Perrens and Trustman (*6*). The use of subsidies to encourage farmers to build terraces has been a standard approach used by the extension component of the project. A subsidy is normally prescribed by the economist in the initial stages of technology diffusion to promote growth and equity among a target population. This form of transfer payment reduces the construction cost and encourages farmers to terrace land. Since material costs are limited to hauling stones, the labor cost has a distributive benefit because payment is made for hired labor.

However, why target transfer payments only to support a long-term goal such as terracing? What if the farmer had an option to use an amount equal to the terrace subsidy as he pleased? What portfolio mix would he chose? The answer lies in the comparative rate of return expected from various alternatives. After the initial period of a new practice fertilizer, pesticide, machinery, or soil conservation method, there is little economic justification to provide a subsidy. Continuation of such transfer payments then becomes more a political and social issue than one that requires further

Table 3. Price and rental value of upland and lowland in Gunungsari, DAS Jratunseluna, Central Java, 1988.

Type of Land and Criteria	Number of Samples	Price (000 Rp/ha)	Standard Deviation	Coefficient of Variation (%)	Number of Samples	Rental Value (000 Rp/ha/yr)	Standard Deviation	Coefficient of Variation (%)
Upland*								
1) terraced—I	5	3,430	1,199.22	35.00	-	-	-	-
-II	23	1,700	620.78	36.59	20	42	13.37	31.79
2) not terraced-I	4	2,680	822.09	30.07	-	-	-	-
-II	20	840	469.12	55.68	10	20	10.29	51.09
Lowland	16	7,100	-	20.36	14	164	60.51	36.94

*Criteria of land according to farmer; (1) color of land-black, with no stone problem; and (2) color of land-white with many stones or red clay.
÷1,000 rupiah=0.6 US$.

economic judgment.

Other instruments that could encourage soil conservation include fiscal and monetary measures. Modifying existing tax structures to provide relief from soil erosion and encourage corrective measures warrant attention (*1*). Similarly, soft loans aimed at capital investment in the uplands could be encouraged. An important aspect of micropolicy formulation in Indonesia relates to regulatory power vested in the village leadership that can lead to distortions. This is especially true when village-level studies are generalized to support broad-based policy interventions. Given an authoritarian command system, it is easy to seek cooperation through the village chief. In other words, farmers can be told what to do and, under fear of "unwritten social codes of behavior," will adopt or modify induced change, sometimes only temporarily. Also, when technology testing projects, like the Farming Systems Research Projects, offer attractive test components free of cost, the real impact of the subsidized input needs to be evaluated across several years before valid conclusions can be drawn.

Summary

In the case of Indonesia, upland development activities need to be coordinated with lowland agriculture. Projects that seek to bring change only in the upland component without due consideration of farmers' needs for lowland development will meet with limited success. Furthermore, any conflict in allocation of resources between the uplands versus lowlands imposed by new technology will meet resistance from farmers. Thus, if the government wishes to increase lowland output of rice on farms with both lowland and upland fields, it must carefully weigh the consequences on overall productivity of the farm system and its individual components. At times, regulatory decrees that require local authority to meet certain production targets result in distortions that have a long-term impact on stability and sustainability of the system.

REFERENCES

1. Bunce, A. C. 1950. *The economics of soil conservation.* University of Nebraska Press, Lincoln.
2. Carson, B., and Wani Hadi Utomo. 1986. *Erosion and sedimentation processes in Java.* Kepas, Malang, Indonesia.
3. Farming Systems Research, Upland Agriculture and Conservation Project. 1987. *Research highlights 1985-86.* Agency for Agricultural Research and Development, Indonesia.
4. Food and Agricultural Organization, United Nations. 1979. *Solo watershed and upland development. Some aspects of watershed management economics in Indonesia.* Jakarta, Indonesia.

5. Kartikarn, B. 1988. *Guideline for on-farm horticulture interventions.* Consultants report. Farming Systems Research, Upland Agriculture and Conservation Project, Salatiga, Indonesia.
6. Perrens, J. S., and N. A. Trustman. 1984. *Assessment and evaluation for soil conservation policy.* East-West Environment and Policy Institute, Honolulu, Hawaii.
7. Schoemaker, M. 1988. *Erosion measurements and observations as part of a hydrological monitoring program in upper Konto watershed, East Java.* DHV Consulting Engineers. Project Working Paper Number 21. Ministry of Forestry, Jakarta, Indonesia.
8. Young, Y. K., and P. Amir. 1988. *Village marketing systems in selected FSR sites in Central and East Java: A case study.* Farming Systems Research, Upland Agriculture and Conservation Project, Salatiga, Central Java, Indonesia.

PRODUCTIVITY PATTERNS
OF TREE-CROP
SMALLHOLDINGS

U. R. SANGAKKARA

Sri Lanka, an island of 65,415 square kilometers in the Indian Ocean, has a prominent hill country in its central region. This area, approximately one-fourth of the country, contains cultivated perennial and annual species as well as forests. A large part of this area can be considered the steep lands of Sri Lanka.

The hill country is divided into mid-country (300 to 1,500 meters elevation, 10 to 20 percent of the area) and up-country (1,500 meters and above). The mid-country realizes more than 2,000 millimeters of annual rainfall, and the soils are Ultisols with medium fertility (1). In the mid-country, the perennial crops are rubber and tea. Tea occupies the upper, steeper slopes, while rubber is grown at lower elevations. The smaller tea plantations cover 5 to 20 hectares. Management is poor, with high soil erosion. Coupled with low-quality planting material, this results in low production.

In addition to tea, perennial mixed gardens are grown; these consist of food and fruit crops and spices and timber. These smallholdings range from 0.5 to 4.0 hectares and average 1 hectare (2). Forests make up 5 to 6 percent of the area in contrast to the national average of 25 percent. Rice predominates in the valleys under rainfed conditions and on selected slopes of well-terraced fields. Production of vegetables and tobacco has resulted in a high degree of erosion.

The pressure of urbanization and expanding population has forced agriculture onto steep lands. Destruction of forest cover has caused heavy erosion and changes in microclimate. Emphasis has been placed on development of marginal tea lands on the steep lands. These tea lands are characterized by high erosion, sparse vegetation, and high weed population. They are abandoned as production falls below a certain level. Erosion continues after abandonment, resulting in sedimentation problems downslope.

A program was implemented to replace the uneconomic tea production with high-income perennial crops (mainly spices) in mixed gardens (4). Surveys have been undertaken by the Department of Minor Export Crops of Sri Lanka (3). Plant densities vary from 70 to 1,700 plants per hectare. A very important feature of these perennial mixed gardens is the absence of soil erosion, due mainly to plant canopy.

The study summarized here was undertaken to evaluate the characteristics of selected mixed gardens to determine the species, plant densities, and other important agronomic parameters that determine their adaptability to steep lands.

A Study Initiated

The study was carried out over a period of 1 year to encompass the northeast (October-January) and southwest (May-July) monsoons that bring rainfall to the region. The selected holdings were in the Kandy District (an area of 215,770 hectares). Ten owner-cultivated mixed gardens were selected within a 20-kilometer radius from the University of Peradeniya. The land area, species, and plant densities were determined for each holding. The farmers kept records of products consumed, exchanged, or sold; fertilizer and other agrochemicals; and hired labor used. Leaf litter accumulation on four 1-meter-square quadrats was weighed monthly. Rainfall was measured both under the canopy and in clear areas. Weeds from five 1-meter-square quadrats were cut and weighed every 3 months. Light penetration through the crop canopy was determined by a Lambda photometer at three levels (6 meters, 3 meters, and ground level) every 3 months.

Some Results

The size of the surveyed holdings ranged from 0.46 to 1.84 hectares, with an average size of 0.78 hectare. Slopes ranged from 5° to 25° (9 to 47 percent). Crops were primarily perennial or semiperennial, with some annual vegetables and tuber crops interplanted. The tree and shrub density ranged from 74 to 344 plants per hectare, with an average of 195 plants. Farmers on the smaller units grew a large number of shrub species, presumably due to the need for a diverse range of crops to sustain the family and to sell.

All units had at least one tree of jackfruit (*Atrocarpus heterophyllus*), the fruit and seed of which are principally consumed by the family, but in some instances were sold. Pepper vines (*Piper nigrum*), coffee shrubs and betelnut (*Areca catechu*) were the most common species. Crop compatibility was noted, where pepper vines were placed adjacent to jackfruit or betelnut for support, and coffee was grown between. Hence, somewhat unintentionally, a multistoried canopy developed. The deep-rooted jackfruit and coffee shrubs used a different part of the soil profile than the shallow-rooted betelnut and pepper vines. Other crops commonly found included coconut (*Cocoa nucifera*), plantain (*Musa* spp), and cloves (*Syzigium aromaticum*). The latter, which is a very high-income crop, was found in 80 percent of the holdings, and all other farmers planned to plant cloves. There was no regular, planned arrangement of crops in any unit. Crops were randomly distributed to use all available land. The compatible canopy structure in each case was attributed to the farmer's experience and intuition.

Each unit had nine crops on average; the range was six to 17. Larger units had fewer cloves, pepper, nutmeg (*Myristica fragrans*), and coffee plants.

The total cash income from the sale of produce ranged from 5,840 Sri Lanka rupees (SLR) (1 US\$=33 SLR, 1988 rate of exchange) to SLR 32,560 annually from the larger, more specialized units. The mean income from sales was SLR 13,242. In addition, home consumption and exchange with neighbors accounted for approximately SLR 1,099 annually.

Family labor is used almost exclusively on the smallholdings. On the larger units, there was some hired labor for maintenance and for harvesting high-income crops, such as cloves, nutmeg, pepper, and coffee. The mean hired labor was 54 percent of the total, ranging from 8 percent to 86 percent between the small and large units. The main purchased item was fertilizer, which was applied regularly to the high-income crops. The cost of fertilizer ranged from SLR 545 to 4,215 between small and large units.

Mean annual leaf fall was 0.94 kilogram per square meter. Light availability for plant growth at the soil surface was minimal, which kept weed growth to a minimum. The taller species, such as betelnut, coconut, and jackfruit, intercepted approximately 16 percent of the incident radiation. Medium-height species, such as cloves, nutmeg, and plantain, intercepted 30 percent, leaving 54 percent for shrub species, such as coffee.

Sixty-seven percent of the rainfall reached the soil surface, virtually all dripping from leaves. The remainder presumably runs down the tree trunks.

Conclusion

The tea lands in the mid-country steep lands were once profitable enterprises. However, poor management and the low price of tea has made them unprofitable. These lands are now being developed using sustainable crop-ping systems that seek to stop erosion (with canopy), improve soil (with leaf recycling), provide income for the farmers (with high-value crops), and improve forest cover. The study showed that the perennial, tree-crop smallholdings studied were generally achieving these desired goals.

Acknowledgement

Thanks is expressed to A.S.M. de Zoyza and E. R. Piyadasa for their assistance with this research.

REFERENCES

1. Domros, M. 1974. *Agroclimate of Ceylon.* Springer Verlag, West Germany. 265 pp.
2. Jacob, V. S., and W. S. Alles. 1986. *Kandyan gardens of Sri Lanka.* Agroforestry Systems 5: 123-137.
3. McDonnel, D. G., and K.A.B. Dharmapala. 1973. *The economic status of Kandyan forest farms.* The Management Report 7, U.N. Development Program/Food and Agricultural Organization. Agricultural Development Project, Peradeniya, Sri Lanka. 125 pp.
4. Sappideen, T. B. 1987. *The spice industry of Sri Lanka.* Economic Review (Sri Lanka) 13(1): 4-15.

ALLEY CROPPING
AS A SUSTAINABLE SYSTEM

B. T. KANG and B. S. GHUMAN

World population could stabilize at 10.5 billion people by the year 2110 (*13*), compared to 4.4 billion during the early 1980s. The portion of world population living in developing countries will also increase to 87 percent in the year 2110. Proportionally, population increases of three and five times, respectively, are expected in Asia and Africa.

Production of adequate food to meet the demand of the rapidly increasing population in the developing countries, particularly those countries with limited resources, is a major challenge. According to Dudal (*1*), there are three options for increasing food production in developing countries: (1) land use intensification, (2) land expansion, or (3) both. Because most fertile and easily accessible land in the humid tropics has already been brought under cultivation and the remaining land is either too steep, too remote, or subject to nutritional and physical limitations, the most logical option is, therefore, to intensify production on existing land rather than clearing new forest land for cultivation. Even in Africa and Latin America, where large-scale agricultural land expansion is still possible (*1*), vast areas have already been cleared and used for low-intensity, traditional farming in recent times. The greatest potential for increasing food production lies in these areas, provided that agricultural production can be intensified through the use of more productive, sustainable, and ecologically viable farming methods.

Over the last 4 decades, a number of crop and soil management systems have been tried, with mixed results, in an attempt to increase crop production in the humid tropics. More recently, research has indicated that a more productive, sustainable, and low-input food production system may be attained by intercropping food crops with perennial woody species, particularly legumes that can biologically fix nitrogen. One such technology based on this principle is alley cropping (*4, 5*).

Alley Cropping

During the past 2 decades, there has been increasing interest in promoting agroforestry as a sustainable land use system. Agroforestry systems are perceived to improve soil physical properties, maintain soil organic matter, and promote nutrient cycling with the presence of woody species (*16, 17*). Woody species protect the soil against raindrop impact, runoff, and erosion through their canopy cover and particularly through the surface litter layer (*17*). For generations, traditional farmers have been exploiting the benefits of woody species by including them in shifting cultivation and related bush-fallow production systems.

As part of efforts to improve the traditional bush-fallow, slash-and-burn cultivation system, investigations were undertaken at the International Institute of Tropical Agriculture (IITA) in Ibadan, Nigeria, to assess the potential of intercropping woody species with food crops as a system for managing fragile uplands dominated by low-activity clays for more productive and sustainable food production. This has led to the development of the alley cropping system (*6*).

Alley cropping is an agroforestry production system in which food crops are grown in alleys formed by hedgerows. These hedgerows preferably are comprised of legume species that can biologically fix nitrogen. The hedgerows are cut back at planting and periodically pruned during the growing season to prevent shading and to reduce competition with the associated food crops. The prunings are used either as a surface mulch or as green manure. The hedgerows are allowed to grow freely to cover the land when there are no crops.

Research results obtained from the alley cropping of food crops with *Leucaena leucocephala* and *Gliricidia sepium* on nonacid soils have shown that the system is beneficial for nutrient cycling, as a biological nitrogen source, for weed supression, and for sources of fodder, stakes, and firewood. The system can, therefore, be used as a sustainable and low-input production system (*6, 7*). In addition, the planting of woody hedgerows has been reported in several instances to reduce runoff and soil erosion (*9, 10, 12, 14*).

A long-term trial was established in 1982 at Ibadan to evaluate the effect of alley cropping and tillage on soil properties, water runoff, soil loss, and crop performance. Reviewed here are the results obtained during the 1988 cropping season.

Experimental Methods

Plot Layout and Management. The experiment was conducted at the IITA farm near Ibadan in southern Nigeria. Mean annual rainfall at the farm is 1,280 millimeters. The rainfall follows a bimodal distribution, with peaks in June and September and a period of lower precipitation in August. The dry season lasts from November to February. The soil at the experimental site is classified as an Oxic paleustalf (*11*); average slope is about 7 percent.

The experimental treatments consisted of:
* *Leucaena leucocephala* with a 4-meter interhedgerow spacing, tilled.
* *Leucaena leucocephala* with a 2-meter inherhedgerow spacing, tilled.
* *Gliricidia sepium* with a 4-meter interhedgerow spacing, tilled.
* *Gliricidia sepium* with a 2-meter interhedgerow spacing, tilled.
* No-tillage control.
* Tilled control.

Each unreplicated runoff plot was 10 meters wide and 70 meters long. A sill and apron was constructed at the lower end of the plot to concentrate runoff water into the measuring system. An earthen embankment was built around each plot. There was a buffer zone of 1 meter between adjacent plots.

In 1982, *Leucaena* and *Gliricidia* hedgerows were planted across the slope at spacings described above. More detailed information of the trial plot was provided by Lal (*10*). Missing *Leucaena* and particularly *Gliricidia* plants were replanted in 1987. Hedgerows were allowed to grow freely in the dry season of 1987 to 1988. The hedgerows were pruned in March 1988 prior to planting maize (*Zea mays* L.) in April. Preplanting land preparation for all treatments, except the no-tillage control treatment, was performed manually using a handhoe to a depth of 15 centimeters. After pruning the hedgerows, leaves and small twigs were separated from the woody stems and spread as mulch in the alleys. The stems were collected and placed against the upslope side of the hedgerows. One week after pruning, all plots were sprayed with paraquat and primextra. Compound fertilizer (45-20-36 in kilograms per hectare) was also applied to all plots. Maize (TZSR-W) was planted in each of the six plots at a 25 x 100-centimeter spacing in the control plots and at a 25 x 80-centimeter in the alley-cropped plots to yield a population of 40,000 plants per hectare. Narrower spacing in alley-cropped plots was used to ensure a uniform maize population in alleyed and control plots. The alley-cropped and tilled control plot were hand-weeded about 4 weeks after planting maize. In the no-tillage plot, weeding was performed by slashing weeds with a machete. The maize crop was sidedressed with 30 kilograms of nitrogen per hectare applied as calcium ammonium nitrate at 5 weeks after planting. During maize cropping, the hedgerows were pruned twice (May and July), each time to a 0.75 meter height to prevent shading of the maize.

Cowpea (*Vigna ungurculata*, IT 81D-994) was planted in September in all the plots during the second season at 25 x 80-centimeter spacings in the control plots and at 25 x 75-centimeter spacings in the alley-cropped plots, yielding a population of 50,000 plants per hectare. Before planting, plots were sprayed with paraquat and the hedgerows pruned. No fertilizer was applied to the cowpea crop. Additional handweeding was performed at four weeks after planting cowpea. Hedgerows were pruned again in October.

Maize was harvested in August 1988 and cowpea in November 1988 for yield measurements.

Observations. Composite surface soil samples were collected from each plot prior to the first pruning of the hedgerows for soil characterization. Analysis was performed using the procedure described by Juo (2).

• Maize and cowpea yield and hedgerow biomass growth and yield were determined using four samples taken in the upper, upper middle, lower middle, and lower portions of each plot. Statistical analysis was completed for each of these parameters.

• After maize harvesting in August, soil bulk density in the 0- to 5-centimeter layer was determined at 16 points in each plot using 250-cubic-centimeter cores.

Experimental Results

Soil Properties. Data on chemical properties of the experimental plots at the start of the cropping season are shown in table 1. The soil properties reflect the effect of various treatments applied during the previous 6 years. Continuous addition of prunings from the hedgerows in alley-cropped plots lowered soil pH compared to the nonalley cropping treatments. The control tilled plot showed the lowest level of organic carbon, which was less than 60 percent of that obtained in the other treatments. In addition, this plot also showed lower levels of potassium, calcium, and magnesium than the alley-cropped plots. There was no effect of alley cropping on the texture of the surface soil.

Table 1. Some chemical properties of the surface soil (0-15 cm) at the start of the trial.*

Treatment	pH-H₂O	Organic C (%)	Extractable Bray-1 P (ppm)	Exchangeable K	Ca	Mg
				— (me/100g) —		
Without alley cropping						
Tilled control	5.3	0.5	8.6	0.2	2.2	0.4
No-tillage	5.4	0.9	7.3	0.3	2.2	0.6
Alley-cropped						
2-m *Gliricidia*	5.2	0.8	9.6	0.4	2.3	0.5
4-m *Gliricidia*	5.1	0.8	9.9	0.4	2.4	0.5
2-m *Leucaena*	5.1	0.9	9.8	0.4	2.6	0.5
4-m *Leucaena*	5.1	1.1	9.4	0.5	2.8	0.6

*All treatments were sandy loam texture.

Table 2. Plant height, dry pruning biomass, and wood yield from hedgerow prunings during first and second season.

Treatments— Interhedgerow Spacing	Plant Height* (cm)	First Season†	Biomass Second Season‡	Total	Wood§
			—————— (t/ha) ——————		
Gliricidia					
2-m spacing	281a‖	5.40b	1.38b	6.78b	3.14a
4-m spacing	303a	3.25a	0.52a	3.77a	1.67a
Leucaena					
2-m spacing	336a	7.22c	2.54c	9.76c	6.52b
4-m spacing	397b	6.13bc	1.45b	7.58b	4.73b

*Measured in March 1988. Hedgerows were last pruned in October 1987.
†Pruning done in March, May, and July.
‡Pruning done in September and October.
§Mainly from first-season pruning done in March.
‖Figures within column followed by the same letter are not significantly different (P=0.05) according to Duncan's multiple range test.

Table 3. Grain and stover yield of maize (TZSRW) with and without alley cropping and tillage.

Treatment	Grain Yield	Stover Yield
	—————— (t/ha) ——————	
Without alley cropping		
Tilled control	2.27a*	3.10a
No-tillage	2.40ab	3.23a
Alley-cropped		
2-m *Gliricidia*	3.24cd	4.57bc
4-m *Gliricidia*	2.83bc	4.19b
2-m *Leucaena*	3.45d	4.94c
4-m *Leucaena*	3.13cd	3.94b

*Figures within column followed by the same letter(s) are not significantly different (P=0.05) according to Duncan's multiple range test.

Table 4. Cowpea (IT8ID-994) plant biomass, nodulation, and grain yield with and without alley cropping and tillage.

Treatment	Plant Dry Weight*	Nodule Dry Weight*	Seed Yield (Kg/ha)
	——— (g/plant) ———		
Without alley cropping			
Tilled control	11.6a†	0.09a	408a
No-tillage	15.8ab	0.27b	590ab
Alley-cropped			
2-m *Gliricidia*	19.8bc	0.25b	707b
4-m *Gliricidia*	17.2ab	0.19ab	754b
2-m *Leucaena*	16.0ab	0.16ab	580ab
4-m *Leucaena*	25.0c	0.17ab	779b

*Sampled at 7 weeks after planting.
†Figures within column followed by the same letter(s) are not significantly different (P=0.05) according to Duncan's multiple range test.

Biomass Yield and Crop Performance. *Leucaena* and *Gliricidia* hedgerows showed substantial growth during the dry season. On average, *Leucaena* and *Gliricidia* grew to about 3 meters and 2 meters in height, respectively, in less than 5 months (Table 2) using subsoil moisture. The first pruning before cropping also produced large quantities of wood, particularly with *Leucaena*, which produced over twice as much as *Gliricidia*. The pruning biomass also showed large differences among species, spacing, and season. For example, *Leucaena* produced about 40 percent more pruning biomass than *Gliricidia*. More biomass was produced with a 2-meter than with 4-meter interhedgerow spacing.

The effect of various treatments on the maize crop is shown in table 3. As expected, the control plots showed the lowest maize grain and stover yields. Plants in the control plots showed distinct symptoms of nitrogen stress. Significantly higher maize grain and stover yields were obtained in alley-cropped plots. Except for the 4-meter *Gliricidia* treatment, maize grain yields in alley-cropped plots were significantly higher than in control treatments. Stover yields in alley-cropped plots were also significantly higher than in control treatments. Maize grain yields in plots alley cropped with *Gliricidia* and *Leucaena* were 33 percent and 45 percent higher, respectively, than in the tilled control treatment and 26 percent and 37 percent higher than with no-tillage. The highest maize yields were obtained in alley cropping with *Leucaena* at 2-meter interhedgerow spacing, followed by *Gliricidia* treatment at the same spacing.

Cowpea plant biomass, nodule, and seed weights were lowest in the control tilled plot (Table 4). Higher plant biomass and seed yields were observed with alley cropping compared with no-tillage treatment, except for the 2-meter *Leucaena* treatment in which cowpea biomass and seed yields were depressed mainly due to shading by the hedgerows.

Effect on Runoff and Erosion. Effect of alley cropping on runoff and soil erosion during the first season is shown in table 5. As expected, the highest runoff (9.4 percent of rainfall) occurred in the control tilled plot. Treatment with 2-meter *Leucaena* hedgerows resulted in minimum runoff (0.4 percent of rainfall). Runoff from other plots followed the order: 4-meter *Gliricidia* greater than 4-meter *Leucaena* greater than no-tillage greater than 2-meter *Gliricidia*. These results show a positive role for alley cropping in reducing runoff compared with nonalley cropping. Alley cropping with *Leucaena* was more effective than with *Gliricidia* in reducing surface runoff, probably due to the more dense hedgerow formation, because this species established better than *Gliricidia*. In addition, *Leucaena* seeded

Table 5. Water runoff and soil loss under maize grown with and without alley cropping, and tillage from March to July, 1988 (first season).

Treatment	Runoff* [mm (percent of rainfall)]	Soil Loss (t/ha)
Without alley cropping		
Tilled control	66.0 (9.4)	6.18
No-tillage	5.6 (0.8)	0.43
Alley-cropped		
2-m *Gliricidia*	4.8 (0.7)	0.57
4-m *Gliricidia*	23.1 (3.3)	1.44
2-m *Leucaena*	2.6 (0.4)	0.17
4-m *Leucaena*	10.7 (1.5)	0.82

*Rainfall (March-July 1988) = 704.2 mm.

Table 6. Bulk density (on fine soil fraction basis) of the 0-5 cm layer at the end of a first season maize crop.

Treatment	Bulk Density (g/cm^{-3})	
	Upslope	Downslope
Without alley cropping		
Tilled control	1.38b*	1.36b
No-tillage	1.35ab	1.43b
Alley-cropped		
2-m *Gliricidia*	1.27a	1.24a
4-m *Gliricidia*	1.24a	1.44b
2-m *Leucaena*	1.34ab	1.37b
4-m *Leucaena*	1.39b	1.24a

*Figures within column followed by the same letter(s) are not significantly different (P=0.05) according to Duncan's multiple range test.

more easily than *Gliricidia*. The *Gliricidia* hedgerows showed many gaps and were, therefore, less effective as a physical barrier against runoff water.

Soil erosion related to runoff. Minimum soil loss (0.17 ton per hectare) resulted in the plot with 2-meter *Leucaena* hedgerows, whereas maximum soil loss (6.18 tons per hectare) resulted in the control tilled plot (Table 5). Soil loss from other plots was in the order of 4-meter *Gliricidia* greater than 4-meter *Leucaena* greater than 2-meter *Gliricidia* greater than no-tillage.

Surface-soil bulk density was measured in each plot at the end of the maize growing season (Table 6). Upslope bulk density was lower in the 2-meter and 4-meter *Gliricidia* treatments than in other plots (Table 6). Downslope bulk density was significantly lower in the 4-meter *Leucaena* and 2-meter *Gliricidia* plots. No plausible explanation exists for these differences as yet. There was no difference in bulk density values in the other treatments.

Nutrient Loss. Total nutrient losses in runoff water were proportional to surface runoff and were, therefore, affected by soil and crop management treatments. Total nutrient losses were in the order: control tilled treatment greater than 4-meter *Gliricidia* greater than 4-meter *Leucaena* greater than no-tillage greater than 2-meter *Gliricidia* greater than 2-meter *Leucaena*) (Table 7). Similar trends also were observed for the losses of the individual plant nutrients from the various plots. The greatest loss of most nutrients occurred from the control tilled plot and the least from the 2-meter *Leucaena* plot. However, in the case of nitrate nitrogen, the greatest loss (0.291 kilograms per hectare) occurred from the 4-meter *Leucaena* plot.

Discussions and Conclusions

Experimental data presented herein show that sustainable crop production can be achieved on erodible and sloping land using an alley cropping system

Table 7. Nutrient loss in runoff water for various treatments during a period from March to July.

Treatment	NO_3-N	NH_4-N	PO_4-P	Ca	Mg	Na	Total
				(kg/ha)			
Without alley cropping							
Tilled control	0.247	1.092	0.096	1.900	0.569	2.016	5.920
No-tillage	0.027	0.027	0.011	0.212	0.063	0.146	0.486
Alley-cropped							
2-m *Gliricidia*	0.014	0.030	0.005	0.181	0.055	0.121	0.406
4-m *Gliricidia*	0.206	0.280	0.033	0.965	0.253	1.270	3.007
2-m *Leucaena*	0.011	0.011	0.002	0.107	0.025	0.085	0.241
4-m *Leucaena*	0.291	0.058	0.014	0.445	0.107	0.462	1.377

that includes woody legumes.

After 6 years of intensive cropping, the alley cropping plots, particularly those with *Leucaena* hedgerows, maintained higher organic matter and nutrient levels than the control tilled treatment (Table 1). Similar results were reported by Kang and associates (*4*). Although *Leucaena* and *Gliricidia* prunings have relatively fast decomposition rates (*15*), both species also produce large amounts of pruning biomass (Table 2), which result in the high soil organic matter status. In addition, the slowly decomposing woody materials (e.g., stems) also can serve as a source of slow release nutrients.

The low pH of the surface soil with alley cropping may be the result of high amounts of cations retained in the plant biomass, which includes plant stumps and woody material (Table 2). Further investigation is being undertaken to better elucidate the factors involved.

The large maize grain and stover yield differences among treatments observed in the seventh cropping year are significant (Table 3). Grain yield of maize in the alley-cropped treatments was more than 30 percent higher than in the nonalley-cropped treatments. The higher maize grain yield with alley cropping can, in part, be attributed to nutrient contribution from the prunings. Kang (*3*) reported that alley cropping with *Leucaena* and *Gliricidia* contributes 42 kilograms of nitrogen per hectare to the associated maize crop. An important aspect of the results is that, with equal fertilizer input, higher return in maize grain yield was obtained with alley cropping. The effect of alley cropping on cowpea seed yield is, however, not as pronounced.

The effect of alley cropping and tillage systems on water runoff and soil erosion and nutrient loss (Tables 5 and 7) was similar to previous years' results reported by Lal (*10*), except that, in 1988, runoff, erosion, and nutrient loss were lowest with the two-meter *Leucaena* treatment. Placement of stems along hedgerows after the first pruning, as was done in 1988, may have reduced runoff and erosion and nutrient loss on the 2-meter *Leucaena* plot over that on the no-tillage plot.

The slightly lower runoff, erosion, and nutrient-loss values observed (Tables 5 and 7), compared with those reported by Lal (*10*), may be due to the rainfall distribution in 1988. There were several rainstorms, which were widely spaced in time, but the amount of rainfall received was lower than that mentioned during the observation period reported by Lal (*10*).

The positive effect of alley cropping in reducing runoff, soil erosion, and nutrient losses in water runoff, as shown in tables 5 and 7, may be due to the combined effects of (a) physical presence of hedgerows, which form a barrier for runoff, allowing runoff water to stand longer in the plot and thereby increasing infiltration and deposition of soil between the hedgerows, and (b) the addition of surface mulch from the prunings. Mulch has been shown to effectively reduce runoff and erosion (8). As a result of physical barrier by the hedgerows, minibench terraces also are visible in the alley-cropped plots after 7 years of tillage cropping.

Although there was no physical tree barrier in the no-tillage treatment, runoff and erosion were effectively checked. This likely was due to the plot's high infiltration rate and undisturbed surface. In contrast, surface soil in the control tilled plot was disturbed by tillage and easily eroded with runoff water.

Because nutrient losses in runoff water were low (Table 7), it appears that leaching losses of nutrients, particularly nitrogen, can be considerable in these soils. Variable phosphorus concentrations ranging from 0 to 1.2 parts per million were observed in runoff water. However, a relatively lower phosphorus concentration was measured in runoff from alley-cropped plots with 2-meter *Leucaena* and *Gliricidia* hedgerows, with higher concentrations from the tilled plot. Therefore, nutrient loss and, hence, pollution of water supplies could be checked to a certain extent with appropriate soil and crop management practices, for example, no-tillage and alley cropping systems that minimize runoff and encourage water retention and infiltration.

REFERENCES

1. Dudal, R. 1982. *Land resources and production potential for a growing world population.* In *Optimizing Yields: The Role of Fertilizers.* International Potash Institute, Bern, Switzerland. pp. 277-288.
2. Juo, A.S.R. 1979. *Selected methods for soil and plant analysis.* International Institute for Tropical Agriculture, Ibadan, Nigeria.
3. Kang, B. T. 1987. *Nitrogen cycling in multiple cropping system.* In J. R. Wilson [editor] *Advances in Nitrogen Cycling in Agricultural Ecosystems.* Commonwealth Agricultural Bureaux International, Wallingford, England. pp. 333-348.
4. Kang, B. T., and G. F. Wilson. 1987. *The development of alley cropping as a promising agroforestry technology.* In H. A. Steppler and P.K.R. Nair [editors] *Agroforestry a Decade of Development.* International Council for Research in Agroforestry, Nairobi, Kenya. pp. 227-243.
5. Kang, B. T., G. F. Wilson, and L. Sipkens. 1981. *Alley cropping maize (*Zea mays L.*) and Leucaena (*Leucaena leucocephala*) in southern Nigeria.* Plant and Soil 63: 165-179.
6. Kang, B. T., G. F. Wilson, and T. L. Lawson. 1984. *Alley cropping a stable alternative to shifting cultivation.* International Institute for Tropical Agriculture, Ibadan, Nigeria.
7. Kang, B. T., H. Grimme, and T. L. Lawson. 1985. *Alley cropping sequentially cropped maize and cowpea with leucaena on a sandy soil in southern Nigeria.* Plant and Soil 85: 267-276.
8. Lal, R. 1974. *Role of mulching techniques in tropical soil and water management.* Technical Bulletin 1. International Institute for Tropical Agriculture, Ibadan, Nigeria.
9. Lal, R. 1987. *Managing the soils of sub-saharan Africa.* Science 236: 1,069-1,076.
10. Lal, R. 1988. *Soil erosion control with alley cropping.* In Proceedings, Fifth International Soil Conservation Conference. Soil and Water Conservation Society of Thailand, Bangkok.

11. Moormann, F. R., R. Lal, and A.S.R. Juo. 1979. *The soils of IITA.* Technical Bulletin 3. International Institute for Tropical Agriculture, Ibadan, Nigeria.
12. Pacardo, E. P. 1985. *Soil erosion and ecological stability.* In E. T. Craswell, J. V. Remenyi, and L. G. Nallana [editors] *Soil Erosion Management.* Australian Center for International Agricultural Research, Canberra. pp. 82-85.
13. Salas, R. M. 1981. *The state of the world population 1980.* United Nations Fund for Population Activities, New York, New York.
14. Vega, E., C. van Eijk-Bos, and L. A. Moreno. 1987. *Alley cropping with* Gliricidia sepium *(Jacq.) Walp. and its effect on the soil losses on hillslopes in Uraba, Columbia.* In D. Withington, N. Glover, and J. L. Brewbaker [editors] Gliricidia sepium *(Jacq.) Walp. Management and Improvement.* Nitrogen Fixing Tree Association, Waimanalo, Hawaii. p. 68.
15. Wilson, G. F., B. T. Kang, and K. Mulongoy. 1986. *Alley cropping: Trees as sources of green manure and mulch in the tropics.* Biological Agricultural Horticulture 3: 251-267.
16. Young, A. 1985. *The potential of agroforestry as a means of sustaining soil fertility.* Working Paper No. 34. International Council for Research in Agroforestry, Nairobi, Kenya.
17. Young, A. 1986. *The potential of agroforestry for soil conservation. Part 1. Erosion control.* Working Paper No. 42. International Council for Research in Agroforestry, Nairobi, Kenya.

SOIL CONSERVATION PRACTICES 5

ORIGIN, APPLICATION, AND DESIGN OF THE FANYA JUU TERRACE

D. B. THOMAS and E. K. BIAMAH

T he fanya juu terrace is a structural method of soil conservation that has been widely practiced on small, labor-intensive farms in Kenya. Attempts have been made to introduce it elsewhere as well. "Fanya juu" is the Swahili expression for "make it up." The term refers to the practice of digging a ditch on the contour and throwing the soil uphill to form an embankment, which is subsequently stabilized by planting grass. Although the system has been popular, particularly in semiarid areas, it has not been critically studied and evaluated, and there is considerable argument about design principles and applications. There is also some confusion about the subject in the literature. For example, Morgan (4) confuses fanya juu terraces with the traditional ladder or step terraces that are found in some parts of Tanzania, and Hudson (1) refers to them as a type of intermittent terrace, which does not clarify the issue.

Origin of Fanya Juu Terraces

The fanya juu terrace came into use in Kenya during the early 1950s when erosion problems were causing a great deal of concern. The system of graded channel terraces made by digging a channel and throwing the soil downhill, which was common in the United States, had proved inadequate because of the rapid siltation of channels. The need to keep channels desilted involved considerable labor and prevented their use for other purposes, such as growing bananas. The local people felt that too much land was taken out of production with this system (D. Nzioka, 1988, personal communication). The cultivation of steep slopes and erodible soils for annual crops, which left the land bare or thinly covered at a time when the heaviest rains were likely to occur, was responsible for high rates of erosion and siltation. Bench terracing was seen as one solution to this problem and the fanya juu terrace was encouraged because it allowed the natural process of erosion to assist in the formation of benches. The term, fanya juu terrace, therefore, refers to a method of construction. It does not adequately describe the resulting structure, which changes with time and may become a forward- or outward-sloping bench terrace, or even a level bench terrace, and may or may not retain some capacity to store runoff and sediment. The rate of change from the original conformation will depend, first, on the rates of soil movement and deposition above the bank, due to erosion and cultivation, and, second, on the efforts that the farmer may make to increase the height of the embankment. This is accomplished by throwing more soil up from the lower side so that the storage capacity is not diminished.

Application of the Fanya Juu System

Kenya. The application of the fanya juu system in Kenya has been widespread. Prior to independence, it was promoted mainly in the Machakos District of eastern Kenya, which is characterized by steep slopes, erodible soils, and a subhumid to semiarid climate. In this area, there was considerable support for terracing because of the realization that erosion control is critical to survival. Furthermore, where the terracing led to the formation of level benches, the benefit to crop production from stored rainfall was noticeable. The Akamba tradition of community work through self-help "Mwethya" groups made an important contribution to the early successes in conservation in this part of the country.

In central Kenya, under better rainfall conditions and less erodible soil, the need for conservation was less clearly perceived, the benefits of terracing were less conspicuous, and growing nationalism brought conflict with the colonial authorities over conservation measures that were enforced.

The lull in conservation activities on small-scale farms after independence was broken in 1974 with the initiation of a soil conservation program by the Ministry of Agriculture, with assistance from the Swedish International Development Authority (SIDA). Under this program, pilot projects were started in many districts. Initially, these projects concentrated on laying out cutoffs and fanya juu terraces. The digging of cutoffs was subsidized, while terrace construction was carried out by the farmers without assistance, except in some instances in which tools were given to a group of farmers as an incentive.

Although the fanya juu system of terracing has been widely adopted in the drier areas east of the Rift Valley, it has not been as popular elsewhere. In some areas, farmers have opposed it, probably due to the labor involved and the lack of immediate and visible benefits. Therefore, it is necessary to take a look at the advantages and disadvantages of this system and to compare it with the conventional narrow-based channel terrace, which involves throwing soil downhill (fanya chini). Even before independence, there was considerable argument about the merits of the alternatives systems (L. H. Brown, 1977, personal communication), and the debate continues.

Suitability for Erosion Control. The fanya juu terrace leads to a *decrease* in the slope of the cultivated land. Because the erosion slope relation is exponential, reducing slope by 50 percent may lead to a 75 percent reduction in erosion. The conventional narrow-based channel terrace, made by throwing soil downhill, can sometimes lead to an *increase* in the slope of the cultivated land (Figure 1).

Suitability for Steep Slopes. On steep slopes, over 15 to 20 percent, the fanya juu terrace involves some risks because runoff is held by an embankment above the ground surface, which is sometimes poorly consolidated and likely to break if a heavy storm occurs before stabilization with grass has taken place. In contrast, the narrow-based channel terrace stores much of the runoff in a channel excavated from consolidated material. It is, therefore, more stable. On slopes of 55 percent or more, the fanya juu terrace is definitely unsuitable and, for most crops, with the notable exception of tea, properly constructed bench terraces are the only solution.

Suitability for Various Soils. The fanya juu terrace is suited to most soils, although difficulties may arise with Vertisols, certain Andosols, and soils that are shallow. The problem with Vertisols arises because they crack easily when dry and a loose bank is likely to be breached by a heavy storm at the start of the rainy season. Some Mollic Andosols formed from recent volcanic ash, with a high silt content and low cohesion, are also prone to slumping when wet. Shallow soils are generally unsuitable for fanya juu terracing because of the difficulty of digging a ditch where there is a stone layer or rock close to the surface and the lack of soil to form the embankment.

Suitability for Areas of Low Rainfall. The fanya juu system is suitable for areas of low rainfall. If the terraces are at zero gradient, all the rain that does not infiltrate during a storm is retained and spread over a larger area than would occur with the conventional channel terrace (which is usually graded). Furthermore, as the process of benching proceeds, the excess rainfall is spread over an increasingly large area (Figure 2). Therefore, the fanya juu terrace is just as important for water conservation as for soil conservation.

Suitability for Mechanized Farming. The fanya juu system has not been used on mechanized farms in Kenya, although it is, in principle, similar to the steep, grassed-backslope terraces that have become popular on mechanized farms in parts of the United States, such as western Iowa (*3*). However, in western Iowa, very deep loess soils are common, with more or less uniform fertility throughout the profile. It is, therefore, possible to push up large banks with bulldozers without affecting soil fertility. In Kenya, soils are less deep and fertility usually declines with increasing depth. Furthermore, equipment for throwing soil uphill is not readily available on large farms.

Suitability for Various Crops. The fanya juu system leads to the accumulation of sediment and runoff at the front (outer edge) of the terrace. The amount of either will depend on the nature of the storm, the steepness of the land, and the spacing between the terraces. In the worst situation, one or two rows of an emerging crop could be buried by sediment or suffer from waterlogging. If there is a serious risk of waterlogging, it may be possible to plant crops that are less easily affected [e.g., sorghum (*Sorghum*

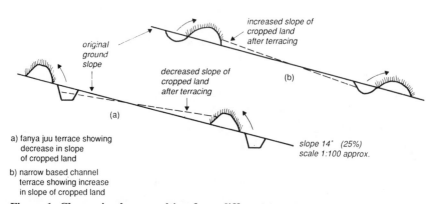

Figure 1. Change in slope resulting from different terraces.

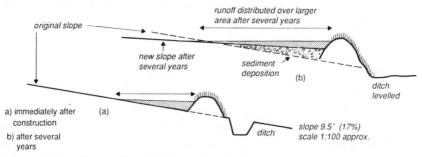

Figure 2. Runoff spreading with fanya juu terrace.

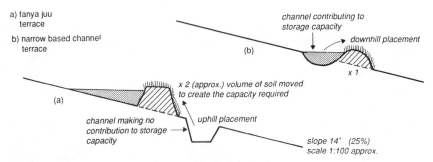

Figure 3. Labor requirement for different terraces.

bicolor) or sweet potatoes (*Ipomoea batatas*)], near the terrace embankment and to plant other crops [e.g., maize and beans (*Phaseolus vulgaris*)] where there is no such risk. The risk of waterlogging will be greatest with terraces that are level (zero gradient) and designed to retain water, but the risk decreases as benching proceeds (Figure 2).

Wastage of Land. The land taken for terraces is sometimes considered by farmers to be wasted. But if fodder is grown on the embankments; if there are good quality, stall-fed livestock that can use the fodder; and if there is a good market for the produce, such as milk, there need be no loss of output or income. Furthermore, integration of livestock into the farming system leads to a more balanced and stable farming system, provided manure is returned to the land.

Complaints are sometimes made about the waste of land occupied by the ditch from which soil was excavated in constructing the embankment. If the ditch does not serve a useful purpose in controlling runoff, it can either be leveled or used for fruit trees. One attraction of the fanya juu system when it was first introduced was that the ditch could be used for growing bananas, unlike the channel of narrow-based terraces, which required constant desilting. Therefore, less land was taken out of production (D. Nzioka, 1988, personal communication).

Labor Requirement. One objection to the fanya juu system is that it initially requires more labor to achieve the same degree of runoff control, assuming that the terrace is designed and constructed to prevent overtopping and the ditch is leveled off to provide more room for cropping. With the conventional channel terrace, both the excavated channel and the downhill bank contribute to the terrace capacity. Furthermore, it is easier to throw soil downhill than uphill (Figure 3). Roughly twice as much soil has to be moved to create the same storage capacity when using the fanya juu system.

Maintenance Requirements. In the fanya juu system, the sediment brought into the channel area contributes to the benching process and need not be removed. All that is required is to raise the height of the embankment by adding more soil from the lower side, paying particular attention to low spots so that overtopping does not occur. In practice, this is not always done, and overtopping does sometimes take place. Failure to maintain terraces, with consequent overtopping, seriously reduces the effectiveness of the system. If runoff passes over the embankment and is not trapped by the ditch, it will pass on downslope and cause rilling and failure of successive terraces. Stabilization of embankments with grass is particularly important, but the need is often overlooked. This is possibly due to fears of competition between the grass and the crop, which can be serious if high-yielding grasses, such as Napier (*Pennisetum purpureum*), are grown and terraces are closely spaced.

Ethiopia. Hurni (2) provided recommendations both for contour (zero gradient) fanya-juu terraces and for graded fanya-juu terraces. He indicated that the ditch below the bank plays an important role in collecting overflow; and, where terraces are on the contour, he recommends cross ties to prevent lateral movement of water. Graded terraces can be graded at 1 percent to facilitate drainage. Sediment that fills the ditch should be dug out periodically and used to raise the bank. Hurni suggested that fanya juu terraces be used on slopes of 3 to 50 percent, although experience in Kenya indicates that there is considerable risk of failure on the steeper slopes. Thirty percent would be a more reasonable figure for the upper limit.

Design and Construction.

General specifications for fanya juu terraces are given in the Ministry of Agriculture Soil Conservation Handbook (6) but design principles for different situations have not been given detailed consideration. Thomas and associates (5) attempted to provide a rational basis for the design of fanya juu terraces in low rainfall areas where water conservation is required. However, there is a need for more research on terrace design and for the use of computer modeling to facilitate the process. Whether terraces are designed for discharge or retention of water, the following points should be considered.

Design Storm. Terraces should be designed to cope with the heaviest storm, of given duration, that is expected in a 10-year return period. The duration of the storm will depend on whether the terraces are designed for discharge or retention of runoff. Where terraces are designed for discharge, the rainfall intensity appropriate to the time of concentration can be used in the rational formula to estimate peak discharge in cubic meters per second. Because terraces are often closely spaced and short, a storm of 15 minutes may be appropriate. Where terraces are designed for retention, an estimate is needed of the total quantity of water to be stored in cubic meters per meter of terrace, that is, the cross-sectional storage area required. This can be derived from the maximum difference between the cumulative curves for rainfall and infiltration for storms of different durations. For a terrace that is designed to retain runoff, a storm period of 1 hour or even 3 hours may be appropriate, depending on the infiltration rate of the soil (5).

Runoff Control. The design of the terrace requires decisions on whether runoff is to be discharged or retained and on where it is to be held prior to discharge or infiltration. If runoff is to be discharged, a gradient of between 0.4 percent and 1 percent can be used, depending on the soil's erodibility, but a discharge area or a waterway must be available. If runoff is to be retained, terraces with zero gradient are required. As a safety precaution in the latter situation, the ends can be left open to allow some discharge during peak storms and to reduce the risk of overtopping. There are three possible alternatives for holding runoff prior to discharge or infiltration: (1) above the embankment, (2) below the embankment in the ditch from which soil was excavated, and (3) in both places. There are advantages and disadvantages to each approach, which should be considered before a final decision is reached.

Holding Runoff Above the Embankment. If runoff is to be prevented from overtopping the embankment, then sufficient capacity must be maintained by raising the embankment periodically with soil dug from the lower side. This is necessary because of the erosion and deposition of sediment, which is part of the process of benching. Runoff passing over the embankment should be avoided, if possible, because of the damage it may cause in the process. Furthermore, runoff that infiltrates above the embankment will aid production of fodder grasses that are used for stabilization. However, there are some problems that can arise with a fanya juu terrace that is designed to retain runoff above the embankment. The first problem is that breakage can occur if the structure is not well consolidated and stabilized with grass. The risks arising from breakage of terraces on steep land or long slopes should be treated seriously. Second, if the excavated ditch below the bank is not used, the labor demands for creating the necessary storage capacity on the upper side is increased. However, in areas where rainfall is normally deficient and slopes not more than approximately 15 percent, it is advisable to make terraces that retain runoff above the embankment. Design procedures for this are given by Thomas and associates (5).

Holding Runoff Below the Embankment. Holding runoff below the embankment has one major advantage in that runoff is trapped in an excavated ditch that is stable and is unlikely to break. Runoff held in this way can be used to improve the growing conditions of bananas (*Musa* Sp.), pawpaws (*Carica papaya*), or other fruits planted in the ditch. The only problem is that runoff passing over the embankment will cause erosion in the process and will fill the ditch with sediment which has to be dug out from time to time if the structure is to remain effective. The natural process of benching, which takes place if runoff and sediment is held above the embankment, will be delayed. A ditch not used for fruit is considered wasted land and generally unacceptable to small farmers.

Combined Solution. The third alternative, holding runoff partly above and partly below the embankments, has certain advantages. In a light storm, runoff will be held before it passes over the embankment, whereas in a heavy storm, part will pass over the embankment and be caught in the ditch. Problems arise where there is no clear policy and there is insufficient capacity either above or below the embankment. Such a situation is common in the field.

Gradient. Graded fanya juu terraces that are designed to discharge runoff can have smaller capacity than contour terraces and, therefore, involve less labor for construction. They can be justified in areas where there is normally sufficient rainfall and where there is a safe place to discharge water. They may also be desirable on steep slopes with unstable soils where a terrace that is designed on the contour to retain runoff could lead to a risk of mass movement. In areas where there is normally a shortage of rainfall, terraces with zero gradient are recommended.

Terrace Spacing and Ground Slope. Terrace spacing may be determined by the presence of some existing structures but it is normally based on slope. The following formula has been used in Kenya for determining vertical interval, $VI = as + b$, where VI is vertical interval between terraces in meters; a is a rainfall factor (usually 0.075); b is a soil factor (usually 0.6); and s is percentage slope. If fanya juu terraces are placed too far apart, the development of bench terraces will be slow and will involve risers that are higher or steeper than is desirable.

Soil Depth and Erodibility. The depth of soil will also influence the spacing of terraces. There should still be adequate rooting depth at the foot of the riser even after the benching process has led to the formation of level or nearly level benches. Where there is no expectation or intention of creating level benches, Hurni's approach (2) is appropriate, whereby the vertical interval between terraces should be two and one-half times the depth of the easily reworkable soil on slopes over 15 percent or 1 meter on gentler slopes.

Construction. Construction is carried out after laying out pegs on the contour or at a gradient as required. A trench is dug and soil thrown uphill, leaving a berm of 20 centimeters to prevent the soil from falling back. The loose soil should be thoroughly compacted to reduce the risk of breakage, and the slope of the embankment should conform to the recommendations of Wenner (6). After completion, the top of the bank should be resurveyed to ensure that it conforms with the required gradient, although this is rarely done. The farmer should also check for low spots or weakness after rain and complete any necessary repairs. Grass should be planted on the embankment as soon as possible after construction. Elephant grass (*Pennisetum purpureum*) or Guatamala grass (*Tripsacum laxum*) are very productive, but also competitive and should not be used in dry areas or where terraces are close together. Alternatives include such species as signal grass (*Brachiaria decumbens*) or donkey grass (*Panicum trichocladum*) for humid areas and Makarikari grass (*Panicum coloratum var Makarikariensis*) for dry areas.

Conclusions and Recommendations

The fanya juu terrace has been accepted as the best conservation structure by many farmers in dry areas of Kenya. It is particularly valuable for water retention in semiarid and subhumid areas and where benching is required to reduce the problems associated with the annual cropping of erodible soils on sloping land.

The method of handling runoff must be planned from the start, and the options of discharge or retention of runoff above or below the embankment should be carefully considered before reaching a decision.

Where slopes are steep, consolidation and stabilization of the embankment is particularly important, and establishment of grass should be given priority.

Where labor is scarce, the narrow-based channel terrace can be used as an alternative. Past experience indicates, however, that sedimentation of the channel is a major problem where erosion rates are high.

Recommendations for terracing should be tailored to local conditions of rainfall, soil, slope, and farming system. Full account must be taken though of the farmer's own needs and preferences, the resources available, and the constraints under which he or she is operating.

Acknowledgement

The authors thank Professor Norman Hudson for the useful comments he made on the original draft of this chapter.

REFERENCES

1. Hudson, N. W. 1981. *Soil conservation.* Batsford, London, England.
2. Hurni, H. 1986. *Soil conservation in Ethiopia.* Ministry of Agriculture, Addis Ababa, Ethiopia.
3. Jacobsen, P. 1976. *New developments in land-terrace systems.* Transactions, American Society of Agricultural Engineers 9: 576-577.
4. Morgan, R.P.C. 1986. *Soil erosion and conservation.* Longman, London, England.
5. Thomas, D. B., R. G. Barber, and T. R. Moore. 1980. *Terracing of cropland in low rainfall areas of Machakos District, Kenya.* Journal of Agricultural Engineering Research 25: 57-65.
6. Wenner, C. G. 1981. *Soil conservation in Kenya.* Ministry of Agriculture, Nairobi, Kenya.

MULCH EFFECTS
ON SOIL AND WATER LOSS
IN MAIZE IN INDIA

M. L. KHYBRI

Maize is commonly grown in
the Himalayan region on sloping land and in adjoining valleys. Cultivation
of this crop without soil conservation measures causes heavy erosion losses
on the sloping land in the Doon Valley (*3*). Use of atrazine to keep the
fields free of weeds results in even greater erosion (*1*).

Mechanical erosion control measures, such as bunding and terracing,
although used, are sometimes not feasible and expensive. Mulching effectively reduces erosion. Khybri and associates (*2*) found that grass mulch
applied to maize at a rate of 4 tons per hectare effectively reduced soil
and water losses on an 8 percent slope.

The study reported here was undertaken to determine the effectiveness
of lesser amounts of mulch. Also, because the peak rainy season lasts to
the middle of August, the effect of removal of mulch then, for other uses
by the farmer, on crop yield and soil and water loss was studied. The work
was undertaken at the research station of the Central Soil and Water Conservation Research and Training Institute, which represents the northwestern
outer Himalayan and Valley regions.

The Experimental Design

The experiment consisted of eight runoff plots, 22 meters x 1.8 meters,
on deep silt-loam soil with an 8 percent slope. Runoff was collected in
tanks with multislot dividers. The study was conducted for 3 years
(1982-1984). Maize (*Zea mays* L, Ganga-5) was planted in rows 60 centimeters apart. Fertilization consisted of 100 kilograms of nitrogen, 60

kilograms of phosphate, and 40 kilograms of potash per hectare without irrigation. The nitrogen application was split; half was applied at planting and half 1 month later.

Treatments included (1) maize planted up-and-down slope, (2) maize planted on the contour, (3) maize planted on the contour with 2 tons per hectare of mulch up to mid-August, (4) maize planted on the contour with 2 tons per hectare mulch during the entire crop period, (5) maize planted on the contour with 4 tons per hectare of mulch up to mid-August, (6) maize planted on the contour with 4 tons per hectare of mulch during the entire crop period, and (7) cultivated fallow.

Locally available grass was applied immediately after maize planting. During the winter, a uniform crop of wheat was grown on all plots.

Mulch Saves Soil and Water

Rainfall, runoff, and soil loss data are given in table 1. Runoff and soil loss from maize planted up-and-down slope were 64 percent and 33 percent, respectively, of that from cultivated fallow. Runoff and soil loss from contouring were 85 percent and 75 percent, respectively, of that from up-and-down slope planting. Runoff and soil loss from contoured maize with 2 tons per hectare of mulch were 54 percent and 41 percent, respectively, of that from contoured maize with no mulch. Runoff and soil loss from contoured maize with 4 tons per hectare of mulch were 43 percent and 31 percent, respectively, of that from contoured maize with no mulch. Runoff and soil loss when mulch was removed in mid-August were essentially the same as when mulch was left on the entire crop period for both 2 and 4 tons per hectare of mulch. Yields of maize (2,800 kilograms per hectare) and wheat (3,000 kilograms per hectare) were essentially the same regardless of slope direction or mulching treatment.

Conclusion

Continuous fallow loses much more soil and water than cropping to maize. Contouring is helpful in reducing soil and water loss compared with up-and-down hill planting. Mulching reduces soil and water losses still further. Adding 2 additional tons of mulch per hectare reduced runoff 18 percent and soil loss 25 percent compared to the first 2 tons per hectare. Also, the farmer may remove the mulch in mid-August without changing soil and water loss, compared to leaving it on during all of the crop period. Crop yields are not affected adversely by mulching.

Table 1. Effect of amount and duration of mulch on runoff, soil loss, and yield of maize.

Runoff and Soil Loss	Maize Up-and-Down Slope	Maize on Contour	Mulch at 2 t/ha up to Mid-August	Mulch at 2 t/ha During Crop Period	Mulch at 4 t/ha up to Mid-August	Mulch at 4 t/ha During Crop Period	Cultivated Fallow
Runoff as a percentage of rainfall							
1982 (rainfall 836 mm)	49.3	41.8	18.1	15.9	12.4	13.2	60.5
1983 (rainfall 1,095 mm)	36.2	31.9	19.1	19.8	16.1	16.2	60.6
1984 (rainfall 899 mm)	31.7	25.8	16.4	16.2	14.2	14.1	60.9
Average (rainfall 943 mm)	39.1	33.2	17.9	17.3	14.2	14.5	60.7
Soil loss (t/ha)							
1982	17.5	13.8	6.2	6.4	4.5	4.2	58.9
1983	26.1	17.8	7.2	7.3	5.7	5.4	70.7
1984	23.6	19.0	7.2	7.0	5.7	5.5	74.2
Average	22.4	16.9	6.9	6.9	5.3	5.0	67.9

REFERENCES

1. Bhardwaj, S. P., M. L. Khybri, O. P. Gupta, and R. N. Rai. 1979. *Effect of atrazine application in maize on soil and water losses.* Indian Journal of Soil Conservation 7(1): 5-9.
2. Khybri, M. L., S. P. Bhardwaj, S. N. Prasad, and Sewa Ram. 1984. *Effect of minimum tillage and mulch on soil and water loss in maize on 8 percent slope.* Indian Journal of Soil Conservation 12(2&3): 65-69.
3. Tejwani, K. G., S. K. Gupta, and H. N. Mathur. 1975. *Soil and water conservation research in India 1956-71.* ICAR Publications, New Delhi, India.

CULTURAL PRACTICES
FOR EROSION CONTROL
IN CASSAVA

S. JANTAWAT, V. VICHUKIT, S. PUTTHACHAROEN, and R. HOWELER

Cassava (*Manihot esculenta* Crantz) is grown extensively in eastern and northeastern Thailand. It is a major economic crop for the country. The cultivated area for cassava was 1.4 million hectares in 1987, with an export value of $760 million in 1986. More than 10,000 families earned their living from cassava, which is grown mainly on highly erodible soils. It was recently reported that the quantities of plant nutrients lost by erosion were greater than those taken up by the cassava plants (*1*).

Little research has been done on soil erosion control under cassava. Therefore, considering the problem, research on cultural practices that minimize erosion is badly needed.

Two Experiments

From 1987 to 1989, two experiments were conducted at the Sriracha Research Station, Sriracha District, Chonburi Province, on a soil classified as an Oxic paleustult (fine loamy mixed) on an 8 percent slope. The soil texture was 68 percent sand, 13 percent silt, and 19 percent clay, with 0.82 percent organic matter, 19.5 parts per million available phosphorus (Bray II), 172.5 parts per million exchangeable potassium, 232.8 parts per million exchangeable calcium, and 44.1 parts per million exchangeable magnesium. The pH was 5.9. Average annual rainfall at the site is 1,200 millimeters.

In 1987, 14 runoff plots were established for this study. Each plot, 15 meters long and 10 meters wide, was surrounded by earthen ridges. Below each plot was a channel of 40 x 40 centimeters, 15 meters long, covered by a polyethylene sheet with small holes to allow the water to seep through. At monthly intervals the sediment was weighed for calculation of soil losses.

The treatments are described in table 1. All crops—cassava, maize (*Zea mays* L.), groundnut (*Arachis hypogaea*), and grass (*Brachiaria humidicola*)—were planted May 15, 1987. Cassava roots were harvested March 24, 1988. Groundnuts were harvested October 12, 1987. The maize crop failed because of the long, dry period in July 1987. Rainfall during the experiment is shown in table 2.

In 1988, the experiment, with changes, was repeated at the same site using eight treatments with two replications. Repeated treatments are shown

Table 1. Description of 14 treatments used in the erosion control experiment with cassava.

1. No land preparation, preplant application of Gramozone; cassava planted in holes made with pointed stick.
2. Plowing only, one time with 4-disk plow.
3. Two plowings with 4-disk plow followed by two diskings with 7-disk plow.
4. Two plowings and two diskings followed by contour ridging.
5. Two plowings and two diskings followed by up-and-down ridging.
6. Strip preparation with 4-disk plow, preparing 2-meter contour strips, alternated with 1-meter unprepared strips; cassava planted 100 x 67 centimeters.
7. Live barrier of *Brachiaria* grass (*humidicola*), 2-meter-side contour strip every 8 meters of cassava.
8. Live barrier of elephant grass (*Pennisitum purpureum*), two-meter-wide contour strips every 8 meters of cassava.
9. Treatment 3, but without fertilization.
10. Treatment 3, but planted at 80 x 80 centimeters (15,625 plants/hectare).
11. Treatment 3, but cassava planted in double rows (150 x 80 x 87) intercropped with two rows of ground nuts, 50 centimeters between rows.
12. Treatment 3 with cassava in double rows and intercropped with 1 row of maize.
13. Treatment 3, but with chemical weed control: preemergent application of Diuron and Lasso, postmergent application of Diuron + Gramoxone.
14. Subsoiling at 40-centimeter depth, and 80-centimeter row width, cassava planted at 80 x 125 centimeters.

Note:
(1) Cassava fertilized with 625 kilograms 15-15-15 NPK/hectare except in Treatment 9. Live barriers and intercrops were fertilized additionally as needed.
(2) Cassava (Rayong 1) planted at 100 x 100 centimeters (10,000 plants/hectare), except in Treatment 10; in Treatments 11 and 12, cassava was planted in double rows with 150 centimeters between double rows, 80 centimeters between rows, and 87 centimeters between plants to maintain a population of 10,000 plants/hectare.
(3) Manual weed control with the hoe was performed in all treatments except Treatment 13, in which herbicides were used preemergent, followed by hand weeding with a knife, and postemergent herbicides after 3 months.

Table 2. Monthly rainfall at the experimental site in the Sriracha District, Chonburi Province, Thailand, during the study period.

Month	Number of Rainy Days			Rainfall (mm)		
	1987	1988	1989	1987	1988	1989
May	9	9		135.0	112.0	
June	13	8		96.4	125.0	
July	7	8		35.6	195.0	
August	12	14		78.2	195.0	
September	16	13		183.8	282.0	
October	16	15		219.5	374.0	
November	17	3		374.9	13.0	
December	-	-		-	-	
January	-	-	3	-	-	56.0
February	-	3	3	-	115.1	12.0
March*		1	1		1.3	126.0

*Up to March 12 in 1989.

in the results for 1988 (Table 3). An additional treatment consisted of two plowings and two diskings, with a contour bank every 10 meters planted to *Leucaena leucocephala*. Cassava and groundnut were planted May 25, 1988. Cassava was harvested March 13, 1989, groundnut on September 8, 1988.

Soil Loss and Crop Yield: A Summary

In 1987 to 1988, soil losses from no-tillage were more than double or triple those of all the tilled treatments. Subsoiling reduced soil loss from 53 to 73 percent of the other tilled treatments, whereas contour ridging reduced soil loss to half of subsoiling, the next lowest treatment. Intercropping with groundnut reduced soil loss from 33 to 56 percent of the other intercropping and live-barrier treatments, whereas fertilization reduced soil loss to approximately half that without fertilization. In all of these treatments, only the two plowings and disking with contour ridging resulted in soil losses below 12 tons per hectare, or what many consider acceptable limits.

The high soil losses from no-tillage resulted from an unusual set of circumstances—a heavy rain following a preemergence herbicide application, rendering it ineffective, followed by hand weeding and a great deal of bare soil. The bare surface sealed, greatly reducing infiltration and resulting in high runoff. The following year no-tillage was an effective treatment. The tilled soil (1987-1988), especially subsoiling, had a high infiltration rate immediately after tillage. Contour ridges, which reduced runoff, were effective in reducing soil loss.

Lower soil losses from intercropped groundnuts were believed to be due

Table 3. Effect of soil and crop management on cassava yield and soil losses due to erosion in two experiments in Sri Racha, Thailand.

Soil and Crop Management	1987		1988	
	Casava Yield	Dry Soil Loss	Cassava Yield	Dry Soil Loss
		t/ha		
A. Soil preparation practices				
No tillage (1)*	30.7	93.8	26.2b†	5.7c†
Strip preparation, alternating prepared and unprepared strips (6)	26.7	42.1		
One plowing with four-disk plow (2)	22.3	37.5		
Two plowings followed by two diskings (3)	25.8	30.5	31.1ab	11.1b
Two plowings and disking followed by up-and-down ridging (5)	25.6	35.4	33.2a	11.8b
Two plowings and disking followed by contour ridging (4)	35.5	11.1	29.6ab	5.1c
Subsoil only (14)	34.3	22.2	22.5b	4.6c
Treatment (2), but with contour bank‡	–	–	27.4b	17.7a
B. Intercropping and live barriers§				
No intercropping or live barriers (3)	25.8	30.5		
Intercropping double-row cassava with maize (12)	22.5	44.9		
Intercropping double-row cassava with ground nuts (11)	22.8	17.2	26.4b	4.7c
Live barrier of *Brachiaria* grass (7)	22.6	52.7		
Live barrier of elephant grass (8)	23.3	36.5		
C. Crop management practices§				
With fertilization, low population, hand weeding (3)	25.8	30.5		
Without fertilization (9)	18.8	54.9	24.1b	16.7a
Higher plant population (10)	25.4	24.4		
Chemical weed control (13)	30.9	25.7		
LSD (P<0.10)			5.3	2.7

*Treatment numbers from table 1 shown in parentheses.
†Average of two replications.
‡New treatment in 1988.
§All had two plowings followed by two diskings (Treatment 3).

to earlier canopy closure, which reduced the impact of falling raindrops. Failure of the first planting of *Brachiaria* explains the poor results from these strips. Poor growth and inadequate canopy closure explains the high soil losses from unfertilized cassava.

In the 1988-1989 experiment (Table 3), all soil losses, except strip preparation with contour banks every 10 meters and unfertilized cassava, were below 12 tons per hectare. Soil losses were essentially the same from the noncontouring treatments 3 and 5. Soil losses from contoured treatments and subsoiling were approximately half those from noncontouring and were approximately the same as double-row cassava intercropped with groundnut. Improper design and construction of the contour banks were responsible for the higher soil losses with this treatment.

Cassava yields ranged from 18.8 to 35.5 tons per hectare in the 1987-1988 experiment (Table 3). Maximum yield resulted from the tilled plot with contour ridging, whereas the lowest resulted from the nonfertilized plot. The yield on the contour ridging can be attributed to prevention of water, soil, and nutrient losses. Higher yield on the subsoiled plot can be attributed to better root penetration, and conservation of water and nutrients.

The 1988 to 1989 growing season was much different from the 1987 to 1988 season in that rainfall was much higher in the June through October period. In 1988 to 1989, water conservation was not as important as in the previous season, and up-and-down-hill-treatment yields were comparable to those with contour ridging. Cassava yield on the subsoil treatment was significantly lower than up and downslope ridging in 1988 to 1989. Cassava yields with intercropping and live barriers were generally lower than with the tillage treatments.

Acknowledgement

The authors thank the Centro International de Agricultura Tropical for its financial support of this study and Chamlong Cheimchamnanja, chief of Sriracha Research Station, for making available the necessary facilities for conducting this experiment.

REFERENCE

1. Luangsarard, S. 1987. *Effects of soil and water conservation practices on the fertility loss and cassava yield on Map Bon series in Kae Lae Watershed, Amphoe Ban Kali, Rayong.* M.S. thesis. Kasetsart University, Bangkok, Thailand.

TERRACING SYSTEMS
FOR OIL PALMS

SOON LEONG NEOH

The oil palm (*Elaeis guineensis Jacq.*) is one of the world's major oil crops. The palm oil it produces represented about 18 percent of world trade in edible/soap fat and oil in 1987 (*2*). Malaysia is the leading producer of palm oil, with 75,710 hectares in palms in 1964, increasing to 1.5 million hectares by 1986.

This phenomenal rate of expansion has pushed the planting of oil palm onto steeper and steeper terrain in this relatively small, hilly country of 330,433 square kilometers. In Malaysia, a majority of the steep-land oil palm is planted on mechanically leveled contour terraces. These terraces are spaced to accommodate each row of palm trees (Figure 1).

Palm oil yields are strongly correlated with moisture. Runoff water held by the terraces contributes significantly to yields. However, most terraces are relatively narrow (3 meters) and shallow (0.4 meter). As such, they are susceptible to erosion. Also, because they are so narrow and fragile, they are incapable of supporting mechanized vehicles.

In previous work (*3*), I argued that, in terms of erosion control, water containment, and vehicular access (tractors), it would be advantageous to have fewer but more substantial terraces of at least 5.5 meters wide, with large stop bunds at regular intervals to contain runoff water (Figure 2). These stop bunds also double as individual planting platforms for the oil palms. Palms grow well on these platforms because of their proximity to the captured runoff water. However, construction of 5.5-meter-wide terraces is costly and brings a high proportion of infertile subsoil to the surface (Figure 3). In addition, vehicular traffic tends to compact the soil to the detriment of the palms (*1*).

204

Figure 1. The usual 3-meter terrace width with one terrace per row of oil palms.

Figure 2. A 5.5-meter terrace width with stop bunds.

Present studies demonstrate the practicality of a slightly narrower terrace (4.2 meters), optimized for erosion control and vehicular access. Palms are planted on platforms immediately above and below the terrace. There is only one terrace for two rows of palms. One row is above the terrace and one row is below. Planting platforms are constructed out of the terrace wall (Figure 4). By virtue of their position on the terrace, these platforms also serve as a series of stop bunds to capture runoff in individual ponds adjacent to and below the palms growing on the platforms (Figure 5). The platforms below the terrace are constructed from undisturbed soil immediately below the outer edge of the terrace. Water behind the stop bunds subirrigates the palms by seepage.

The 4.2-meter terraces are wide enough to accommodate tractors. They are linked to one another with vehicular paths to form a road network covering the entire field. Harmful effects of vehicular soil compaction are minimized because the palms are planted above and below the terraces, and the terrace is used exclusively for vehicular movement.

Generally, it is not believed to be possible to have terraces of 4.2 meters in such numbers if the slope is greater than 25 degrees (46.6 percent). For slopes steeper than this, it may be possible to have one terrace for every four rows (Figure 6). From experience, it is more beneficial to the palms

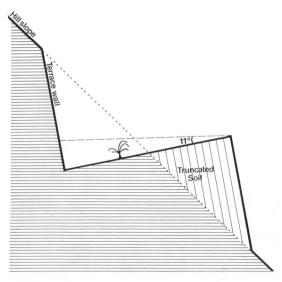

Figure 3. Cross-sectional view of a planting terrace with palm.

Figure 4. A 4.2-meter system with platform constructed out of terrace wall.

Figure 5. A 4.2-meter system with a series of stop bunds adjacent to and below the palms growing on platforms.

Figure 6. Terrace 4.2 meters wide on land steeper than 46 percent slope—one terrace for four rows.

Table 1. Costs of construction, labor, and harvesting on three widths of terraces.

Type of Terraces	I Narrow (3 m)	II Wide (5.5 m)	III Wide (4.2 m)
Cost [Selected items only (US$)]			
Construction			
Terrace	$1.80/10 m	$5.50/10 m	$3.50/10 m
Stop bund cum	$0.40 each	$1.50 each	$1.00 each
Planting platform	(Stop bund only)		
Planting platform on unterraced rows		$1.00 each	$1.00 each
Total cost/hectare	$240.00	$435.00	$330.00
Labor charges in field maintenance			
Weedicide spraying	Manual pump $7.00/ha	Self-propelled motorized pump $3.00/ha	Self-propelled motorized pump $3.00/ha
Harvesting			
Labor cost of collecting the fresh fruit bunches (FFB)	FFB manually wheeled to road side in wheelbarrow: $4.00/ton	FFB collected by tractor equipped with dumper: $1.50/ton	FFB collected by tractor equipped with dumper: $1.50/ton

to have one wider and functional terrace every three to four rows than to have a badly eroded terrace for every row. It should be pointed out, however, that it is costly to construct 4.2-meter terraces on such steep slopes. Planting platforms must be virtually carved out of the steep wall (Figure 6). Detailed cost analysis shows, however, that maintenance and cultivation expenses for oil palms are lower on the wider terraces than on the narrow (3-meter) terraces (Table 1). Furthermore, narrow terraces hinder use of machinery and force planters to rely increasingly on scarce and expensive manual labor for planting, maintenance, and harvesting.

REFERENCES

1. Greacen, E. L., and B. G. Richards. 1983. *Soil mechanical problems associated with the agricultural use of soils.* In E. T. Craswell and R. F. Isbell [editors] *Proceedings of the International Workshop of Soil.* The Australian Center for International Agricultural Research, Canberra. pp. 149-159.
2. Information Malaysia. 1987. Berita Publishing, Kuala Lumpur, Malaysia. 362 pp.
3. Neoh, Soon Leong. 1987. *Planting of oil palm on steep land.* In *1987 International Oil Palm/Palm Oil Conferences.* Palm Oil Research Institute of Malaysia, Kuala Lumpur.

REHABILITATION
OF DEGRADED LAND
IN INDONESIA

H. SUWARDJO, AI DARIAH, and A. BARUS

Degraded land is defined as soil with little productivity or no productivity for agriculture activity, caused by management and land use that allowed excessive erosion (6).

Land degradation in Indonesia is a serious problem in upland agriculture. It is caused by such activities as shifting cultivation, volcanic eruption, erosion, improper land use, land clearing, mining, etc. These activities tend to increase because of population pressure, but, so far, soil erosion has been the most serious problem. The most common land degradation in a densely populated area, like Java, is due to improper land management that causes soil erosion.

In Java, where agricultural land is very limited, many farmers plant steep land with annual food crops. Soil erosion and declining organic matter content cause deterioration of soil physical properties. Most farmers do not use proper soil conservation and management. Soil degradation is accelerated by intense rainfall and the high temperatures of the tropical climate. Land degradation in densely populated areas decreases soil productivity. This and poor water relations in the soil results in widespread poverty.

In the framework of the transmigration program between 1980 and 1986, about 120,000 familes per year resettled from Java to the outer islands (3). One family needs 2 hectares of land, which means at least 250,000 hectares of forest must be cleared for agricultural land annually. Use of heavy machinery for land clearing sometimes creates problems. The correct choice of land clearing method and implements used are important decisions (8).

Land clearing with heavy machinery is fast, but improper machinery increases soil compaction and bulk density, with reductions in macroporosity, infiltration capacity, available moisture, and soil aeration (5, 9). The present land clearing leaves the soil bare and the subsoil exposed to high-intensity rainfall. This mechanical land clearing results in severe soil compaction and low infiltration and increases soil erosion. Furthermore, the effects of soil compaction persist for many years, with root penetration adversely affected. This results in low or even no soil productivity.

In 1982, land clearing experiments were begun, and some studies have since been conducted on rehabilitation of degraded land caused by mechanical land clearing and soil mismanagement.

An estimated 12 million people in Indonesia are dependent on shifting cultivation (2). Shifting cultivation is a traditional farming system in which forest is cleared by the slash-and-burn method. The soil is not tilled, and the crop is planted directly. This method requires a long fallow period before the land can be returned to cropping. Increases in population density and the desire of people to raise their standard of living by changing from subsistance farming to cash crops causes even greater pressure on the land. Reducing the fallow period causes serious problems and promotes land degradation.

Severely eroded land is classified as critical land. In Indonesia, there are 24 million hectares of critical land that is unproductive, and 8 million hectares of these are severely eroded. The question is, what rehabilitation measures are justified on this unproductive, critical land (4)?

The land that requires rehabilitation is easily recognized in the field by poor vegetation, very low productivity, no response to fertilizer, low infiltration, high runoff and erosion. This is due to poor soil physical properties and unstable soil structure.

High runoff and erosion can be prevented by growing better vegetation. The problem is how to turn these poor conditions into a better crop cover that can conserve more moisture.

Some restoration measures have been undertaken by the Indonesian government through a regreening movement and soil conservation program. For the regreening movement, forest trees are used. However, because some of the land is owned by farmers who prefer to grow food crops, even on steep land, the regreening program was not accepted by many farmers. To support the rehabilitation program, some studies on rehabilitation of degraded upland have been conducted.

Rehabilitation Study for Improving Soil Productivity

To overcome the problem of degraded land, studies on the use of inedible legume cover crops have been conducted by many researchers (1, 7).

Five cover crop species have been tested for 2 years on a degraded Oxisol in West Java. The results show that soil physical properties, which include aeration porosity, permeability, and soil aggregate stability index, were consistently improved (Table 1). Legume cover-crop treatments greatly increased the yields of the subsequent soybean [*Glycine max* (L.) Merr.] and cowpea crops (Table 2).

Centrocema (*Centrocema pubescens*) was considered to be the best legume cover crop for improving soil productivity (Tables 1 and 2). This plant has been tested with different degrees of erosion damage. Results show that rehabilitation of degraded land requires at least 1 year under a cover crop. The more serious the erosion, the longer the rehabilitation period needed. The low production on eroded land is due to higher aluminum content, lower cation exchange capacity, lower nutrient content, and poorer soil physical properties (Table 3).

Although inedible legume crops, such as centrocema and capologonium, have shown good results for improving soil productivity, it is difficult to encourage their use by farmers because they do not obtain a direct yield from the crop. Therefore, attention should be given to finding other legume crops that produce a direct harvest and are accepted by farmers.

Four edible legume crops have been tested for rehabilitation of degraded land caused by improper land clearing and erosion in a transmigration area in Jambi. These legume crops are Cowpea, *Dolicus lab lab, Mucuna* sp.,

Table 1. Effect of cover crop on soil physical properties.

Treatment	Soil Bulk Density (gm/cm³)	Aeration Porosity (% volume)	Permeability (cm/hour)	Aggregate Stability
Bare soil (natural grass)	1.01a*	15.1b	0.6c	34.1c
Setaria conjugula	0.93bc	20.7a	3.5bc	36.8bc
Crotalari ussaramoensis	0.89bc	23.6a	5.1bc	41.1bc
Pueraria javanica	0.94b	20.6a	3.9bc	43.8ab
Centrocema pubescens	0.87c	24.3a	12.7a	51.1a
Psophocarpus palustris	0.93bc	21.3a	6.7b	37.3bc

*Numbers followed by the same letter are not significantly different.

Table 2. Effect of cover crop on subsequent soybean and cowpea crops

Treatment	Soybean (t/ha)	Cowpea (t/ha)
Bare soil (natural grass)	0.06d*	0.07e
Setaria conjugula	0.76b	1.83b
Crotalari ussaramoensis	0.41c	0.72d
Pueraria javanica	0.73b	1.08c
Centrocema pubescens	1.02a	2.26a
Psophocarpus palustris	0.13d	0.64d

*Numbers followed by the same letter are not significantly different.

Table 3. Effect of land rehabilitation, using *Centrocema pubescens* on different degrees of erosion, on soil properties and maize production.

Symbol	Treatment	Permeability (cm/hour)	Aeration Porosity	Organic C	CEC	Exchangeable Mg	Al	Maize Yield Straw	Grain
			(%)	(%)		(me/100g)		(ha)	
T1	Erosion 5 cm, rehabilitation	1.55	21.0	1.83	17.6	1.1	0.16	8.03a*	1.67a
T2	Erosion 6-10 cm, no rehabilitation	1.29	19.2	1.22	16.3	0.7	2.10	2.70bc	0.16c
T3	Erosion 6-10 cm, 6 months rehabilitation	2.71	19.7	1.35	-	0.1	-	3.50bc	0.92bc
T6	Erosion 11-15 cm, 1 year rehabilitation	1.69	13.5	1.03	-	0.1	1.00	4.17b	1.36b
T1	Erosion 16-20 cm, 6 months rehabilitation	1.57	16.8	1.61	11.0	0.6	-	1.68c	0.21c
T1	Erosion 16-20 cm, 1 year rehabilitation	2.99	13.0	1.52	-	0.9	-	2.77bc	0.30c

*Numbers followed by the same letter are not significantly different.

and mungbean. Results show that *Mucuna* sp. had the most positive effect on soil physical properties (Table 4). This effect is also shown on the crop production after *Mucuna* sp. (Table 5).

The greater effect on soil properties by *Mucuna* was due to its higher biomass production (9.2 tons per hectare), compared to *Dolicus lab lab,* which produced only 4.5 tons per hectare; cowpea, 5.9 tons per hectare; and mungbean, 2.3 tons per hectare. Also, the rooting depth of *Mucuna* was greater than 32 centimeters, compared to *Dolicus lab lab,* which was only 19 centimeters.

A similar experiment also was conducted on a critical limestone-derived soil in Java. This experiment showed likewise that *Mucuna* sp. was most promising.

Mucuna sp. is an edible legume crop grown as a home garden plant, especially in central Java. The seed is commonly used for making fermented cace (tempe) or is mixed with cassava, a secondary staple food. It has high nutritive value, characterized by its high protein content. However, it requires a pretreatment, soaking in water for at least 24 hours, to leach its high hydrocyanic acid (0.13 parts per million).

The use of *Mucuna* sp. as an edible legume crop has been studied in a crop rotation and rehabilitation on an Oxisol in a transmigration area in Jambi Province. The results shows that the yield of soybeans grown after *Mucuna* sp. was significantly higher than that after either groundnut or

Table 4. Effect of legume crops on soil physical properties at the 0- to 10-cm depth.

Legume	Bulk Density (gm/cm^{-3})	Aeration Porosity	Water Storing Porosity
		(%)	
Mucuna sp.	1.05	30.8	11.7
Dolicus lab lab	1.06	30.6	9.2
Cowpea	1.22	20.0	10.7
Mungbean	1.22	22.7	9.6

Table 5. Effect of legume used for soil rehabilitation on soybean and maize production.

Treatment	Soybean Dry Grain	Maize Grain Production
	t/ha	
Mucuna sp.	0.66a	2.88a
Dolicus lab lab	0.27b	0.94b
Cowpea	0.29b	0.92b
Mungbean	0.27b	0.45b

*Numbers followed by the same letter are not significantly different.

Table 6. Effect of *Mucuna*, groundnut, and grass on the yield of soybean and maize.

Treatment	First Crop (Soybean)		Second Crop (Maize)	
	Green Manure	Seed	Green Manure	Seed
		t/ha		
Mucana	1.261a*	1.150a	2.356b	1.461b
Fresh crop residues removed				
Mucuna	1.374a	1.259a	4.630a	2.251a
Fresh crop residues returned†				
Groundnut (limed at 2 ton/ha)				
All crop residues returned	0.992b	0.756b	4.022b	1.282b
Grass	0.722b	0.561c	1.626b	1.097b

*Numbers followed by the same letter are not significantly different.
†Mulching of *Mucuna* also improved the soil condition (Table 4).

Table 7. Effect of *Mucuna* in combination with tillage treatment on the seed yield of soybean and maize.

Treatment	Soybean	Maize
	t/ha	
Tilled, no fertilizer, *Mucuna* removed	0.693c	0.538c
No-tilled, fertilized *Mucuna* mulched	1.100a	2.209a
Tilled, fertilized, *Mucuna* incorporated	0.997b	1.811b

*Numbers followed by the same letter are not significantly different.

Table 8. Effect of organic manure on the soybean production on degraded land.

Treatment	Soybean Production	
	SD*	SH†
	kg/ha	
Control	406	276
Cattle dung at 10 ton/ha	636	492
Forest humus at 10 ton/ha	797	919
Green manure of legume cover crop at 20 ton/ha	842	950

*SD represents degraded land caused by clearing with a straight blade.
†SH represents degraded land caused by clearing with a rake-and-rome harrow.

grass (Table 6). Table 6 also indicates that *Mucuna* sp. increased the yield of soybeans and of maize planted after the soybeans.

As shown in table 1, legume cover crops improved soil physical properties. Use of mulched *Mucuna* can also reduce tillage frequency (Table 7).

Some rehabilitation studies on degraded land using organic manure, such as forest humus and green cover crops, were conducted. Results show that 10 tons of forest humus are similar to 20 tons of cover crop biomass in improving soil productivity of degraded land caused by land clearing using a straight dozer or a rake-and-rome harrow (Table 8). Forest humus is better than cattle dung.

Conclusion

Degraded land in Indonesia is a serious problem in upland agriculture. This land degradation is mostly caused by serious erosion and decreasing soil organic matter. The problem arises because of population pressure, improper land management and soil conservation, improper land clearing, mining, and shifting cultivation.

There are 24 million hectares of unproductive, critical land, 8 million hectares of which are severely eroded. It will be impractical and uneconomical to use this degraded land without rehabilitation measures.

Some restoration measures using forest trees were not fully successful because they were not accepted by farmers who prefer to grow food crops.

Rehabilitation studies of degraded land show that *Centrocema* sp. is the best inedible legume to restore the soil physical properties and, at the same time, improve soil productivity. Other species range from somewhat lower to considerably lower in effectiveness than *Centrocema* sp.

Mucuna sp. is the most promising edible legume crop for rehabilitation of soil physical properties and for improving soil productivity of degraded land. The effect of the legume not only increases the yield of soybeans but also the yield of the next crop planted after soybeans. The use of *Mucuna* can also reduce tillage frequency.

Rehabilitation of degraded land requires at least 1 year under a cover crop. The more serious the erosion, the longer the rehabilitation period needed.

REFERENCES

1. Barus, A., and H. Suwardjo. 1987. *Effect of topsoil loss and cover crops on soil productivity of Haplorthox at Citayam, Bogor.* Pemberitaan Pen. Tanah dan Pupuk. No. 5, 1986. Puslittan, Bogor, Indonesia.
2. Dent, F. J. 1984. *Land degradation, present status, training and education needs in Asia and the Pacific.* In Proceedings, International Workshop on Soil Erosion and Its Countermeasures. Chiangmai, Thailand.
3. Djatijanto Kretosastro, and S. Rawidjo. 1988. *The role of agricultural research on the second stage development of transmigration program.* In Proceedings, Workshop on Farming System Research. Central Research Institute for Food Crops, Bogor, Indonesia.
4. Hudson, N. 1971. *Soil conservation.* B. T. Batsford Limited, London, England.
5. Lal, R., and D. J. Cummings. 1978. *Clearing a tropical forest: Effects on soil and microclimate.* Field Crop Research 2: 91-107.
6. Muljadi, D., and M. Soepraptohardjo. 1975. *The problem of data acreage and distribution of degraded land.* In Proceedings, Symposium, Rehabilitation and Protection of

Degraded Land for Regional Planning. Centre for Soil Research, Bogor, Indonesia.

7. Sumanti, S. 1984. *The role of organic matter on the upland farming system.* Agriculture Faculty, Gajah Mada University, Yogjakarta, Indonesia.

8. Suwardjo, H. 1986. *Land development for transmigration areas in Sumatera and Kalimantan.* Land Clearing and Development. Agency for Agricultural Research and Development, Jakarta, Indonesia.

9. Suwardjo, H., and A. Barus. 1986. *The effect of land clearing on soil tilt and soil physical properties.* In Proceedings, National Congress. Indonesian Soil Science Society, Bogor, Indonesia.

RESEARCH 6

FARMERS AND SCIENTISTS:
A JOINT EFFORT

S. FUJISAKA and D. P. GARRITY

Some 118 million hectares of the uplands in Southeast Asia are characterized by sloping land, high soil erodibility, strong acidity, and low available phosphorus. Millions of small-scale farm families have settled in these once-forested areas to practice shifting cultivation until increasing populations dictate changing to permanent field cultivation. Many of the resulting cereal-based farming systems in such areas are unsustainable because of soil erosion and soil nutrient depletion. Although the principles of soil conservation and nutrient management are well known, formal scientific research has not successfully developed land management systems suited to upland farmers' actual circumstances.

A joint effort was initiated in which researchers from the International Rice Research Institute (IRRI) and farmers from an upland community of the Philippines worked to adapt and transfer a system of technologies for soil conservation. Specifically, the effort sought to determine or to achieve the following: (a) farmer practice and knowledge concerning soil erosion, (b) farmer-to-farmer training in the use of contour hedgerows, (c) farmers' and researchers' adaptive research, (d) farmer technology dissemination and adoption, and (e) lessons for the development of an agronomic research agenda.

The Farm Environment

IRRI's key on-farm research site for improving upland, rice-based systems is located in Claveria in northern Mindanao, Misamis Oriental province, the Philippines. Most Claveria farmers are from the Visayan Islands and have migrated since the 1940s seeking a broader land base. The municipal population has doubled since the 1960s, reaching almost 30,000 by the early 1980s (*3*). The settlers' semi-shifting cultivation and logging resulted in conversion of virtually all forest land to cropland and grassland. Although there are pasture leases of up to 1,000 hectares, farm sizes of most owners, tenants, and land-reform beneficiaries are less than 3 hectares.

Small-scale farmers are faced with making a living in a difficult upland area typical of Asia. Acid, infertile soils (Ultic haplorthox, and Oxic dystropepts) predominate. They are characterized by moderately well-drained clays of pH 3.9 to 5.2. More than half of the land has a slope greater than 8 percent and is severely eroded. Although mean annual rainfall is 2,200 millimeters, most falls from July to December, leaving a dry season from October to March. Weeds and diseases, especially blast, are also major upland rice production problems.

Farmer Practice and Knowledge

Initial interviews were conducted with 55 farmers. They shared their knowledge about the local environment, identified crop production problems, discussed related changes in lands and soils, and described their attempts to solve the problems. Although they came originally from another area of the country, the farmers had acquired a knowledge base pertaining to local conditions. They tested many land, soil, crop, cultivar, and input combinations. Lands were classified locally by slope and elevation and soils by fertility, color, texture, acidity, and friability. For example, red (*puwa puwa*) soils were considered poor (*niwang*, "thin"), and acidic (*aslom*, "sour") (Table 1).

Soil erosion was considered a major problem. Ninety percent of the respondents reported yield declines of rice (*Oryza sativa* L.) and maize (*Zea mays* L.) due to soil erosion (Figure 1). They discussed the erosion caused by rainfall runoff, called attention to parts of fields and crops damaged, and identified different types of erosion in local terms. About 15 percent said that the prevalence of noncontour plowing contributed to the problem. Respondents welcomed eroded nutrients from upslope, particularly from pastures.

Many farmers said their soils initially had been dark on top and reddish underneath, but over time the top layer had eroded away. The infertile, red subsoils were increasingly exposed. Farmers estimated that erosion reduced the depth of the darker soil from 50 centimeters in 1976 to 10 centimeters in 1986.

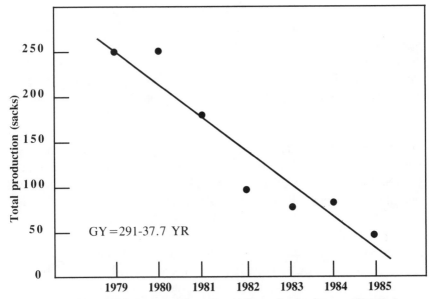

Figure 1. Typical record of the trend in maize grain production by a small-scale farmer in Claveria, Misamis Oriental province, Philippines. One caven=50 kilograms.

Table 1. Farmers' land and soil categories in Claveria, Misamis Oriental province, Philippines.

Soils		Lands	
Name	*Description*	*Name*	*Description*
Undesirable Characteristics			
Puwa puwa	red	Bakilid	sloping
Niwang, umau	poor, thin	Buntod buntod	hilly
Walay sustancia	nothing left	Baton	rocky
Aslom	"sour" or acidic	Nagasgasan	washed out, literally
Pundok pundok	spotty fertility		"scratched"
Pagkumot magbuwag/ Magkabuwag	disintegrates when held		
Desirable Characteristics			
Tambok tambok	fertile, rich	Patag patag	flat
Itom itom	black, dark	Bunkag	newly opened
Bukakhaon	absorbs/holds water	Kabugon	low-lying area
Madali madayao	not easily dried	Basak	waterway/lowland
Pughay na, humok	friable		
Balason	sandy		
Medyo mopilit	quite sticky		
Bonbon	silt (rich)		
More Neutral Characteristics			
Mogahi, mobagtik	crusty	Nahanay hay,	
Tibuok	coarse	nahandig	gently sloping
		sakom	*kaingin*

Farmers' methods of erosion control, cited by 50 percent of those interviewed, were diversion canals, planting perennials on upper slopes, and bananas planted in gullies to trap soil and utilize eroded nutrients. Some 20 percent named such priorities as grassy strips across slopes or along field borders, *Leucaena leucocephala* strips, weed or crop residue piled across gullies, contour plowing, and cover crops.

One-fifth of the farmers interviewed had constructed diversion canals. Others left weedy strips between plots, piled weeds and crop residues across their fields, or planted bananas in channels. Farmers, however, did not practice all of the soil conservation measures they named as being effective. Only a few landowners planted perennials on slopes; no one planted trees in strips or on upper slopes; and while some left trees on fallowed areas, most farmers reported that they lacked enough land to plant trees.

Of the 55 informants, 96 percent claimed that inorganic fertilizers, lime, and chicken manure are needed to boost production and to maintain or improve soils, but, they said, these inputs were wasted on slopes because of erosion. In practice, few purchased inputs are used for the main crops. Plot selection, however, is carefully considered; traditional maize is planted on better soils and upland rice or cassava (*Manihot esculenta*) on poorer soils. Highest levels of inputs are applied to tomatoes (*Lycopersicon esculentum*) because of the potentially high returns. Lower levels of inputs are applied to hybrid maize and an improved upland rice cultivar (UPL RI5).

No farmer used green manures, and no one who had grown a legume experienced soil nutrient benefits from the crop or biomass. Eight farmers had switched from burning to crop residue incorporation. Some 70 percent mentioned compost benefits, but only six farmers had compost pits. Labor (including hauling water) and lack of raw materials limit compost production. Although farmers thought animal dung increased soil fertility, they generally grazed draft animals and did not use the manure.

Farmers knew that field fallows usually led to nutrient regeneration (Table 2), but they had observed few positive effects of fallows in Claveria. We analyzed fallow weeds and soils and concluded that farmer perceptions were essentially correct. Vegetative succession no longer proceeds after grasses (*Imperata cylindrica, Saccharum spontaneum, Paspalum* spp.). Soil organic matter was increased by fallowing, but levels of nitrogen and phosphorus remained low.

Farmer-to-Farmer Knowledge Transfer

Claveria upland farmers had adapted their farming practices to local conditions. Those with sloping land were concerned about soil erosion. They knew of several ways to conserve soils and had tried a few. They were knowledgeable about soil nutrient management alternatives, but faced cash and labor constraints.

Table 2. Examples of Claveria farmer concepts/statements concerning aspects of sustainable crop production.

Crops and soil nutrients
 "Cassava adds soil acidity."
 "Cassava gobbles up soil nutrients."
 "Rice is more tolerant of acidic soils than is maize."
 "Rice is more vigorous on an area previously planted in tomato."
 "Intercropping is good only if there are complete chemicals."

Nutrient depletion
 "Soil fertility has been used up."
 "The soil is weak."
 "Fertility is spotty."
 "Soils are overtrained."
 "The soils are getting older."
 "Poor, but not used up, in the sense of the hardest part within a log."

Fallows
 "The decomposing leaves of the weeds help to enrich the soil."
 "The land is resting so the soil can store some nutrients."
 "Rich because it is rested."
 "Fertility is added and the soil is made cool."
 "The soil is slightly enriched if left a short time."

Weeds
 "Rice was harmed by *cogon* (*I. cylindrica*) roots."
 "Poor soil if *cogon* dominates."
 "*D. longiflora* and *cogon* consume soil nutrients and destroy soil quality."
 "Acidity increases where *cogon* dominates."
 "Weeds are thin on infertile soils."
 "*R. cochinchinensis* rapidly produces seed; thus, easily soars in population; if not weeded, it exceeds the height of rice or corn."
 "Fertility is added and the soil is made cool" (re. *Calapogonium* spp.).
 "Soil is good where there are weeds/grasses with nodules."

Soil erosion
 "Soil slides down and floats away."
 "Nutrients are drawn down."
 "Plants are eroded along with soil."
 "Soil was drawn down and fertility was washed out."
 "The land was shaven and eroded after trees were removed."
 "Fertilizer is collected (on lower plots) due to rain."

Erosion control
 "Banana and coconut are better because they hold the soil."
 "Contour plowing reduces downslope erosion losses."
 "Weedy strips can decrease erosion effects."
 "Trees planted above and below fields can decrease erosion effects."
 "Banana planted above and below fields can decrease erosion effects."

Based on such findings and on researcher and farmer discussions, we felt agroforestry-based technology was potentially appropriate for soil erosion control (*1*). This technology involves contour ditches and bunds that are planted to hedgerows. The hedgerows form terraces of graded material between the planted strips and are appropriate for areas with sloping land, permanent plow agriculture, intense rainfall, and land scarcity. Contour hedgerows have been tried in various countries (*5*), including the Philippines (*4*). It also seemed appropriate and cost-effective to link farmers from different areas into a system of "farmer-to-farmer" communication rather than to follow standard technology transfer procedures.

World Neighbors, a nongovernmental organization working with upland farmers in Cebu (an island with high population and very eroded uplands), successfully employed a "menu" of contour technologies by facilitating farmer participation, group cooperation, and minimal farmer subsidies. In response to a request by the IRRI research team, farmers from Cebu agreed to teach contour farming to a group of farmers from Claveria.

The Claveria participants were those who had described soil erosion and nutrient depletion, had tried to address the problems, and did not want degraded land to (again) force them to migrate to a new area. With fares paid by IRRI, they traveled to Cebu for hands-on training in establishment of contour bunds, ditches, and hedgerows of fodder grasses (napier, *Pennisetum purpureum*) and legume trees (*Gliricidia sepium*).

Upon their return, the farmers worked as a cooperative group during the period prior to the rains. Local sources of *G. sepium* and *P. purpureum* cuttings were located and planted on the contour bunds. Neighboring farmers joined the group. Heavy storms damaged some of the newly constructed bunds, but farmers had learned in Cebu that substantial bund maintenance was needed for about 3 years.

The first group established almost 7,000 meters of hedgerows on 10 parcels with a mean size of 0.8 hectare. The average labor requirement to develop 1 hectare of hedgerows was 30 person-days per hectare. The labor varied with differences among the fields in slope and in the distances between strips (Table 3). Differences in soil compaction and ground cover resulted in a range of 17 to 57 meters per person-day of planted strip established.

Farmers' Adaptive Research

Farmers immediately started to experiment with the technology. They tested combinations of other hedgerow species, including grasses (e.g., *Panicum maximum*), trees (local *Cassia spectabilis*), cash perennials [coffee (*coffea arabica* C. Indica), cacao (*Theobroma cacao*), fruit], wild

Table 3. Labor (hours) and outputs for establishment of 10 contour parcels in Claveria, Misamis Oriental province, Philippines, 1987.

Farm	1	2	3	4	5	6	7	8	9	10	Average
Slope (%)	12	27	18	19	14	22	16	11	9	5	15
Operations: (hours/ha)											
Survey	11.8	30.0	10.0	20.0	20.0	8.6	10.0	11.4	12.5	6.6	14.1
Plow	9.1	22.5	15.0	20.0	20.0	10.0	12.5	8.6	9.2	7.5	13.4
Shovel	72.7	125.0	56.6	165.0	160.0	92.9	105.0	80.0	62.5	51.6	97.1
Cut/gather	21.8	12.5	3.3	60.0	40.0	11.4	45.0	17.1	8.3	6.6	22.6
Haul cuttings	0.9	2.5	0.8	5.0	10.0	1.4	2.5	1.4	1.6	0.8	2.7
Chop/plant	16.4	57.5	25.0	60.0	20.0	25.7	60.0	17.1	20.0	15.0	31.7
Total	132.7	250.0	110.7	330.0	270.0	150.0	235.0	135.6	114.1	88.1	181.6
Person-days/ha	22.1	41.6	18.4	55.0	45.0	25.0	39.2	22.6	19.0	14.7	30.3
Meters of hedgerow/ha	501	1,340	845	1,555	770	1,339	1,478	673	937	702	1,014
Meters of hedge-row/person-day	23	32	46	28	17	57	37	29	49	47	37

sunflower (*Helianthus anuus*), and weeds that are otherwise competitive with field crops (*D. longiflora, Paspalum conjugatum*). Grasses appeared to provide more effective and faster terracing than trees. Grasses, however, may exacerbate problems of root aphids (*Tetraneura nigriabdominalis* or *Rhophalosiphum rufiabdominalis*) and white grubs (*Holotrichia* spp. or *Leucopholis irrorata*), which are important problems in upland rice areas (2).

Some farmers added hedgerows between initial strips for more terracing and erosion control. Farmers noticed that *G. sepium* suffered from competition when napier grass was planted on the upper side of the bund. A row of trees above and grass below provided a compatible alternative. Many farmers planted napier grass on the hedgerow for ruminant forage.

Obtaining high survival of *Gliricidia* stem cuttings was a problem. Farmers tried different ways of planting *G. sepium* cuttings after termite damage and poor rooting. Farmers and researchers built a small nursery to supply and test *G. sepium* and *C. spectabilis* seedlings. Seed germination of *C. spectabilis* was low. Timing of seed gathering and sowing and practical scarification techniques are currently being investigated to make use of seed produced on the farm.

As their land terraced, the Cebu farmers had switched from cereal crops to flowers or vegetables and started to use manure and fertilizer for these cash crops. Claveria farmers expect to be able to do the same.

Farmers were willing to solve problems over time. A field with broken bunds was temporarily abandoned, but then terraced well as weeds and napier grass took over the bunds. Napier grass on the bunds proved competitive with crops planted in the alleys. Farmers then tried other grasses or legumes as well as penned goats. A range of forage grass and legume varieties are being screened as noncompetitive hedgerow components. Goats are being tested as components of an improved nutrient cycling system.

In addition to contour bunds and ditches planted to trees and grasses, some of the more experimental forms include grassy hedgerows formed by laying down crop and weed residues along the contour, stone-walled bench terraces, and even contours planted to cassava with rice in the alleys.

Evolution of an Agronomic Research Agenda

Agronomic research at Claveria was initiated in 1985 on the flat land units (less than 8 percent slope) that occupy a small percentage of the agricultural area but are more productive than the more sloping land. Soil fertility maintenance was the dominant issue addressed. Included were studies of how fertilizer and lime could increase or sustain yields and how grain legume crops could be integrated into rice or maize monocrops.

Agronomic research attention began to shift to the sloping land in 1986. Nutrient depletion was the focus of initial research on hedgerows. Experiments were initiated to test the efficacy of green leaf manure from nitrogen-fixing tree hedgerows on the yields of rice and maize in adjoining alleys. Weed and insect pest dynamics of alley-cropped cereals also were investigated.

Concurrently, farmer experiments revealed several important technical problems. Erosion control was the farmers' primary motivation for hedgerow development. Cycling nitrogen to the cereal crop was a lower priority.

Farmers' fields with contour hedgerows gave an opportunity to study soil erosion rates for contour-bunded and nonbunded areas and effects on rice and maize yields over time with contour bunding and green leaf manures.

Five farmers agreed to participate in an experiment superimposed on their contour-bunded fields on which they had planted the local variety of *G. sepium*. Each contour-bunded field was treated as a main plot and compared to the adjacent unbunded area, which was divided into two management systems: conventional (uncontoured) tillage and contour cropping. Each main plot was divided into four subplot treatments. Nutrient management was varied to determine the response to nitrogen and phosphorus interacting with the three management systems. The five farms served as replications.

Soil erosion was monitored in the three land management systems using wires attached to buried concrete disks. The device does not hamper field operations. Soil loss with conventional land management averaged 304 tons per hectare per year, which results in a lowering of the surface soil level of 3.0 centimeters per year. Net soil loss in the cropped area of the contour-bunded fields was 64 percent lower than with conventional management.

The hedgerows were not pruned during the first year after establishment. They were pruned from one to three times during the rice-maize crop cycle in the second year, depending on the growth differences of the trees among the test fields. The aluminum saturation of the cation exchange complex of the surface soil varied from 2 to 75 percent among the five hedgerow experimental farms. Annual hedgerow green-leaf manure production was observed to be related to aluminum, varying from greater than 4.0 tons per hectare to less than 0.1 ton per hectare as aluminum saturation increased. The hedgerows contributed an average of 53 kilograms of nitrate per hectare and 4 kilograms of phosphorus per hectare during the second year.

Researchers initially favored a double row of nitrogen-fixing leguminous trees (the locally available *G sepium* and *C. spectabilis*) for hedgerows. Farmers also began to use *P. purpureum* (as in Cebu) and perennials, such as coffee and fruit trees. Researchers then investigated how cash and forage crops could be intercropped in the hedgerows with the least competition to generate the greatest economic value.

Although trade-offs are involved in intercropping nitrogen-fixing trees with grasses or perennial crops, it appeared that productivity and stability could be improved. Trials were designed to quantify species' interactions in hedgerow associations of napier grass with *Gliricidia* and coffee with *Gliricidia* at different input levels (using chicken manure and lime). Performance criteria to judge these treatments are being established.

A problem in hedgerow establishment involved the low survival of stem cuttings of trees. Locally available stem cuttings were the major source of planting materials because seed was not available. Research to solve the low survival problem included depth of planting of cuttings, use of commercial root-inducing hormone, and pre-preparation of a planting hole. The data indicate that the interaction of these factors significantly improved cutting establishment, particularly of *C. spectabilis*.

More than half the labor in establishing contour hedgerows on a farm involved shoveling soil to shape and heighten the bund. Farmers and researchers tested alternatives to reduce labor requirements. One farmer placed a line of *Paspalum conjugatum* grass residue (with roots) along the contour. The resulting grass bund rapidly stabilized into an effective soil trap. Researchers also investigated nonbunded hedgerows. Double rows of cuttings of several species were planted on the contour in fallowed grassland. Once the trees were established, a contour hedgerow remained after the field was plowed and planted. Experiments also evaluated the seeding of grass species in contour strips in cultivated fields. All of these methods appear to be promising alternatives to bund construction.

Farmers' Technology Dissemination and Adoption

The Philippine Department of Agriculture and IRRI are working to develop methods that can be used by national agricultural programs to facilitate contour hedgerow technology adoption. The conventional extension approach has involved farm demonstrations on sloping land next to well-traveled roads and featured fixed technology packages extended through lecture-based training courses presented by extension technicians. The IRRI team explored an approach that involved (a) the participation of farmers selected on the basis of their concern about soil loss, (b) farmer-to-farmer training, and (c) farmer participation in technology generation.

By early 1989 the Claveria farmers had trained five more groups of farmers from nearby areas who would eventually train others. A model is being developed for a regional farmer-to-farmer training program that could enable a large farmer population to be reached. The process begins with a few farmers from one community who participate in farmer-to-farmer training in another community. Upon their return, these farmers develop their own contour farming systems with periodic exchange with their trainers. They, in turn, will become farmer trainers within their own communities, guided by extension technicians linked to the research base.

The research program to develop sustainable cereal-based farming systems for sloping, acid upland ecosystems provided a unique opportunity for a joint effort by farmers and researchers. The farmer-initiated experimentation increased the efficiency of three aspects of the program: First, it led to a more relevant research agenda. Second, it influenced the design of the agronomic research trials and farmer feedback on experimental results. Third, the sharing of knowledge through direct farmer-to-farmer exchange proved effective.

For on-farm research at Claveria, efforts to improve cropping systems were broadened to address the critical farmer problem of soil erosion. Farmers learned about contour hedgerows from other farmers, and the farmers' experimental adaptation of the hedgerow system became closely tied to the formal research work. Innovations by the researchers were farmer tested and evaluated for local adaptation.

IRRI is currently developing methods that factor farmer knowledge and related technology adaptation and dissemination into work conducted by national agricultural programs. The approach of learning from farmers is also being applied to establishing priorities for collaborative rice research in other countries.

The case presented here suggests that on-farm research can link the contributions of farmers and scientists in the development, adaptation, and dissemination of appropriate innovations. The process includes:

• Understanding existing farmer practice for adaptation to local agroecosystems.

• Problem identification based, in part, on such understanding.

• Learning from farmers' knowledge and their problem-solving adaptive experimentation.

• Substantial participation by farmers who are interested in problem-solving.

• Research using rigorous experimental methods.

• Technology transfer from adaptor-adoptors to other farmers.

• Development of methods for national programs.

Farmer knowledge and researcher experience can be used to identify and set research priorities. Farmers and researchers can then participate in the design, testing, and adaptation of appropriate technologies. It appears that such knowledge can be shared via farmer-to-farmer technology transfer, with the organizational guidance and technical support of a committed national research and extension program.

REFERENCES

1. Fukisaka, S., and D. P. Garrity. 1988. *Developing sustainable food crop farming systems for the sloping acid uplands: A farmer-participatory approach.* In Terd Charoenwatana and A. Terry Rambo [editors] *Sustainable Rural Development in Asia. Selected papers from the Fourth SUAN Regional Symposium on Agroecosystems Research.* Farming Systems Research Project and Southeast Asian Universities Agroecosystem Network, Khon Kaen, Thailand. pp. 181-193.
2. Litsinger, J. A., A. T. Barrion, and D. Soekarna. 1987. *Upland rice insect pests: Their ecology, importance, and control.* IRRI Research Paper Series No. 123. International Rice Research Institute, Los Banos, Philippines pp. 1-41.
3. National Census and Statistics Office. 1980. *Census of population: Preliminary report.* Manila, Philippines.
4. World Neighbors. No date. *Simple soil and water conservation methods for upland farms.* World Neighbors, Cebu City, Philippines.
5. Young, A. 1987. *The potential of agroforestry for soil conservation. Part I. Erosion control.* Working paper 43. International Council for Research in Agroforestry, Nairobi, Kenya.

HILL COUNTRY
EROSION RESEARCH

J. G. HAWLEY

In New Zealand, "farming on hill-slopes" means grazing sheep and cattle. Orchards are to be found on hillslopes in a few places but, by Asian standards, hillslopes are not farmed intensively in New Zealand.

Pasture, improved by topdressing (from light aircraft), is dominant on the more gentle slopes. Steeper areas and areas with lower potential for grass production or higher erosion potential are commonly used for forestry, the most common species being Monterey pine *(Pinus radiata)*. In many parts of the country, there are areas of mountainland above and beyond the slopes used for forestry. Some of these areas are given over to extensive grazing, that is, grazing with small (if any) inputs of fertilizer, fencing, etc. Other such areas are regarded as "protection land" and left undeveloped, both for their own sake and for the protection of areas downstream. Tramping and mountaineering are permitted and, indeed, encouraged in many areas of "protection land." Some such areas include skifields.

The influence of grazing on the soils of hill country and mountainland has been a subject of research since the first decades of this century. In some situations, most notably in the high mountainlands, recent research has shown that the influence of man and his grazing animals on erosion rates has been much less than previously thought and less significant when compared with natural erosion rates. In other situations, the influence of introduced grazing animals on soil depletion rates has been shown to be measurable and serious.

In New Zealand, individual research and survey projects attempt to answer one of the following eight questions:

- What erosion is occurring, has occurred, or may occur and where?
- How much does it matter?
- What are the implications if current rates and trends continue?
- What causes erosion?
- What can be done to repair erosion damage?
- How effective are such repair and control measures?
- Is soil conservation economic, and who should pay?

Erosion Mapping

Erosion mapping is undertaken in response to question 1. A system involving a multifactor land resource survey was developed in New Zealand in the 1950s. In the 1960s and 1970s, this was refined in the course of widespread application. It allows observed erosion type and severity to be recorded, along with the key physical attributes, rock type, soil, slope, and vegetation cover (current land use) (4).

The area being mapped is divided into map units. A map unit is an area that, at the scale of mapping, may be regarded as a single entity with regard to rock type, soil, and slope. Map units may be regarded as the geomorphic units within a landscape. The vegetative cover and erosion (type and severity) information is then added for each map unit.

All of New Zealand has been mapped in this fashion at a scale of 1:63,360. More than 90,000 map units appear on this survey, which is called the New Zealand Land Resource Inventory (NZLRI). Although every map unit could conceivably be regarded as unique, the map units are grouped into approximate 680 land use capability units or types of land. Map units assigned to a particular land use capability unit may be regarded as the same type of land from a soil conservation point of view and for most other practical purposes.

The NZLRI data base is being upgraded from the 1:63,360 scale to a 1:50,000 scale as it is updated (i.e., in the course of its maintenance). This is far from a trivial change because there is 60 percent more paper used to show detail at the 1:50,000 scale.

This NZLRI data base has been recorded on computer files. Several programs were developed for storing, sorting, and presenting the data. The geographic information system software ARC/INFO, supplied by the Environmental Systems Research Institute, is now used.

The multifactor mapping system described above is also used at more detailed scales for soil and water conservation planning on individual properties. These properties are large by Asian standards—hundreds and even thousands of hectares, rather than 1 or 2 hectares.

Considerable progress has yet to be made in mapping basic erosion indicators, such as "denudation rate" and "rate of loss of potential productivity" (4). At present, skills for mapping the "percent bare ground" and "difficulty of repair" indicators are more highly developed.

What Use is Multifactor Mapping? More than 1,000 users have paid to use the NZLRI computerized data base. The number of users of the data in its printed map form can only be estimated, but they must number many thousands.

Approximately 5,000 soil and water conservation farm plans are in operation, based on the multifactor land use capability Land Use Capability (LUC) system applied at scales of 1:5,000 to 1:20,000.

The mapping system makes it possible for central government to establish soil conservation (and other) policies for specific types of land, with full knowledge of how much land each policy applies to, or could be applied to, and where such land is located. Examples of such policies include subsidies for soil conservation work on particular types of land, prohibition of tree felling, control of burning, and funding of local pest-destruction boards.

Types of Erosion. Twelve types of erosion are shown in the NZLRI: sheet, wind, scree, soil slip, earth slip, slump, rill, gully, earthflow, tunnel gully, stream bank, and debris avalanche. All of these erosion types are found on hillslopes, although debris avalanche is mapped almost exclusively on slopes of such steepness as to be confined to areas more properly described as mountainlands.

Erosion Mapping. When in March 1988 a major tropical cyclone (Cyclone Bola) remained stationary for 3 days over New Zealand's most erodible hill country, the landslip and flooding damage was so severe that it called for special attention by the government. Compensation grants were paid to farmers according to the amount of damage done to their properties.

Because satellite coverage (SPOT) taken before the cyclone was obtainable, this and complementary post-cyclone coverage was obtained. The bare ground areas on two sets were compared and measurements of bare ground due to Cyclone Bola were determined.

Slips in the finer grained siltstones and the jointed mudstones had larger debris tail/slip scar ratios than those in the volcanic ashes and the coarser grained sandstones. Areas of debris tail are less serious for a farmer than areas of slip scar. This is because areas of debris tail recover their capacity to grow grass more quickly and more completely. Because the NZLRI includes discrimination between these rock types, it was possible to obtain more true values of damage than would have been possible otherwise. This involved using the raster satellite images and the computerized vector NZLRI (*14, 16*).

This work was performed on a farm-by-farm basis for 100 farms of the 1,100 farms on which compensation payments were made.

This work illustrates well the integration of (a) digital image analysis; (b) the use of raster images (satellite), together with computerized vector information (NZLRI and property boundaries); and (c) the use of land resource information and skills in a situation of importance to the central government.

This adds up to a high degree of sophistication and efficiency in answering the question "What erosion is occurring or has occurred recently?" More finely focused studies, of erosion processes and engineering geology, are required in order to produce good answers to the question "What erosion is likely to occur as a result of proposed changes to land use?" However, the multifactor land inventory can provide a first approximation if areas with similar rock type, slope, and climate exist with the proposed land use already in place.

How Much Does Erosion Matter?

Pastoral Hillslopes. Shallow landslides on pastoral hillslopes are a major soil conservation problem in New Zealand. This type of erosion is widespread, particularly on seasonally dry hill country (*2*).

Over the last 10 years, the cost of this erosion, in terms of reductions in potential pastoral productivity, has been measured. These reductions in (dry matter) productivity can be expressed as reductions in carrying capacity (sheep and cattle numbers per hectare). These, in turn, can be converted to dollars per annum. This is one of the few mass-movement soil conservation problems in which the effects can be expressed in dollar terms, based on measurement.

This work has been published (*10, 17, 18, 20*). It is now being extended (a) into areas with different geology, soils, and rainfall patterns; (b) to obtain more quantitative information on the effect of initial forest clearance 100 years ago (*12, 19*); and (c) to advance understandings of rates of change in the soil and the topography over longer time spans, on the order of a few thousand years.

Earthflow, sometimes referred to as creeping earthflow, is a major erosion form on New Zealand's tertiary hill country. Recent research has shown that these features are pre-European and probably pre-Polynesian, that is, more than 150 years and probably more than 700 years old.

What Are the Implications for the Future?

The results of these studies, researching what is occurring now and what has occurred in the past, are being used to predict the future: the geomorphic future of catchments and the future productivity of hillslopes. This work raises the question of sustainability of productive land use. It also leads to the introduction of a degree of measurement to the definition of (discrimination between) different LUC units (different types of land).

What Causes Erosion?

The shallow landslips, which are the subject of the work referred to above, occur in rashes as a result of either very intense rainfall or prolonged absence of drying days. It follows that the magnitude and frequency relationships for erosion are closely related to the magnitude and frequency relationships of intense rainfall (and flooding) event periods of 2 months or more without drying days.

Obtaining (or at least looking for) magnitude and frequency relationships is enlightening scientifically, and results are valued by the community, from the individual farmer to the politicians. This is because such relationships can influence land use decisions, and vice versa, with regard to the erosion magnitude and frequency relationships. The quest for such magnitude and frequency relationships is a very real link between this work on hillslopes and the work in the mountainlands (*22, 23*).

Intense rainfall and absence of drying days are triggering events (*11*) rather than root causes of failure. A look behind the triggering events commonly reveals inappropriate land management or even inappropriate land use as causes. Looking behind these causes, the reasons why the land management or use is inappropriate may be found. These causes usually involve either decreases in strength or increases in stresses. The processes causing these increases or decreases may be identified (Table 1).

What Can be Done to Repair the Damage and Inhibit Erosion?

The oversowing and topdressing of slip scars and debris tails have been undertaken experimentally and operationally, both with and without government subsidy. These are the primary means of repairing damage already done.

Erosion control measures can be successful only if they inhibit the processes leading to the development of failure conditions within the soil mass (5). These processes are listed in table 1. The most common erosion control measures involve tree planting.

A major accomplishment of the Plant Materials Group at Aokautere over the last 20 years has been to collect, select, propagate, and establish trees suitable for stabilizing pastoral hillslopes. Before being released by the researchers, a new species must have the qualities shown in table 2. The quality of dual-purpose tree species (Table 2) has been taken up by many landholders, and the New Zealand Tree Crops Association is very active in promoting it.

Over the last 15 years, 12 poplar and 13 willow cultivars (varieties), as well as a range of eucalypts, acacias, shrubs, herbs, grasses, and legumes, have been released for use on pastoral hillslopes. A *Plant Materials Handbook for Soil Conservation* was published in 1986 (*13, 21*). Several other soil conservation measures are undertaken on pastoral hillslopes (Table 3).

How Effective Are Repair and Control Measures?

Staff members in the Land and Soil Sciences Division are working on the question of repair and control in three ways:

Table 1. Processes leading to development of failure within a soil mass.

1. Mechanical weathering
   a. Shear and/or tensile failure due to
      i. freeze/thaw of water, and growth of other crystals. e.g., gypsum
      ii. rapid temperature change
      iii. shrinkage or swelling
      iv. mechanical slaking
      v. unloading
      vi. loss of soil water (e.g., prior to wind erosion of "cohesionless" soil)
   b. Dilatancy-increase in moisture content due to a decrease in dry density induced by shear strain.
2. Chemical weathering
   a. Oxidation (and reduction)
   b. Hydration and hydrolysis
   c. Solution
   d. Chemical slaking (dispersion)
3. Biological weathering
4. Increased pore water pressure
5. Processes leading to increased shear stress
   a. Due to tetonic distortion/tilting/uplift
   b. Due to river downcutting
   c. Increased loading due to growth of trees or increase in soil water content

Table 2. Desired qualities for trees used for slope stabilization.

Resistant to diseases
Resistant to insect pests
Rapid rate of growth
Deciduous or lightly shading evergreen
No adverse effect on stock health (seedfall, pollen, etc.)

No adverse effect on wool quality (leaves, berries, etc.)
Reasonable longevity
Erect and narrow crown
Early rough bark development
Extensive strong root system

Unpalatable to possums
High transpiration rates
Easy to propagate
Easy to establish
Easy to protect from grazing animals

Adapted to particular site conditions
Wind resistant
Drought resistant
Does not foul pasture
Does not acidify soil

Does not harbour pests harmful to stock, other crops or humans
Does not become a fire hazard (e.g., accumulation of dry litter)
Preferably dual purpose (e.g., timber, fodder for stock, food for birds, food for bees,
    and amenity (appearance, fruit, nuts, etc.)

Table 3. Common soil conservation measures for pastoral hillslopes.

Reforestation (typically 400-1,500 trees/ha)
Agroforestry (typically 100-200 trees/ha)
Spaced planting of trees (typically 50 trees/ha strategically planted)
Control of grazing densities and grazing styles
Careful placing of fences, stock ponds, farm tracks, etc.

Planting of shelter-belts
Planting on stream banks
Improving ground cover and productivity (fertilizers, grasses, legumes, etc.)
Recontouring (smoothing) of ground surface
Adoption of special cropping practices (e.g., minimum disturbance of soil, contour
    cultivation)

Installation of bored-in underdrains
Construction of debris dams
Control of burning of scrub, stubble, etc.
Adotpion of wise land-use options—type and intensity (forestry, pastoral, horticulture,
    cropping, etc.)

1. Surveys are made of the effectiveness of soil conservation works (a) in small areas after major storm events (9) and (b) over large areas several decades after application.[1]

2. Examination of "engineering geological" factors and what influence these factors may have on the success or other results of soil conservation works (15).

3. Development and application of a method based on the spatial relationship between trees and slip scars (7, 8).

Is Soil Conservation Economic and Who Should Pay?

This last of the eight questions is one that is raised every few years in New Zealand in connection with government subsidies for soil conservation works. If soil conservation works were discontinued because they were "shown to be uneconomic," the value of soil conservation research would be greatly reduced.

Four currently fashionable tenets are used by economists against funding for soil conservation:

• Beneficiaries of soil conservation works are identifiable individuals (the farmers); they should pay the full cost.

• A farmer can judge best how he should spend his money; he should not have his judgment distorted by subsidies.

• Market forces will sort everything out for the best.

• Future benefits should be discounted to present value.

The reasons why these are inappropriate arguments were discussed by Hawley (6).

Two Settings of Interest

Most of the above has been written with New Zealand's dominant hill country in mind—pastoral hillslopes with rainfall in excess of 800 millimeters per acre. Most soil erosion research in New Zealand has been directed toward such land. There are at least two other settings that deserve mention, however. First is the high country, and second are other arable hillslopes.

---

[1]Dixie, R. C. 1982. "A reconnaissance of soil conservation and water control techniques: Review and recommendations." Unpublished report. National Water and Soil Conservation Authority, Wellington, New Zealand.

Rowell, A. 1983. "Reconnaissance of techniques applied to soil conservation in the South Island over the period 1942-1982." Unpublished report. National Water and Soil Conservation Authority, Wellington, New Zealand.

The High Country. New Zealand's high-country, semiarid pastoral land is a subject in itself. Conservation research has been directed toward improving groundcover (and thereby reducing soil movement/loss, while improving productivity). The introduction of nonindigenous, drought-tolerant, grazeable shrubs, herbs, grasses, and legumes has led to the identification of several lines that are proving beneficial. The introduction of these plants has been facilitated by the development (under contract to universities) of minimum cultivation machinery, which allows seeds to be introduced with little disturbance of the existing, protective indigenous grass cover. Control over the number of rabbits remains a challenge in the most drought-prone areas.

Research has led to a reappraisal of the role of humans in erosion in the steeper (South Island) high country. Early surveys reported significant human-induced erosion throughout the region. Subsequent work allows the human influence to be viewed in context with the more significant and more extensive natural erosion. The highest sediment yields and erosion rates in the Alps are within the wetter and, in some places, well-forested areas in the west, rather than in the drier, depleted eastern ranges. Some barren screes have changed little over centuries, and even very active, unstable screes may be old landforms. Soil stratigraphy reveals a long history of episodic stability and instability. Dated charcoals provide a fire history spanning more than 40,000 years. More frequent fires between 500 and 1,000 years ago (i.e., since the arrival of the Maori) resulted in widespread deforestation. There probably were regional increases in erosion while forest soils adjusted to loss of tree-root strength. Early pastoralists further increased the frequency of fires and grazed sheep, greatly modifying the grassland and shrubland vegetation in both height and composition. Erosion rates would have increased because sheet erosion is more than 10 times greater from bare soils than from those with intact tussock, scrub, or scree cover. Repeat photographs, however, show both increases and decreases in bare ground, rather than a general trend over the past 90 years. Widely distributed grassland transects also show little consistent change in bare ground in the past 10 to 35 years. Knowledge of tectonic uplift rates has improved markedly in recent years. These typically range from 10 to 16 millimeters per year in alpine regions. Average denudation rates have not been ascertained accurately, but available information suggests that these are of the same order: 10 to 16 millimeters per year. These lines of evidence suggest that the added component of human-induced erosion in the last 1,000 years has been small in comparison to the high natural rates of erosion in the area.

That most of the erosion of the mountainland may be natural and not human-induced, however, does not make any of it less of a problem for the management and use of the land. Both components constrain the available options for land use and limit the intensity at which these options may be undertaken.

Arable Hillslopes. Slopes less than 15° to 20° (27 to 36 percent), depending on lithology and climate, are regarded as arable land. On such land, landslips are rare, and attention is appropriately focused on surface erosion, including sheet, rill, gully, and wind (Table 1).

Research into these erosion types is now gaining momentum in New Zealand (*1*). Studies are beginning on measuring soil movement and loss from ^{137}Cs isotope levels (*4, 16, 22*); assisting catchment authorities with the design, construction, and operation of rainfall simulators to be used for demonstration of the influence of management on soil movement; and measuring deposition volumes in (natural) sediment traps after major rainstorm events.

Conclusions

Concerning soil conservation measures that developing countries can afford, this concept may be valid for civil engineering structures for controlling debris avalanches, but it does not apply to the use of plants, or even terraces, for soil conservation. The cost of planting trees for soil conservation on hillslopes is of the order of $10.00 per tree. In developing countries, it may be $1.00. The costs are almost entirely labor costs. As the standard of living rises, costs of tree planting will rise. Tree planting should not be postponed. It will only get more and more costly.

All research proceeds by fits and starts. Erosion research is no exception. Advances at any one time occur more often as side effects of advances in technology in other disciplines than in response to needs and priorities recognized by users or research advisory committees. Examples are the influence of remote sensing on erosion and land use mapping and the influence of low-cost electronic dataloggers on studies of rainfall and river flows.

REFERENCES

1. Basher, L. R. 1989. *Surface erosion: A review of techniques for assessing the magnitude of soil loss.* Technical Record CH1. Division of Land and Soil Sciences. 26 pp.
2. Eyles, G. O. 1983. *The distribution and severity of present erosion in New Zealand.* New Zealand Geographer 39: 12-28.
3. Eyles, G. O. 1989. *The New Zealand Land Use Capability System: Techniques and applications.* Proceedings, Fifth Australian Conference on Soil Conservation, Perth.

4. Hawley, J. G. 1985. *Concepts of erosion severity.* Proceedings, Soil Dynamics and Land Use Seminar (Blenheim). New Zealand Association of Soil Conservators and New Zealand Society of Soil Science, Lower Hutt.

5. Hawley, J. G. 1985. *Relating soil conservation measures to erosion type.* Proceedings, Soil Dynamics and Land Use Seminar. New Zealand Association of Soil Conservators and New Zealand Society of Soil Science, Lower Hutt.

6. Hawley, J. G. 1987. *Soil conservation: Should the user pay?* Soil and Water Magazine (Autumn 1987): pp. 4-7.

7. Hawley, J. G. 1988. *Measuring the influence of trees on landslip.* Proceedings, Annual Conference. New Zealand Association of Soil and Water Conservation. pp. 67-76.

8. Hawley, J. G., and J. R. Dymond. 1988. *How much do trees reduce landsliding.* Journal of Soil and Water Conservation 43(6): 495-498.

9. Hicks, D. L. 1989. *Soil conservation in the Waihora Catchment, East Coast—an assessment in the wake of Cyclone Bola.* Technical Record PN3. Division of Land and Soil Sciences, Wellington, New Zealand.

10. Lambert, M. G., N. A. Trustrum, and D. A. Costal. 1984. *Effect of soil slip erosion on seasonally dry Wairarapa hill pastures.* New Zealand Journal of Agricultural Research 27(1): 57-64.

11. Northey, R. D., J. G. Hawley, and P. R. Barker. 1974. *Classifications and mechanisms of slope failures in natural ground.* Proceedings, Symposium (Nelson). New Zealand Institution of Professional Engineers and New Zealand New Zealand Geomechanics Society, Wellington.

12. National Water and Soil Conservation Authority. 1987. *Farming the hills: Mining or sustaining the resource.* Streamlands No. 62. Department of Scientific and Industrial Research, Wellington, New Zealand.

13. Pollock, K. M. 1986. *Plant materials handbook for soil conservation, Volume 3: Native plants.* Water and Soil Miscellaneous Publication Number 95. Soil Conservation Center, Aokautere, MWD, Palmerston North, New Zealand.

14. Stephens, P. R., C. M. Trotter, R. C. DeRose, P. F. Newsome, and K. S. Carr. 1988. *Use of SPOT satellite data to map landslides.* Proceedings, Ninth Asian Conference on Remote Sensing. Asian Association on Remote Sensing.

15. Thompson, R. C. 1989. *Summary of engineering geological characteristics in assessing soil conservation work effectiveness in the Gisborne-East Coast region.* Interim report. Department of Conservation, Wellington, New Zealand.

16. Trotter, C. M., P. R. Stephens, N. A. Trustrum, M. J. Page, K. S. Carr, and R. C. DeRose. 1989. *Application of remotely sensed and geographic information system data to quantitative assessment of landslide damage.* Proceedings, 12th International Symposium on Geoscience and Remote Sensing.

17. Trustrum, N. A., and J. G. Hawley. 1985. *Conversion of forest land use to grazing—A New Zealand perspective on the effects of landslide erosion on hill country productivity.* Proceedings, Seminar on Land Use Planning in a Watershed Context.

18. Trustrum, N. A., M. G. Lambert, and V. J. Thomas. *Erosion—a drop away in production.* Soil and Water 19(1): 11-19.

19. Trustrum, N. A., and R. C. DeRose. 1988. *Soil depth: Age relationship of landslides on deforested hillslopes, Taranaki, New Zealand.* Geomorphology 1: 143-160.

20. Trustrum, N. A., V. J. Thomas, and M. G. Lambert. 1984. *Soil slip erosion as a constraint to hill country pasture production.* Proceedings, New Zealand Grasslands Association 45: 57-64.

21. van Kraayenoord, C.W.S., and R. L. Hathaway. 1986. *Plant materials handbook for soil conservation, Volume 1: Principles and practices. Volume 2: Introduced plants.* Water and Soil Miscellaneous Publication Numbers 93 and 94. Soil Conservation Center, Aokautere, MWD, Palmerston North, New Zealand.

22. Whitehouse, I. E. 1984. *Erosion in the eastern South Island high country: A changing*

perspective. Tussock Grasslands and Mountain Lands Review 42: 3-23.
23. Whitehouse, I. E. 1987. *Geomorphology of a compressional plate boundary, Southern Alps, New Zealand.* In V. Gardiner [editor] *International Geomorphology 1986.* John Wiley and Sons, Chichester, United Kingdom. pp. 897-924.

TRACING SOIL
EROSION SOURCES

T. C. JUANG

Sedimentation of eroded soil in reservoirs greatly affects water resources conservation, electric power transportation, flood control, and irrigation management. The Teh-Chi Reservoir has been key to the multipurpose development of the Ta-Chia River Basin in Taiwan. Economic development in central Taiwan depends heavily on the effective life and proper management of the reservoir.

During the 20 years after construction of the east-west cross-island highway, the ecosystem of the area was disturbed because of intense land use, overcutting of forests, burning, road construction, and poor management of soil and water resources on orchard land. Soil erosion and landslides increased because of the land's steepness, high rain intensity, thin soil layer, and improper construction of debris dams. This increased the amount of eroded soil entering the river and being deposited in the reservoir; it also limited the efficiency and life of the reservoir (9, 10).

A comprehensive soil and water conservation plan for the Teh-Chi Reservoir watershed has been implemented in recent years, and erosion throughout the watershed and sediment deposition in the reservoir have decreased. However, it is necessary to trace soil erosion sources in the watershed to understand more precisely the potential damage to the reservoir and to better manage the reservoir and the watershed.

A considerable amount of radionuclides escaped into the atmosphere when nuclear tests were conducted in the past at the ground surface or in the atmosphere. In radioactive fallout, atmospheric radionuclides fall to the ground and are widely distributed in the environment. Their distribution and accumulation are influenced by the topography, hillside slopes, rain

245

intensity, vegetative situation, and thickness of the soil. The half-life of both cesium 137 and strontium 90, the major products of nuclear testing, is about 30 years. However, the movement and diffusion of cesium 137 is slower than strontium 90 because of stronger adsorption of cesium 137 by soil (2, 5). The adsorption of cesium is highly correlated with clay content, type of clay minerals, pH, and organic matter content in soils (7). The method of analysis used for determination of cesium 137 is much simpler than that for strontium 90. Therefore, determining the radioactive activity of cesium 137 is a better method of tracing soil erosion sources in the reservoir watershed area.

Mineral resistance to weathering depends on the intensity of chemical weathering, crystal structure, composition of the mineral, and the environment causing the weathering (4). Jackson and Sherman (4) reported a mineral weathering sequence suggesting that feldspar is more susceptible and muscovite is more resistant to weathering than quartz. A weathering stability series proposed by Goldich (1) suggests a sequence in order of increasing stability as follows: anorthite, calc-alkalic feldspar, albite, orthoclase, microcline, muscovite, and quartz (1). The residual minerals in soil depend not only on the parent material and its weathering stability but also on the climate, topography, permeability, chelation, oxidation-reduction reaction, and ionic concentration in soil water in the area. Kiely and Jackson (6) suggested that a quartz/feldspar ratio could be used as a weathering index.

This study describes and discusses the methodologies of using a low-background Geiger-Müller (G-M) counter to determine the activity of cesium 137 from radioactive fallout, and using chemical dissolution and X-ray diffraction (XRD) methods to measure the quartz/feldspar ratio in soils collected from the upper watershed of the Teh-Chi Reservoir and their possible use in tracing the source of soil erosion.

Geologic and Soil Environment at the Research Area

The research area is surrounded by the mountains of Tse-Gou, Tao, Nan-Hu, Chung-Yang-Gien, Wu-Ming, Bee-Lu, and Ho-Huan. Elevation of these mountains is about 3,000 meters. The major rivers in the area are the Chi-Chia-Wan, Se-GeeLung, I-Ka-Wan, Nan-Hu, Er-Wu, Bee-Lu, Ho-Hwan, and Ta-Chia (9, 10).

Rock strata in the area were formed between the eocene and oligocene of the tertiary period. The dominant constitutive rocks are clay slate and quartzite. The clay slate is grey-black and exhibits plate structure. Silty clay slate is more resistant to weathering than stony clay slate, which readily slides away from quartzite surface if it is stratified with quartzite. The major rock strata are from a northeast to a southwest direction with substantial fault and fold. In the clay slate area, cleavage structure often mixed with the stratum surface to form blocky rock.

Soils in the watershed investigated were mostly clay and clay loam, with a thin soil layer. The plane area along the riverside and some platforms and low slope hillsides had a thicker soil layer, but clear horizons were not evident. Podzolization was found in some soils because of low temperature and high rainfall, while laterization was found in some soils because of high solar radiation. Soils in the area include (1) red-yellow podzolic soil, including two soil series; Chia-Yang light clay and Chia-Yang sandy clay loam; (2) alpine meadow soil; and (3) Lithosols.

Materials and Methods

Determination of Cesium 137 Radioactive Activity. The method used was based on the method described by the U.S. Environmental Protection Agency (*11*). Air-dried soil was ashed at 450°C for 15 hours, 40 grams of ashed soil were digested with three-normal hydrochloric acid, and a cesium carrier and ammonium molydbenum phosphate were added to the soil extract to form a cesium compound precipitate. After centrifugation, the precipitate was dis solved by six-normal sodium hydroxide. Calcium chloride was added to form a $CaMoO_4$ precipitate, and the cesium ion was precipitated by adding H_2PtCl_6 to form Cs_2PtCl_6. The golden Cs_2PtCl_6 was collected by filtration, washed with water and one-normal hydrochloric acid, and dried until there was no weight change. Beta radiation activity of cesium 138 was determined by a low-background G-M counter (background was about three cpm). Specific activity of cesium 137 beta radiation was calculated as follows:

$$Acs = \frac{N}{2.22 \ YEW} \ \times \ \frac{W1}{W2}$$

where Acs is specific activity of cesium per kilogram fresh weight ($\mu\mu$Ci/kg); N is the counting rate (cpm); Y is the chemical yield fraction; E is the counting efficiency; W is the weight of ashed soil used for analysis (gm); W1 is the soil weight after ashing; and W2 is fresh soil weight (1,000 gm).

Determination of Feldspar and Quartz Content. The sodium pyrosulfate fusion method (*6*) was used to determine the feldspar and quartz content in the soil samples. High-temperature sulfuric acid, produced by fusing sodium pyrosulfate with the soil sample, was used as a dehydroxylating agent. Mica, kaolinite, and chlorite were dissolved by three-normal hydrochloric acid. Other layer silicates were dissolved by hot one-half-normal sodium hydroxide. Finally, the feldspar and quartz left in the residue were digested by $HF-HClO_4-H_2SO_4$ solution (6), and K_2O, Na_2O, and CaO contents were measured. By using the conversion factors, the contents of microcline-orthoclase, anorthite, and quartz in the soil sample could be calculated (6).

Determination of Minerals in Soils and Gravels by X-Ray Diffraction. The sample was ground in an agate mortar, further ground in a vibration mill, and passed through a 325-mesh sieve. To remove organic matter, 30 to 35 percent of H_2O_2 was added to the ground sample in a 60 °C water bath until bubbling ceased. To avoid preferred orientation during XRD, the sample was compacted into a powder sample holder, and the surface of the sample was smoothed down using a glass slide for XRD.

The XRD of the sample was set at 30 KV, CuK$\propto$ radiation, 20 mA, a scanning speed of 0.25 ° (2θ) per minute, a chart speed of 10 centimeters per minute, a counting time constant of 0.5 second, and measured from 2θ 2 ° to 70 °.

In the soil fraction, XRD intensity of quartz (100), plagicolasite (002), chlorite (002), and illite (002) was estimated by the peak area, which was calculated by the maximum peak height above the base line multiplied by peak width at half the maximum height.

In the gravel fraction, quartz was estimated by using (112) peak, while the other minerals were the same as in the the soil fraction. Intensity was then measured and calculated by the method of Williams (12).

Results and Discussion

Distribution of radioactive fallout varied with plant community, topography, soil type, and rainfall. Generally, the surfaces of forest and densely vegetated areas are relative flat, thus retaining more strontium 90 and cesium 137 in the soils. In the cultivated area, the crop changed frequently and slope and topography had no special features. Thus, the radioactive fallout in the cultivated area was less than in the forest area. In the rocky or landslide area, radioactive fallout did not accumulate because the surface soil was readily eroded. The average specific activity of cesium 137 in various vegetative areas is shown in table 1.

Table 1 shows that the specific activity of cesium 137 in landslide soils was significantly lower than that in forestland, grassland, and orchard land.

Table 1. The specific activity of cesium 137 in surface soil in various vegetative areas of the Teh-Chi Reservoir watershed.

Vegetative Area	^{137}Cs Activity ($\mu\mu Ci/Kg$)	Comments
Grassland	208	
Forest land	203	
Orchard land	302	High variation, range: 18to 828 $\mu\mu Ci/Kg$.
Landslide area	147	
Sample No. 15	40	Landslide area at the juncture of the HO-Huan River and the cross-island highway.
Sample No. 5	73	Landslide area at the mouth of Nan-Hu River.
Sample No. 33	8	Big landslide area at the Huan mountain.

Table 2. The average quartz/feldspar (QF) and mica/feldspar (Mi/F) ratio of surface soil and gravel in various vegetative areas of Teh-Chi Reservoir watershed.

Vegetative Area	Soil		Gravel	
	Q/F	Mi/F	Q/F	Mi/F
Forestland	2.45	1.04	2.12	1.12
Orchard land	2.57	1.40	6.99	4.78
Landslide area	1.77	-	-	-

Even among four landslide areas, significant difference in cesium 137 activity was evident. The lowest activity (8 $\mu\mu Ci/Kg$) was found in the big landslide area at Huan Mountain because of its magnitude.

Residual minerals in soil could be an index of the degree of weathering of rock, mineral, and soil. Goldich (1) proposed a stability series of coarse mineral, suggesting that quartz was more stable than muscovite (mica) and feldspar. Goldich used a quartz/feldspar ratio or muscovite/feldspar ratio as an index of the relative stability of the soil. Table 2 shows that the quartz/feldspar ratios of the surface soil in forestland (2.45) and orchard land (2.57) were significantly higher than that in the landslide area (1.77), suggesting that the soil in forest and orchard lands was more stable.

The difference in stability between the soils on forestland and on orchard land could be evaluated by examining the quarta/feldspar ratio in the gravel fraction. As mentioned before, quartz and muscovite are more stable than feldspar. A high quartz/feldspar ratio indicates a high stability and high resistance to erosion. In the gravel fraction the quartz/feldspar ratio and muscovite/feldspar ratio were much lower in forestland (2.12 and 1.12, respectively) than in orchard land (6.99 and 4.78, respectively). In the soil fraction, quartz/feldspar ratio and muscovite/feldspar ratio were also lower in forestland (2.45 and 1.04, respectively) than in orchard land (12.57 and 1.40, respectively). The results indicated that the soil in orchard land was more stable than the soil in forest land. Soil erosion was more serious in forestland because of landslides, road construction, and natural weathering. The facts in table 1, showing that the specific activity of cesium 137 in soil was higher in orchard land than in forestland, also indicated more serious soil erosion with a thinner surface soil in forestland.

Results obtained from the radioactive fallout measurement and mineral analysis showed that cesium 137 activity and the quartz/feldspar and muscovite/feldspar ratios of surface soil varied significantly under different vegetative conditions, suggesting that these two methods could differentiate soil, whether eroded from forest, orchard, or the landslide area, and could be used in tracing soil erosion sources.

Using geochemical analysis and an XRD method to determine the content of feldspar and quartz and using chemical analysis and a low-background radioactive detector require special knowledge and techniques. Considerable error might result if care is not taken when these two methods are applied.

REFERENCES

1. Goldich, S. S. 1938. *A study on rock weathering.* Journal of Geology 46: 17-58.
2. Hsu, G. M. 1979. *Radiochemistry.* In *Health Chemistry.* Kuo-Hsing Publishing Company, Taiwan. pp. 156-196.
3. Hutchison, C. S. 1974. *Laboratory handbook of petrographic techniques.* John Wiley & Sons, New York, New York. pp. 145-147.
4. Jackson, M. L., and G. D. Sherman. 1953. *Chemical weathering of minerals in soils.* Advances in Agronomy 5: 221-319.
5. Juang, T. C., C. H. Chang, and T. M. Lai. 1962. *Diffusion of strontium-90 and cesium-137 in soil.* Report of the Taiwan Sugar Experiment Station 27: 55-66.
6. Kiely, P. V., and M. L. Jackson. 1965. *Quartz, feldspar, and mica determination for soils by sodium pyrosulfate fusion.* Soil Science Society of America Proceedings 29: 159-163.
7. Klug, H. P., and L. E. Alexender. 1974. *X-ray diffraction procedures for polycrystalline and amorphous materials.* John Wiley & Sons, New York, New York. pp. 505-556.
8. Muller, R. M., Douglas G. Sprugel, and Barbara Kohn. 1978. *Erosional transport and deposition of plutonium and cesium in two small midwestern watersheds.* Journal of Environmental Quality 7(2): 171-174.
9. Teh-Chi Reservoir Watershed Planning Group. 1975. *Planning report on Teh-Chi Reservoir Watershed.*
10. Teh-Chi Reservoir Watershed Working Group. 1972. *Report on management of Teh-Chi Reservoir Watershed.*
11. U.S. Environmental Protection Agency. 1973. *Procedures for radiochemical analysis of nuclear reactor aqueous solutions.* EPA-R4-73014. Cincinnati, Ohio.
12. Williams, P. P. 1959. *Direct quantitative diffractometer analysis.* Analytical Chemistry 31(11): 1,842-1,844.

FRACTAL DIMENSIONS
OF RILL PATTERNS

TERUO FUJIWARA and MITSUO FUKADA

When rain falls on bare hillslopes, rill drainage patterns are formed on the surface by the water flow. The greater part of eroded soil is carried away through these drainages. Erosion rate increases rapidly as the rill drainage patterns develop. The progress of rill drainage sometimes leads to serious damage.

Rill patterns are just as complicated as cloud formations, river networks, and other natural phenomena. The patterns seem to have some relation to the angle of hillslopes and also to soil erosion rate. To analyze these relationships, we first tried to analyze the relationship between rill drainage patterns and the angle of hillslopes using field data.

Highly involved figures, such as the rill drainage patterns, cannot be described by traditional Euclidean geometry, which cannot express the degree of complicated patterns by numerical values. In fractal geometry (*I*), complex patterns can be characterized by the fractal dimension, D, which is generally a noninteger value. In this study, the fractal dimensions were applied to a plane pattern of rills, and the relationship between the fractal dimensions and the angle of hillslopes was determined.

Fractal Dimensions of Rill Patterns

Concept of Fractal Dimensions. The central concept of fractal geometry is the statistical self-similarity of patterns. The essence of this concept is illustrated in figure 1 by successive views of a coastline from the air. A portion of the patterns, as shown in the lowest picture in figure 1, can be magnified to the middle figure; thus, we can see that the figures are similar in a statistical sense. Similarly, each successive magnified figure of a selected portion of coastline has statistical similarity with each other. This is a characteristic of fractal geometry that differentiates it from Euclidean shapes, which become increasingly more simple with magnification. The parameters that characterize such a set of patterns are the fractal dimensions.

Method of Evaluating the Fractal Dimensions of Rill Patterns. The procedure for evaluating the fractal dimension, D, is outlined in figure 2. A

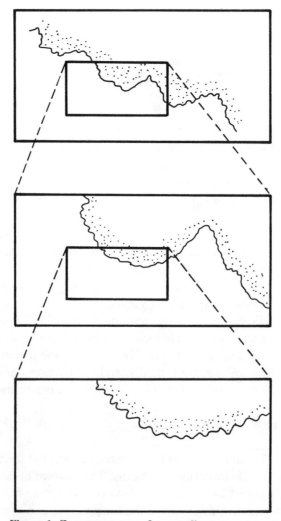

Figure 1. Zoom sequence of a coastline.

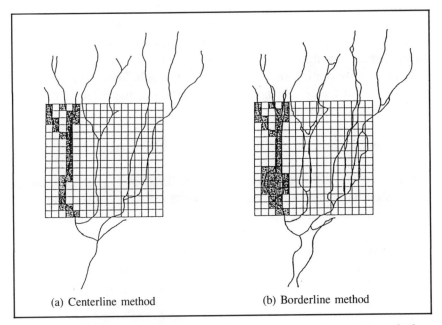

(a) Centerline method   (b) Borderline method

Figure 2. Method of evaluating the fractal dimension using the square method.

plane figure drawn by the centerline or borderline of rills can be divided into small squares, with the length of the sides as r. All squares in the figure are numbered 1, 2, 3,... N(r), even if only a fragment of a line segment is in a square. After plotting the values of r and N(r) on double logarithmic graph paper, a line is drawn to connect these values. If rill patterns have self-similarity, a linear relation is obtained between r and N(r). An absolute value of the slope of this line represents the fractal dimension of the rill patterns. This value is generally a noninteger (e.g., 1.15, etc.) and increases with pattern complexity. Figure 3 shows the evaluated results of D_c by the centerline method of five rill patterns developed on the same hillslope.

Definition of D_c and D_s Based on Two Types of Square Methods.

Centerline Method. The centerline of rills is drawn by connecting the middle points of each rill width. The fractal dimension, D_c, is evaluated by using this centerline. This D_c demonstrates mainly the grade of bifurcation and meandering of rills.

Borderline Method. The borderline of rills is drawn, and the fractal dimension D_s is evaluated by using this borderline. This D_s demonstrates the fractal dimensions, taking the rill area into consideration.

Area Ratio. In well-developed rills, the ratio of the area of rill drainage to the total area of the hillslope generally ranges from 10 to 20 percent. This value is high in comparison with that of river networks. This is another distinguishing feature of rills, along with bifurcation and meandering.

To get the area ratio, we traced the figure of rills from the picture and colored part of the rills black. We then calculated the value of the area ratio by computer graphics.

Evaluation of the Fractal Dimensions of Rill Patterns

Survey of the Rill Drainage Patterns on Hillslopes. The rill drainage patterns on hillslopes of decomposed granite (Masa soil) were surveyed in the downtown area of Ube City, Japan, for 2 months, from November to December 1987. Masa soil, which is widespread in the western part of Japan, is very susceptible to erosion by rainfall. In farmland and roadside cuts, erosion repeatedly occurs, resulting in major damage. The survey analyzed the angle of the hillslopes, the width and length of the slope, and

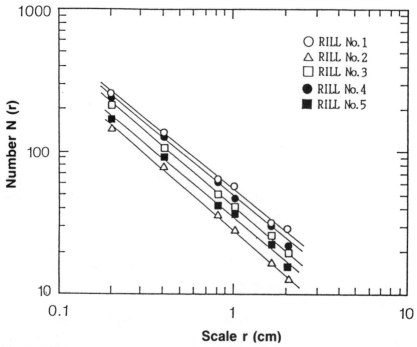

Figure 3. Relationship between *r* and *N(r)* of rills.

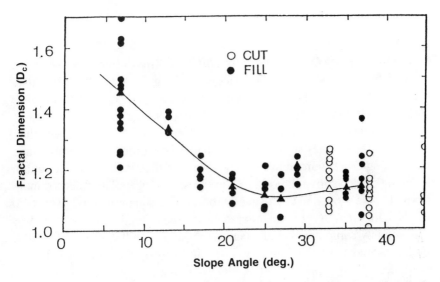

Figure 4. Relationship between D_c and the slope angle (Δ, $\blacktriangle$ represent mean value).

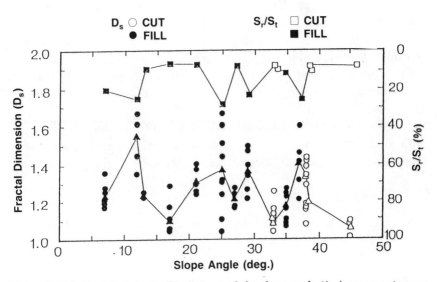

Figure 5. Relationship between D_s, S_r/S_t, and the slope angle (Δ, $\blacktriangle$ represent mean value).

soil properties. Survey data were gathered only from the last-stage rills on the hillslopes.

Relationship of D_c and D_s to the Hillslope Angle. Figure 4 shows the relationship between D_c and the slope angle by using the centerline square method. The solid line in the figure is obtained by the least-squares method. The fractal dimensions, D_c, decrease linearly as the slope angle increases to 25° and then reaches an almost constant value of 1.1. This suggests that, as the slope becomes steeper, the rill pattern becomes more simple, and rilling progresses more in the vertical direction than in the plane direction.

Figure 5 shows the relation of D_s to the slope angle. The fractal dimensions, D_s, were obtained by using the borderline square method. The ratio of the rill area, S_r, to the total area of the hillslope, S_t, which was evaluated by computer graphic analysis, is shown on the same graph. The D_s has a tendency to increase with the increase in the ratio of rill area.

Conclusion

The fractal dimensions of rill drainage patterns that develop on hillslopes at various angles were investigated with use of the fractal dimensions concept. The rill patterns that were chosen for on-site investigations were last-stage rills. The main conclusions from this field study can be summarized as follows:

• The average fractal dimension, D_c, of rill patterns that develop on the hillslopes consist of granite soil in the range 1.1 to 1.4 and decrease in direct proportion to the increase in slope angle, up to 25°. This shows that, if the slope becomes quite steep, rill patterns cannot develop as well, and erosion begins to proceed in a vertical direction from an early stage. If the slope angle ranges from 25° to 40°, the fractal dimension, D_c, has the constant value of 1.1.

• The ratio of rill area to total area of the hillslope does not correlate with slope angle. However, the average fractal dimension, D_s, has a tendency to increase with the increase in the ratio of the rill area.

REFERENCE

1. Mandelbrot, B. B. 1982. *The fractal geometry of nature.* Freeman, San Francisco, California.

CASE STUDIES

7

SLOPELAND
MECHANIZATION
IN TAIWAN

PEN-YU TU

A slopeland mechanization program was implemented in 1970 by the Joint Commission on Rural Reconstruction (JCCR) as part of the Integrated Soil Conservation and Land Use Program, which was described by Koh (3). This program was directed toward the attainment of effective soil conservation and sustained land use through the application of welldeveloped mechanical methods. It covers three major tasks: (1) performing mechanical operations for construction of soil conservation works and improvement of slopeland conditions; (2) modifying and developing suitable farm machines and mechanical installations for promotion of slopeland farm production; and (3) establishing mechanized slopeland conservation farming systems for securing a progressive and permanent slopeland agriculture by integrating soil conservation, crop cultivation, farm installations, and machinery operation. Many advances have been realized over the past 18 years through this program.

Application of Mechanical Operations for Slopeland Conservation

The Mountain Agricultural Resources Development Bureau (MARDB) has been responsible for the mechanical operation work, with technical and financial assistance from the former JCRR and Council for Agricultural Planning and Development (CAPD), now the Council of Agriculture (COA).

Selection and Purchase of Construction Machines. To meet the needs of construction work on sloping land, 31 sets of small- and medium-sized bulldozers were purchased from 1968 to 1987. John Deere's JD-450 and

JD-350 bulldozers were the first choice for their desirable features and adequate capability. Komatsu D314 and E bulldozers have since become the dominant machines.

As the construction work has diversified in recent years, five sets of small- and medium-sized excavators were purchased from 1984 to 1988 for the purpose of improving farming conditions in confined and irregular areas.

Training Operators and Mechanics. The MARDB set up one machinery maintenance shop in 1972 to repair and maintain the construction machines. The shop was adequately equipped with skilled mechanics and necessary repair facilities.

The MARDB has a work force of 27 operators and 10 mechanics for machinery operation and maintenance. To promote their proficiency, the workers were given a seminar every year. The seminar included class instruction, field observation, and the opportunity to exchange work experience.

Management of Mechanical Operations. In the beginning, regulations were drawn up by MARDB, with assistance from the JCRR, for directing the mechanical operations. These regulations prescribed the scope of the mechanical operation, preparation of an annual work plan, assignment of construction machines, management of operators, management of field-operation work, and collection of operation charges.

Work Accomplishment. The important work accomplished through 1986 included annual construction of 2,000 hectares of hillside ditches (including orchard hillside ditches) and about 140 kilometers per year of link roads. The work of bench terracing decreased year by year, while farming path construction greatly increased. The yearly working hours totalled approximately 32,000 (6).

According to a 1979-1985 investigation by MARDB, the average working days for mechanical operations were 189.5 per unit per year, representing an average annual use rate of 51.9 percent per machine. The average working hours were 1,188 per unit per year, or 6.27 per unit per day. The nonuse rate of 48.09 percent was accounted for by 13.94 percent for repair or awaiting repair, 2.3 percent for awaiting land preparation, 13.64 percent for rain days, 10.00 percent for holidays, 2.34 percent for transportation, and 5.86 percent for other reasons.

JD-350 and JD-450 bulldozers were the main machines used on the hillside ditching and bench terracing projects (4). Investigations were made of the performance of these two machines. The results are shown in table 1.

Table 1. General work capacity of the JD-350 and JD-450 bulldozers.

Machine Type	Work Project	Average Length (m/ha)	Work Capacity (m/ha)	Time Requirement (hr/ha)
JD-350	Hillside ditching	450	46-37	7-12(10)*
	Bench terracing	2,000	50-33	40-60(50)
JD-450	Hillside ditching	450	90-50	5-9(7)
	Bench terracing	2,000	71-51	28-40(35)

*Average time requirement is listed in parentheses.

Table 2. Job efficiency of the JD-350 and JD-450 bulldozers.

Machine Type	Work Project	Efficiency Factor
JD-350	Hillside ditching	0.461
	Bench terracing	0.841
JD-450	Hillside ditching	0.572
	Bench terracing	0.839

Table 3. Breakdown of the operation cost of JD-450 (NT$/hr) (7).

Depreciation	Maintenance	Fuel	Allowance	Transportation	Overhead	Total
170	153	87	41	14	50	515
33.01%	29.7%	16.89%	7.96%	2.72%	9.71%	100%

The results in table 1 were estimated from several years of field-work observation on slopes of 15° to 25° (27-47 percent). The major specifications of the JD-350 and JD-450 were 46 net horsepower with a 2.36-meter blade and 64 net horsepower with a 2.69-meter blade, respectively. The average width of the hillside ditch was 2.0 meters (5) and that of the bench terrace 2.5 meters.

The job efficiencies shown in table 2 were calculated from the actual operation in the construction of 50 hectares of bench terraces and 1,634 hectares of hillside ditches (17).

The following formulae were developed through field tests for estimating the time required for constructing hillside ditches and bench terraces using the JD-350 and JD-450 bulldozers on different slopes (17):

$$T(W1M1) = 1.766e^{0.027R} \times R^{0.176} \times A^{0.838}$$

$$T(W1M2) = 1.545e^{0.027R} \times R^{0.176} \times A^{0.838}$$

$$T(W2M1) = 25.880e^{0.027R} \times R^{-0.129} \times A^{0.838}$$

$$T(W2M2) = 22.636e^{0.027R} \times R^{-0.129} \times A^{0.838}$$

where T is operation time (hr), W1 is hillside ditching, W2 is bench terracing, M1 is the JD-350, M2 is the JD-450, R is average slope (degrees), and A is the work area (ha).

Statistics from 15 years of data showed the general life expectancy of the JD-450 to be 10,000 hours, 8,000 hours, and 6,000 hours per unit, respectively, under excellent, average, and severe slopeland work conditions (7). The maintenance cost of the JD-450 was about 90 percent of the depreciation cost (Table 3). The total maintenance cost was composed of repair costs of 45 percent for the undercarriage, 20 percent for the transmission, 12 percent for the engine, 7 percent for the hydraulic system, 3 percent for the electric system, and 13 percent for others (7).

Farmers' Payments and Government's Subsidies for Mechanical Operation. For encouragement of the slopeland mechanical operation, the government gave farmers two types of subsidies. One type was to reduce depreciation cost by 50 percent in payment of the operation charge. The other was to provide farmers with subsidies for mechanical operations. The major subsidies included NT$3,000 per hectare for hillside ditching, NT$4,500 per hectare for orchard hillside ditching, NT$6,500 per hectare for bench terracing, NT$25 per meter for link road construction, and NT$20 per meter for farming path construction. With the reduced depreciation charge and the subsidies, farmers paid only a small amount of the cost and, in some cases, did not need to pay any cost because the subsidy was enough to cover the operation charge.

Improvement of Mechanical Operational Techniques. For efficient and safe operation on slopeland, a set of general operational procedures and a series of improved operating techniques have been developed for machine use:

1. Stake out a central line across the slope.

2. Open an access road to reach the top of the work site.

3. When moving earth or clearing land, work downslope to get greater power.

4. The distance of moving materials should be kept as short as possible, no more than 20 meters up and down the slope or 30 meters across the slope (*15*).

5. The link road should be constructed first, and then the hillside ditching and bench terracing should be constructed from this road.

6. In shaping a slopeland with irregular topography, work should be done section by section, using the slope-dividing lines as the partition for different shaping treatments (*15*).

7. When moving up a steep slope, back the machine and lower the blade to about 30 to 50 centimeters above the ground.

8. When moving down a steep slope, lower the blade so as to readily stop the machine and to avoid turning over in case of an accident.

9. Drive the machine slowly on rugged terrain or steep slopes and never too close to the edge of a cliff or a deep hole.

Improved operating techniques include the following:

1. Angle the blade for side-casting to the lower side of the bench terrace, hillside ditch, or link road and for back-filling ditches or depressions.

2. Tilt the blade for upside slope cutting, digging out rocks and stumps, and, more importantly, for making the reverse-slope bottom of the hillside ditches.

3. Under ordinary slopeland conditions, three passes are adequate to complete the cross-section of a bench terrace, hillside ditch, or link road. The first pass opens the ground to allow the machine to work forward and to cut the upside slope as much as possible for forming the bottom. The second pass constructs the full-width bottom, and the third pass constructs a reverse slope of the bottom and smooths it, especially in building the hillside ditch.

4. In building hillside ditches, the width of cut and the width of fill are about two-thirds and one-third, respectively, of the bottom.

5. In building bench terraces, it is desirable to work from the bottom to the top so the topsoil that is cut from the upper terrace can be turned down to cover the lower terrace.

6. In shaping a large and uniform slopeland, the machine can work across slopes as steep as 15° (27 percent). In doing so, the removed soil is lined on the contour for good soil conservation (15).

7. In shaping steep and irregular slopeland, if the cut amount is insufficient to cover the fill amount, it is better to cut and lower the top to get sufficient fill.

Development of Machinery for Mechanized Slopeland Farming

Slope degree limits the workability of farm machinery on slopeland. The steeper the slope, the more the machinery is limited. When ordinary farm machinery is put to work on slopeland, it works well on slopes below 4° (7 percent); it needs some adjustments and skilled techniques on slopes between 4° to 8° (7-14 percent); it requires certain modifications on slopes between 8° to 12° (14-21 percent); and it won't work properly, if at all, on slopes over 12° (21 percent) (12). In Taiwan, because the average slope of slopeland is over 12° (21 percent), it is necessary to modify and develop slopeland machinery to suit these steep slopes.

A slopeland farm machinery development program was implemented in 1977 under the direction of the former JCRR and CAPD, now COA. This is a research program with participants from concerned universities, colleges, agricultural and livestock research institutes, and district agricultural improvement stations.

Guidelines for Research Work on Machinery Development. Priority should be given to the machinery needed for labor-intensive farm work, such as transportation, pest and weed control, fruit-tree harvest and grading, forage grass cutting, etc. To fit slopeland conditions, cropping patterns, soil conservation, and farm management, the slopeland machinery to be developed can be classified as two types (*11*). One is the self-propelled type, which is to be driven on the slopeland field. The other is the stationary type, which is a set of fixed mechanical installations serving a certain area.

Development of Slopeland Farm Machinery. Experiments were conducted on the performance and behavior of conventional machinery working on slopelands to determine their shortcomings, such as lack of power, low traction, tipping to the downhill side, sliding down the slope, tipping over, etc. (*14, 16*). Based on the performance and behavior of the conventional machinery shown in working slopelands, modification and development should be made with respect to the size of the machine, the structure of the body, the arrangement of wheel and axle, the method of steering, and the power drive, as well as safety features (*9, 16*). Useful methods that can be adopted include lowering the center of gravity, distributing the body weight evenly over the wheels, applying four-wheel drive, using four wide wheels of the same size and low-pressure tires, adopting hydraulic steering of front wheels, adopting the articulated arrangement between the front and rear frames, and installing a safety frame in the middle or rear part of the machine for preventing roll-over (*10, 13, 16*).

Stationary mechanical installations undergoing improvement include the farm cableway, monorail, and ordinary and automatic spraying systems. These mechanical installations have the advantage of speeding up mechanization in transportation, spraying, and irrigation because they can operate in long lines or large areas. Also, they can be installed in a short time with little interference with the existing land use and cropping patterns (*2, 14*). They are especially suited to the steep and irregular slopelands where general farm mechanization is difficult.

The cableway should be located where it can control an adequate area and where there is a sufficient elevation difference between the upper and lower stands for efficient operation. The power drive and automatic control should also be studied.

Emphasis in developing an automatic spraying system should be placed on improving and developing the three main parts of the system, namely, the chemical mixing and pumping station, the time-controlled pipelines, and the self-rotating sprinkler-type spraying head.

With joint efforts by the government and participants, various kinds of slopeland farm machinery and mechanical installations have been improved and developed in the past 11 years. The most significant accomplishments are introduced briefly below:

Wu's articulated-frame and floating-wheel power carts. Among the various types of power carts manufactured by Wu's Company, the newly developed articulated-frame type and floating-wheel type have special features to fit slopeland transportation conditions. The former has an articulated hinge in the center to allow the rear frame, with the two rear wheels, to swing from side to side so that both wheels can rest on the sloping ground for better stability and greater traction. For the latter type, there is a floating frame of four rear wheels on the rear axle to allow the rear wheels to swing upward and downward with the change of ground slope for the same purpose as stated above.

The wheel-adjustment power cart. The wheel-adjustment power cart, developed by Y. S. Lin of the Taitung District Agricultural Improvement Station (Taitung DAIS), has a hydraulic mechanism to change the vertical position of both rear wheels with the change of the groundslope. This maintains the cart body in the level position for more traction and stability.

The cable-drawn monorail. The cable-drawn monorail, developed by K. N. Wang of National Taiwan University, is a combination of the farm cableway and the monorail. It has a carrier on the monorail with a cable-driven mechanism to draw the carrier on the rail for up and down transportation (*1*). Its advantages include greater power with a diesel engine on the ground, greater carrying capacity, less vibration on the rail, and an improved brake system.

The multi-use slopeland machine. This machine, developed by Y. S. Lin of Taitung DAIS, can perform different jobs on slopeland with a variety of attachments. The important features of the machine include wide, low-pressure tires, low center of gravity, hydrostatic drive, evenly arranged attachments, and a roll-over protection frame.

The attached implements and equipment include a flair-type mower, an auger-type digger, a rotary tiller, and a blower-type sprayer. The blower-type sprayer has made the multiuse slopeland machine very popular because of its splendid spraying performance (*1, 16*).

The self-propelled, rope-drawn shaker. This shaker was developed by K. Y. Liu of National Taiwan University for harvesting fruit trees. It is mounted on a slopeland power cart for convenient operation in orchards. The main components include a diesel engine, a reciprocating piston in a square groove, a rotary plate, and the adjustable parallelogram frame. It can work in all directions on complicated slopeland. Field tests show that the shaker is good for harvesting plums, peaches, olive, citrus, etc., with vibration frequencies of 200 to 500 rpm and an amplitude of 5 to 30 centimeters (*1, 16*).

The automatic pipeline spraying system. The automatic pipeline spraying system was first improved by L. C. Chou of the the MARDB Second Work Station to adapt to local slopeland farming conditions. It was then modified by F. T. Kiang of Ta-hu Senior Professional Agricultural and Industrial School in the development of the electronic-controlled operation system, and by Y. J. Huang of Chung-Hsing University, and K. K. Lee and M. C. Hung of Taitung DAIS in the development of the self-rotating spraying head (*1, 16*). Its main components include a deep-well pump to provide larger spraying capacity and higher spraying pressure, a set of electronically controlled operation appliances for automatic operation section by section, and a number of self-rotating spraying heads to provide a steady and uniform mist. The significant advantages are no risk of poisoning, timely pest control, and large-area coverage in a few minutes.

Establishment of the Mechanized Conservation Farming Systems

The Concept of the Systems. Slopeland should be treated for conservation according to its need, and, in the meantime, to achieve sustained slopeland agriculture, the cropping and cultural practices should be fitted to its capability and suitability. For intensifying slopeland conservation farming, we have applied construction machines to perform soil conservation treatments and improve the slopeland conditions, adjusted the cropping pattern to fit the improved land use type, and developed slopeland machinery to mechanize slopeland farming. By integrating these three, the so-called mechanized slopeland conservation farming system is to be established.

Major Systems Developed. Four major mechanized slopeland conservation farming systems have been developed, based on the slopeland use types:

1. *Mechanized system for existing moderate slopelands.* Hillside ditches built across the slope on existing slopeland serve both as a measure for soil and water conservation and as a farming path for small machinery opera-

tion. Link roads are built between hillside ditches to form a road network.

The most useful machine is the slopeland power cart that can be used on hillside ditches for transportation and spraying. The pipeline system can be set up for spraying and irrigation where there is a water source.

This system changed the existing slopeland very little and farming conditions are suited to plantations or orchards under extensive management.

2. *Mechanized system for improved moderate slopelands.* Mechanical operation has been applied to shape the slopeland area-by-area according to slope distribution. Soil conservation and public farm works, such as hillside ditches, irrigation and drainage systems, farm and link roads, etc., have been constructed in accordance with an integrated plan for land use and cropping methods.

Hillside ditches or orchard hillside ditches, which are the skeleton of the system, serve the purposes of soil and water conservation and transportation, as well as machinery operation on the slopelands.

Crops and fruit trees are planted horizontally between hillside ditches. Cover grasses, especially bahiagrasses (*Paspalpum notatum*), are planted on slopes, ditches, and roads. To facilitate mechanized operations, improved cultural practices, such as the use of dwarfstocks, reducing tree size by training and pruning, close planting in rows, etc., should be applied when needed.

This system, which is technique- and capital-intensive, is suited to rather large areas of slopeland farm management and for cooperative, joint, or contract operation.

3. *Mechanized system for existing steep slopelands.* The bench terrace and link road make up the framework of this system. On existing terraced steep slopelands, one farming path should be built between every two terraces to provide a space for transportation or small machinery operation. The tree crops along both sides of the farming path should be heavily pruned to leave adequate space over the farming path.

When new bench terraces are to be built on steep slopeland, the bench should be sloped outward to lower the terrace wall between two neighboring terraces for easy field work and for more useable land area. Tree crops should be planted on the outer side of the bench to leave a space on the inner side for transportation and small machinery operation.

Cover grasses should be planted on the bench and the terrace wall when possible. Pipeline systems are most useful for spraying and irrigation.

This system is only suitable to individual management on a small scale because of the lower land use efficiency and higher terrace construction cost.

4. *Mechanized system for totally shaped slopelands.* This system has special significance in transforming the steep, irregular, and complicated

slopelands into a large, whole piece or several large, connected pieces of gently sloping, even uniform slopelands on which level-land farming techniques can be applied.

A soil and geological formation survey should be made first to decide if the land is capable of withstanding the deep cut and high fill. Then, mechanical operation for shaping the irregular terrain should be well planned for the effective operation, soil conservation, and land use.

Hillside ditching and grass cover are still fundamental soil conservation treatments. Farm facilities and cropping pattern are to be provided and adopted as required.

On land with gentle slopes, all farming practices can be mechanized with large, ordinary farm machinery and mechanical installations. If the land has a steeper slope, slopeland machinery should be used for intensive farming.

Conclusion

A slopeland mechanization program has been implemented in Taiwan to intensify soil conservation and promote slopeland use. The program covers three major activities, namely, applying mechanical operation to enhance soil conservation and improve slopeland conditions, developing slopeland farm machinery to perform mechanized farming practices, and establishing mechanized slopeland conservation farming systems to secure a sustained slopeland agriculture.

The program has produced various accomplishments over the past 18 years. Among the most significant accomplishments are the following:

• Completion of the projected soil conservation and farm installation for about 2,000 hectares per year by mechanical operation.

• A series of practical slopeland machinery and mechanical installations have been developed so that almost all important slopeland farming practices, such as weeding, pest control, pruning, fruit harvesting and grading, irrigation, tilling, and transportation can be mechanized.

• With the establishment of mechanized slopeland conservation farming systems, farmers have a guide to conserve and use the slopeland to the best advantage.

Acknowledgment

The author thanks all of the program participants, including concerned agencies and expert workers, for their dedicated work and contributions in implementing this program. The author is especially indebted to C. C. Koh and M. C. Liao for their foresight and expertise in initiating and guiding the program that the author had the opportunity to carry out.

REFERENCES

1. Department of Agricultural Machinery Engineering, National Taiwan University. 1985. *Research reports on slopeland mechanization* (in Chinese). Taipei, Taiwan. 309 pp.
2. Japanese Institute of Agricultural Machinery. 1980. *Studies on slopeland machinery and installations* (in Japanese). Saitama, Japan. 144 pp.
3. Koh, C. C., M. C. Liao, and S. W. Lee. 1990. *The evolution of conservation farming on hillslopes in Taiwan.* In *Development of Conservation Farming on Hillslopes.* Soil and Water Conservation Society, Ankeny, Iowa.
4. Liao, M. C. 1980. *Soil conservation research and development in Taiwan* (in Chinese). Journal of Agriculture Association of China 112:159-172.
5. Liao, M. C. 1981. *Soil conservation measures for steep orchards in Taiwan* (in English). In Proceedings, South-East Asian Regional Symposium on Problems of Soil Erosion and Sedimentation. Asian Institute of Technology, Bangkok, Thailand.
6. Mountain Agricultural Resources Development Bureau. 1971-1986. *Statistics of mechanical operation in slopeland conservation and use* (in Chinese). Taipei, Taiwan.
7. Mountain Agricultural Resources Development Bureau. 1977-1986. *Statistics of operating costs in slopeland mechanical operation* (in Chinese). Taipei, Taiwan.
8. Mountain Agricultural Resources Development Bureau. 1983. *Taiwan slopeland resources investigation report* (in Chinese). Taipei, Taiwan.
9. Neumeier, K. 1970. *Cross-country vehicle with automatic inclination compensation.* Journal of Terramechanics 7(1): 9-17.
10. Ruhling, W. 1980. *Schlepper fur Weinbau-steillagen, Der Deutsche Weinbau* (in German). No. 112. Organ des Deutschen Weinbauverbans, Weisbaden, West Germany. pp. 522-528.
11. Sano, F. 1985. *Study on mechanized construction works for farmland development* (in Japanese). Journal of Mechanization of Agro-Civil Engineering Practices 16(1): 2-28.
12. Tanabe, H. 1988. *Farming mechanization in slopeland* (in Japanese). Shimane University, Shimane, Japan. 116 pp.
13. Tu, P. Y. 1981. *Development of slopeland mechanization in west Europe* (in Chinese). Journal of Chinese Society Agricultural Engineers 27(2): 54-58.
14. Tu, P. Y. 1983. *Development of slopeland machinery in Japan* (in Chinese). Journal Chinese Society Agricultural Engineers 29(4): 59-67.
15. Tu, P. Y. 1985. *Mechanical operation techniques for slopeland shaping* (in Chinese). Journal Chinese Society Agricultural Engineers 30(4): 35-39.
16. Tu, P. Y. 1986. *Improvement and development of slopeland machinery in Taiwan* (in English). In Korea-China Bilateral Symposium on Reclamation and Soil Conservation of Sloping Farmland. Rural Development Administration, Suweon, Republic of Korea. pp. 167-186.
17. Wu, S. L., C. E. Kan, B. S. Yu, and F. M. Wu. 1982. *Observation on the performance of construction machines in slopeland development and economic analysis* (in Chinese). Taiwan University Agriculture Engineering Department and Mountain Agricultural Resources Development Bureau, Taipei, Taiwan. 112 pp.

WUSHEH WATERSHED MANAGEMENT

YUAN-LIN LIN

Many watershed management programs have been implemented in Taiwan during the past decades. Some programs have improved land productivity and ameliorated sedimentation of reservoirs. The Wusheh watershed management program was the first of these successful programs. The experience of the Wusheh watershed management may provide an opportunity to improve future watershed management planning.

Description of Wusheh Watershed Management

The Wusheh Reservoir was completed in 1959. Its main structure is a curved, gravity-type concrete dam 114 meters in height and 205 meters in width. The storage capacity is 145 million cubic meters, and the effective storage is 127 million cubic meters.

The Wusheh Reservoir is located on Wusheh Creek, the headwater of the Muddy River in central Taiwan (Figure 1). Because it is upstream of the Sun-Moon Lake Reservoir and its Takuan, Chukung power plants, Takuan 2 pumped-storage plant, and Minhu pumped-storage project, the storage of the Wusheh Reservoir has been used by the Wusheh power plant and the Sun-Moon Lake plants. This storage also provides irrigation for paddy and cane fields in the downstream area (*3*).

The Wusheh watershed has been inhabited by aborigine tribesmen who have been accustomed to shifting cultivation and forest burning practices. These practices have caused several problems in the watershed. Because of steep topography, loose geologic formation, earthquakes, and frequent

270

typhoons, soil erosion and landslides have been severe in this area. The initial effort of watershed management was to reduce sediment outflow and thus increase the lifespan of the reservoir.

Before the construction of the Wusheh Reservoir, a land use survey of this area was carried out by the Taiwan Power Company, in 1953. The purpose of the survey was to determine if any conservation practices were needed. This survey was designed to investigate important land use conditions, such as slope, vegetal cover, erosion, soil texture, soil depth, and parent material.

As a result of this survey, the Wusheh watershed management planning was proposed. According to this planning, the Wusheh watershed station was established by the Taiwan Power Company in early 1954. This station was the first of its kind to conduct watershed management in Taiwan.

The Wusheh watershed management program includes watershed protection, training and extension, soil conservation, mountain agricultural improvement, reforestation and nursery, landslide and gully control, and road-slope stabilization. This planning program is long-term. The Taiwan Power Company has been very fortunate to have financial and technical support from other sources during the past decades. This program has im-

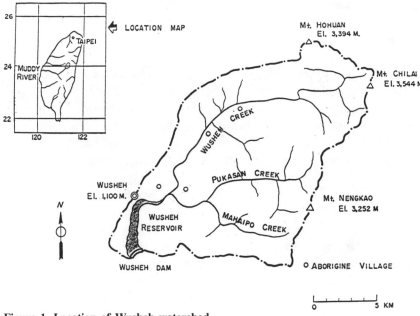

Figure 1. Location of Wusheh watershed.

proved land productivity in the Wusheh watershed and increased the life span of the Wusheh Reservoir.

Watershed Management Problems

The Wusheh watershed encompasses 20,483 hectares. About one-sixth of this area is part of the Aborigine Reservation, where shifting cultivation has prevailed. Shifting cultivation is a land use method in which people with primitive hoes cultivate steep slopes after they burn trees, slash, or grasses. This cultivation shifts from place to place every 2 or 3 years.

Shifting cultivation has caused several problems in this watershed. The aborigine farmers always plant crops on steep slopes. In some cases, the cultivated land is as steep as 35° (70 percent). The preference of people for steep slopes is due to the following factors:

• The severe alpine winters with fairly predictable killing frosts often damage winter crops (i.e., millet, sweet potatoes) if planted on flatter slopes.

• The movement of warmer air currents upslope during the night and overhanging trees that shed frosts are two of the factors in favor of cultivating crops on steep slopes.

• The farming tools usually have short handles, often less than 15 to 30 centimeters in length, so they are more difficult to use on flatter slopes.

• For many generations, the aborigines have been accustomed to upright farming work only.

• The crops need good drainage and loose soil mass, which are always available on steep slopes.

The cultivation of steep slopes has caused soil erosion and sedimentation. Also, the burning of trees, slash, or grass at times causes forest fires.

Maintenance of the Aborigine Reservation is necessary for social and political reasons. The aborigines cannot compete with outside, industrious farmers in producing their crops. Also, there is no other place available for their resettlement. Therefore, there is a need to maintain the reservation and to improve land use methods and farming techniques (*1*).

Land Use Classification and Conservation Needs

According to inventory data from the 1953 survey, the Wusheh watershed was classified into four categories (Table 1). Each class prescribes conservation practice requirements for each range of land use capability.

This classification is necessary for suggesting land use methods and conservation measures in Wusheh watershed management planning. The criteria for this classification are slope, vegetal cover, erosion, parent material, soil depth, and soil texture. Using these criteria, the Wusheh watershed was divided into a relatively stable area, intermediate area, unstable area, and very unstable area (Table 2).

An area is said to be relatively stable if the slopes are gentle, under good vegetal cover, without any perceptible signs of active erosion or erosion features, on very resistant parent rocks, and with deep topsoils. This class requires minor conservation practices. The areas with good forest cover and tall grasses in this watershed are included in this class.

The area classified as intermediate has the following characteristics: 10 percent to 25 percent slope, short grass and/or scattered tree cover, severe surface removal, weathered sandstone with fairly disintegrable or fairly resistant old terrace materials, 0.5 to 1.0 meters of soil depth, and heavy or loamy texture. Minor conservation treatments are needed for this class.

The unstable class represents the group of areas with 25 percent to 70 percent slope, under bushy and scattered trees and/or abandoned for cultivation, with soil depth of 0.25 meter to 0.5 meter and severely eroded, with very highly disintegrable parent rocks. It includes 201.2 hectares of once-cultivated but abandoned area, 26.8 hectares of unclassified area, 1,508.4

Table 1. Land use classification in Wusheh watershed management planning.

Criterion	Relatively Stable	Intermediate	Unstable	Very Unstable
Slope*	S1	S2	S3, S4	S5, S6
Cover†	C1, C3	C4	C5, C7, C8	C6, C9, C10
Erosion‡	E1, E2	E3	E4	E5, E6
Parent material§	P1A, P2A	P1B	P1C, P2B, P3B P4B, P6A, P6B	P2C, P3C, P4C P6C, P5B, P5C
Soil texture#	-	St1, St2	St3	St4
Soil depth‖	Sd1	Sd2	Sd3	Sd4
Conservation treatments needed	few	minor	major	heavy

*S1, less than 10 percent; S2, 10-25 percent; S3, 25-45 percent; S4, 45-70 percent; S5, 70-100 percent; and S6, greater than 100 percent.

†C1, good forest cover; C2, good grass cover; C3, grasses higher than 1.5 meter; C4, grasses shorter than 1.5 meter; C5, bushy with scattered trees; C6, bare ground-no vegetal cover; C7, shifting farms abandoned for more than 3 years; C8, shifting farms abandoned for less than 3 years; C9, hillside area newly burnt; and C10, under active cultivation.

‡E1, no or slight removal; E2, moderate removal; E3, severe removal; E4, very severe removal; E5, slip erosion; E6, slumping bank cutting or landslide.

§P1, sandstone; P2, platy slate; P3, phyllitic slate; P4, alluvial terrace; P5, alluvial fan; P6, talus; A, not easily disintegrable; B, intermediate; C, easily disintegrable.

#St1, clayey or heavy textured; St2, loamy textured; St3, sandy or light textured; St4, stoney gravelly or skeletal soil.

‖Sd1, greater than 1.0 meter; Sd2, 0.5-1.10 meter; Sd3, 0.25-0.5 meter; Sd4, less than 0.25 meter.

Table 2. Land use pattern in Wusheh watershed.

Class	Area (ha)
Relatively stable	11,861.9
Intermediate	1,073.6
Unstable	4,495.5
Very unstable	3,052.4
Total	20,483.5

Table 3. Land use change between 1953 and 1963, in hectares.

	1953	1963	Change
Forest area	14,099.1	15,008.5*	+ 909.4
Grass area	4,205.3	3,019.0	−1,186.3
Cultivated area	856.4	740.5†	− 115.9
Denuded area	1,046.2	1,193.0‡	+ 146.8
Others	276.4	522.5§	+ 246.0
Total	20,483.5	20,483.5	0.0

*Including natural forest, jungle, tree, and bamboo plantations.

†Including 200.5 hectares of area treated with conservation practices, such as bench terraces, hillside ditches, cover crops, drop structures, and grass waterways, and 540 hectares of area to be treated.

‡Including 294 hectares of cutover area, 106 hectares of plantable area, 782 hectares of
unplantable area, and 31 hectares of landslide area.

§Including 67 hectares of orchard farming, 24.5 hectares of paddy field, 63 hectares of
pasture, 50 hectares of urban area, and 318 hectares of water surface and reservoir area.

hectares of area thinly covered by short grass, 2,044.8 hectares of area under
bushy and scattered trees, and 714.4 hectares of area under various covers.
Some major conservation treatments are needed.

The very unstable class area is characterized by steep slopes, above 70
percent or 35°, denuded, with burnt or cultivated surface; active or inac-
tive slip erosion; weak parent rocks of phyllitic slate; consolidated platy
slate, but easily disintegrable, unconsolidated alluvial terraces, riverwash,
or talus deposites; and shallow skeletal soil less than 25 centimeters in depth.
This class consists of 1,012.5 hectares of area with active slip erosion, 1,183.5
hectares of denuded area, and 856.4 hectares of steep slope area under active cultivation. This class requires heavy conservation treatments (1).

Past Land Use Changes

The factors that affected past land use changes include:

• Tree plantation and natural regeneration in the burnt area and cultivated
area increased the amount of forest area. However, hardwood area has been
converted to farming area.

Table 4. Sediment yields from the Wusheh watershed, 1957 to 1985.

Period	Average Annual Sediment Yield (million m³/yr)	Average Soil Loss in Depth (mm/yr)
1957-1959	2.22	10.8
1959-1961	2.04	10.0
1961-1964	0.15	0.7
1964-1966	1.25	6.1
1966-1969	1.49	7.3
1969-1975	0.75	3.4
1975-1985	1.38	6.3
1964-1985	1.22	5.9

- Tree plantation has been successfully developed on the grass area by the Taiwan Forest Bureau. Also, some of the the grass area has been converted to orchard farming, pasture, and reservoir area.
- Total cultivated area decreased by 13.4 percent between 1953 and 1963, while population increased by 27 percent. In order to increase total income, people tended to increase orchard farming area.
- Expansion of the denuded area was an indication of hardwood and softwood removal from the forest area. The denuded area includes plantable and unplantable areas. The plantable area is the steep slope area abandoned from shifting cultivation. The unplantable area consists of roads and landslide areas.
- Expansion of the other area is primarily due to completion of the Wusheh reservoir.

Present Land Use Condition

Since the 1963 survey, more and more tea plantations have been developed in this watershed. This is due to strong demand for tea products in the market in past years. The tea plantations in this area always yield high-quality tea crops, owing to its specific climate and topography. The advantage of local tea plantation has attracted more people to move into this watershed and to convert forest and orchard areas into tea plantations. The tea plantations usually need more extensive conservation treatments to maintain productivity.

Sedimentation

One of the efforts in the Wusheh watershed management is to ameliorate sedimentation of the Wusheh Reservoir. In order to obtain the annual sediment yield from the Wusheh watershed, the Taiwan Power Company has been conducting field surveys since 1956. Table 4 shows this sediment yield data for the Wusheh Reservoir (2).

The period from 1959 to 1961 yielded the highest sediment amount because of the construction of the east-west cross-island highway. This construction induced more sheet and gully erosion and landslides. Concurrently, several typhoons, with high rainfall intensity, passed through this area and caused more erosion.

The period from 1962 to 1964 yielded the smallest amount of sediment because the Wusheh watershed had a long, dry period, and the water storage in the reservoir was lowered to below its dead storage.

At the same time, Sun-Moon Lake needed water, so the reservoir had to open its gate. This operation caused part of the sediment in the reservoir to be transported downstream. Under such conditions the sediment amount obtained did not reflect the actual sediment yield.

From 1964 to 1985, the average annual sediment yield was 1.22×10^6 cubic meters, an average annual soil loss, in depth, of about 6 millimeters.

Conclusions

The Wusheh watershed management program was the first of its kind in Taiwan. It has been successfully implemented over several decades. The initial effort was to reduce the sedimentation rate in the Wusheh reservoir. Through the cooperation of the Taiwan Forest Bureau, Taiwan Forest Research Institute, and the Joint Commission on Rural Reconstruction, the Taiwan Power Company also completed an extensive conservation program. Therefore, the Wusheh watershed management program not only reduced the sedimentation rate for the reservoir but also increased land productivity and the living standard for the aborigines.

Traditionally, watershed management planning considered land use condition and associated conservation treatments. However, economic and social factors may play an important role in the implementation of those programs. These factors must be included in future watershed management planning.

REFERENCES

1. Lin, Ed Y. 1964. *Taiwan Power Company Wusheh Reservoir watershed management.* In Proceedings, The Sixth Regional Conference on Water Resources Development. Economic Commission for Asia and the Far East, Bangkok, Thailand.
2. Lin, Y. L. 1968. *Studies on the past and future management of Wusheh Reservoir watershed.* Journal of Chinese Forestry 1(3): 90-139.
3. Lin, Y. L. 1968. *Watershed management in connection with hydro power in Taiwan.* Journal of Agricultural Association of China, New Series 64: 66-78.

GULLY EROSION CONTROL IN EASTERN TAIWAN

HUEI-LONG WU

The Coastal Range in eastern Taiwan covers a total area of 116,000 hectares. It is the most important agricultural resource in this area. Unfavorable geological conditions and poor soil physical properties tend to cause serious erosion and gully formation during heavy rainfall. In addition, cultivation without proper conservation practices has accelerated soil erosion by water. Rills and gullies are widespread on the hillslopes (16). To reduce erosion and sediment damage and to promote proper land use in these areas, a pilot study to search for appropriate control measures on a small agricultural watershed has been carried out since 1975 by the Fifth Soil Conservation Work Station of the Mountain Agricultural Resources Development Bureau (MARDB) at Fukang.

The watershed is located west of Fukang Air Base, 9 kilometers northeast of Taitung City, in eastern Taiwan. The area covers 420 hectares. Most of the slopeland in the watershed is owned by the Taiwan Sugar Corporation (TSC) and is used as sugarcane plantation. About 120 hectares belong to local farmers who grow sugarcane on contract with TSC and some fruit trees. Elevation rises from 20 meters to 200 meters, and the average slope is about 26 percent.

Soils in this area are mainly shallow, gray, silty clay loams, predominantly formed from highly weathered soft mudstone. They are very erodible and require special treatments for soil conservation. The pH averages 6.5, and the organic matter content averages 1.5 percent (11).

The average annual rainfall for this area is 1,793 millimeters. About 83 percent of the rainfall occurs in summer, especially during the typhoon period from June to September. The rainfall erosivity index in the study

277

area is about 600, based on the rainfall factor of the universal soil loss equation. The average annual temperature is 23 °C.

In past decades, part of the slopeland was used to grow sugarcane and other crops, resulting in severe soil erosion. The tracks of ox-carts and trucks for transporting sugarcane concentrated the runoff and formed gullies all over the fields because no drainage systems were provided. Six huge gullies running down to the Fukang Air Base brought tremendous amounts of sediment after each heavy storm or typhoon. The flooding and siltation damaged the base installations and obstructed regular operations. Typhoons Nana in 1973 and Bess in 1974 produced the most serious damage (10).

Erosion Control Measures

To prevent further flooding and siltation damage to the air base and to ensure the proper use and conservation of the slopeland adjacent to the base, control measures were integrated with the land use of sloping farms. The major treatment consists of conservation practices on cultivated land, waterway stabilization, and gully treatments.

Conservation Treatments on Cultivated Land. The major soil conservation practices used on cultivated land were hillside ditches, which are aimed at reducing slope length, checking and diverting runoff, and serving as paths for small farm machines, thereby avoiding sheet and rill erosion formed by ox-carts and trucks on the hillslopes. The upper and lower sideslopes and the bottom of the ditch were planted separately with bahiagrass (*Paspalum notatum*) (1, 18) and bermudagrass (*Cynodon dactylon*) for stabilizing the sideslopes and checking the soil from moving downward. The vertical interval (VI) of the ditch was determined by the formula adopted from the *Soil Conservation Handbook of Taiwan (1)*:

$$VI = \frac{S + 6}{10}$$

where S is the slope of the land in percent.

In orchards, the interval between ditches has been adjusted in accordance with orchard patterns and requirements of machinery operations. They should be spaced to allow for two to three rows of fruit trees. In addition, cover crop and mulching should be used between fruit trees for two purposes: covering the entire area and establishing strips of grass at intervals between fruit tree rows. Bahiagrass was also recommended. With grass cover and mulching, weeding and herbicides are not necessary, thus eliminating soil contamination. All these make zero tillage possible.

Because the soils are highly erodible, the outlets of hillside ditches are prone to scouring and should be protected. Two treatments are highly recommended:

1. The bottom of the outlet should be level instead of with reverse slope, and the opening should be enlarged outward into a trumpet shape for dispersing water flow. On the slope bottom, bundles of straw should be staked in rows and densely planted with bahiagrass between.

2. With frequent water flow outlets, a pebble-lined ditch or prefabricated chute should be used. Both sides of the ditch should be planted with bahiagrass, forming double cross-sections, which also serve as a farm path.

Waterway Stabilization. Grass waterway is the major form of drainage applied to cultivated land in this area. They are constructed using bulldozers to shape and to smooth the small gullies into a proper cross-section, on which bahiagrass is closely and horizontally planted at an interval of 15 centimeters (*17*). Simple drop spillways are installed to dissipate the energy of flowing water when necessary (*12*). Within 3 months, a dense vigorous cover is established to control erosion.

Rock-laid ditches are built where grass cannot grow normally under the conditions of inadequate sunshine and poor soil. Dips at the juncture of the grass waterways and hillside ditches or link roads allow drainage and the passage of farm machines. They are shallow, wide, and parabolic in shape. Bahiagrass is also densely planted between brick or cobblestone, or the ditches are concrete paved.

Gully Control. In the study area, small and medium gullies prevail over the field. They are still developing progressively and need to be controlled. There were no previous studies conducted to find out which type of control could be adopted for such geologic and soil conditions in this area. Therefore, observations were made on various types of check dams in combination with grass covers on the banks of gullies. The cheapest way to control gullies is to prevent their formation. The small gullies on sloping farms can be smoothed out by a bulldozer when building hillside ditches or by using minimum shaping and some manual labor for constructing grass waterways.

Simple check dams, such as brush dams, sand-bag dams, log-crib dams, loose-stone dams, single-fence dams (*2, 3*), sausage dams, square-box gabion dams, and brick dams, were constructed at suitable locations to stabilize the channel bed and retain eroded soil and other materials. Both banks of the channel were planted with bahiagrass for stabilization, the so-called "systematical treatment" (8). A total of 127 check dams were installed.

There are six large gullies in this study area. Their channel bottoms downstream were previously used as farm paths for transporting farm products using ox-carts. Sediment prevails along these gullies. If check dams were constructed across the gully channels, the paths would be blocked. Thus, stream regulation work, including dikes and sills behind a higher concrete check dam, were installed to protect the channel banks and to stabilize the channel bottom against longitudinal erosion. As a result, the channel beds not only became a well-protected farm road but also provided good gully erosion control.

Results and Recommendations

Project Benefits. Before implementation of erosion control measures, the drainage ditches of the air base were always clogged with a large amount of debris carried in by runoff through enlarged gullies. The consequence was flooding and siltation over the entire area, resulting in great damage (15).

Three years after implementation of erosion control measures, the amount of sediment retained upstream exceeded 38,000 cubic meters. This would cost about NT$2,000,000 to be removed from the base. The total expenditure of the project amounts to NT$9,880,000. The indirect benefits resulting from protection of the base installations and equipment are numerous. The economic analysis of this study indicates a benefit-cost ratio of 1.7 (4).

Conservation Practices on Cultivated Land. Orchard hillside ditches combined with bahiagrass cover and mulching are not only effective in soil and water conservation but can also save considerable labor cost compared with conventional cultivation and weeding practices. This is the key to conservation farming and hillslope landscapes.

The conservation practices recommended for major crops on slopelands in the Coastal Range of eastern Taiwan are listed in table 1 (9).

Waterway Stabilization. Grass waterways established by close planting of bahiagrass may be the best type of drainageway for the soft mudstone region. Small gullies can also be reshaped and planted with grass to establish the waterways. The ease and simplicity of the treatment gives the local farmers confidence to apply the technique to solve the drainage problems in the Coastal Range of eastern Taiwan.

In the past, brick-laid and stone-laid flumes were mainly used for drainage in this area (5, 6). Unfortunately, the clay-rich soils crack during the dry seasons. Planting grass in the waterways not only reduces the drainage cost

Table 1. Recommendations for soil conservation practices for major crops.

Crops	HD* CCP	HD* CCP + SM	OHD* C & M	Bench Terrace
Mangoes			XX†	X
Citrus			XX	X
Mulberry			XX	X
Pineapple		XX		
Sugarcane	XX			
Row crops				XX

*HD, hillside ditch; OHD, orchard hillside ditch; CCP, contour and close planting; SM, stubble mulching; and C & M, cover cropping and mulching.
†XX, very suitable; X, suitable.

Table 2. Cost comparison per hectare of various soil conservation practices.

Soil Conservation Practices	Cost (U.S. Dollars)*	Index (%)
Hillside ditch using bulldozer	199	100
Hillside ditch using manpower	1,093	549
Orchard hillside ditch using bulldozer	259	130
Orchard hillside ditch using manpower	1,420	713
Bench terrace using bulldozer	1,225	616
Bench terrace using manpower	5,143	2,584
Grassed hillside ditch	339	170
Cover crop using bahiagrass	2,296	1,154

*US$1.00 was equivalent to NT$28.00 in 1989.

Table 3. Cost comparison of various types of waterway stabilization works.

Type of Waterway	Unit	Cost (U.S. Dollars)*	Index (%)
Grass	m	7.5	100
Grass-covered concrete	m	16.1	214
Prefabricated chute	m	17.1	229
Concrete ditch	m	19.6	262
Rock-laid ditch	m	17.5	233
Brick ditch	m	18.2	243
Brick drop	unit	42.9	571
Masonry drop	unit	39.3	524

*US$1.00 was equivalent to NT$28.00 in 1989.

Table 4. Cost comparison of building various types of check dams (effective height of the dam is 1.2 meters).

Type of Dam	Cost (U.S. Dollars)*	Index (%)
Concrete gravity	7,423	100
Brick	3,822	51
Sausage gabion	2,142	29
Single-fence	794	11
Loose-stone	685	9
Sand-bag	593	8

*US$1.00 was equivalent to NT$28.00 in 1989.

but also gives the farm a green appearance.

The parabolic cross-section layout or dips at the juncture of the hillside ditch outlet allows easy farm machinery access and can also replace culverts, thus saving considerable money.

Gully Control. The performance of bahiagrass on gully banks to protect the side slopes, in combination with inexpensive check dams to stabilize the gully bottom, is very satisfactory. This practice is much better and more economical than the conventional method of building concrete structures. In addition, a total of 5 hectares of eroded and abandoned land has been reclaimed for farming.

The porous lower check dams, including sausage-gabion dams, loose-stone dams, single-fence dams, and sand-bag dams, have, with the exception of the square-box gabion dam, proved economical and effective for controlling the gullies. Vegetation is also being established in the study region, especially in the area without coarse gravel.

To prevent small gullies from further development, hillside ditching to divert runoff and filling and shaping to establish grass waterways have proved cost-effective.

Construction Cost. There are considerable differences between hillside ditches and bench terraces in the volume of soil to be moved. Assuming that the terraces and ditches have the same width of 2 meters, the soil volume ratio of terrace to ditch varies from 3.9 to 10.5 (*7*). Based on farm records, the earth-moving rates for a John Deere 450 bulldozer used to build terraces versus hillside ditches was 38.8 hours per hectare and 6.3 hours per hectare, respectively. Using traditional manpower of the past, it would take 240 man-days and 51 man-days, respectively, to construct 1 hectare (*9, 13, 14*). The construction costs of various soil conservation practices are listed in table 2.

Waterway Stabilization. The cost comparison of various types of waterways are listed in table 3.

Gully Control. The costs of building various types of check dams are listed in table 4.

In the first 3 years of the project, soil loss has been greatly reduced and gully erosion largely controlled. Grass waterways have been widely used on hillslope farms to the satisfaction of the farmers. Small or medium gullies treated by revegetation and in combination with simple and cheap structures, such as sand-bag dams, loose-rock dams, and sausage-gabion dams, have proved effective. In addition, nearly 11 hectares of badly eroded lands were restored.

REFERENCES

1. Chinese Soil and Water Conservation Society. 1987. *Soil conservation handbook.* Taipei, Taiwan. 121 pp.
2. Heede, B. H. 1966. *Design, construction and cost of rock check dams.* Forest Service Research Paper RM-20. Rocky Mountain Forest and Range Experiment Station, U.S. Department of Agriculture, Fort Collins, Colorado.
3. Heede, B. H. 1977. *Case study of a watershed rehabilitation project: Alkali Creek, Colorado.* Forest Service Research Paper RM-189. Rocky Mountain Forest and Range Experiment Station, U.S. Department of Agriculture, Fort Collins, Colorado.
4. Ho, C. W. 1983. *Effectiveness evaluation of systematic gully control in Taiwan* (in Chinese). National Chung Hsing University, Taichung, Taiwan.
5. Ho, C. W., C. H. Tuan, and J. C. Liou. 1978. *Experimental analysis on gully control and drainage methods in Taiwan* (in Chinese). Journal of Chinese Soil and Water Conservation 9(1): 115-150.
6. Ho, C. W., C. H. Tuan, J. C. Liou, and J. B. Lin. 1977. *A preliminary investigation of gully control and drainage methods in Taiwan* (in Chinese). Journal of Chinese Soil and Water Conservation 8(1): 66-99.
7. Kan, C. E., and M. F. Wu. 1980. *Observation of machinery operations for slopeland conservation and use in Taiwan* (in Chinese). Journal of Chinese Agricultural Engineering 26(2): 44-65.
8. Liao, M. C. 1980. *Soil conservation in Taiwan: Today and tomorrow* (in Chinese). Journal of Chinese Soil and Water Conservation 11(1): 1-8.
9. Liao, M. C., and H. L. Wu. 1987. *Soil conservation on steep lands in Taiwan.* Chinese Soil and Water Conservation Society, Taipei, Taiwan. 112 pp.
10. Mountain Agricultural Resources Development Bureau, Fifth Soil Conservation Work Station. 1979. *Slopeland conservation and utilization project in Fukang* (in Chinese). Taitung, Taiwan. 8 pp.
11. Mountain Agricultural Resources Development Bureau. 1984. *Soil survey in Hwalian and Taitung counties* (in Chinese). Taichung, Taiwan. 241 pp.
12. Wang, H. T., H. M. Chang, M. C. Lee, and J. Chen. 1979. *Observation of grassed waterway* (in Chinese). Journal of Chinese Soil and Water Conservation 10(2): 53-66.
13. Wu, C.K.H. 1971. *Economic evaluation of integrated soil conservation and land use program* (in Chinese). Research Institute of Agricultural Economics, National Chung Hsing University, Taichung, Taiwan.
14. Wu, C.K.H. 1976. *Economics of slopeland utilization in Taiwan* (in Chinese). Journal of Agricultural Economics, National Chung Hsing University, Taichung, Taiwan. 20: 158-176.
15. Wu, H. L. 1980. *A successful soil conservation project in Fukang area.* Chinese Soil and Water Conservation Society, Taipei, Taiwan. 9 pp.
16. Wu, H. L. 1984. *Control of gully erosion in the coastal Range of eastern Taiwan: The Fukang experience.* In Proceedings, Sino-Korea Bilateral Symposium on Soil and Water Conservation of Sloped Farm Land. National Taiwan University, Taipei. pp. 127-131.
17. Wu, H. L. 1984. *Field operation of soil conservation practices* (in Chinese). Department of Agriculture and Forestry, Taichung, Taiwan.
18. Wu, H. L. 1985. *Soil conservation plant: Bahiagrass* (in Chinese). Mountain Agricultural Resources Development Bureau, Taichung, Taiwan. 40 pp.

SOIL CONSERVATION AND THE USE OF HILLSLOPES IN THE SHIHMEN WATERSHED, TAIWAN

YU-YUNG CHU

The Shihmen Reservoir watershed includes the counties of Taoyuan, Hsin-Chu, and I-Lan, 54 kilometers from Taipei, Taiwan. Total area of the watershed is 76,340 hectares. It has 2,527 hectares of cropland, 69,723 hectares of forestland, and 4,093 hectares of other land (*1, 2*).

At present, the use of hillslopes requires extensive cultivation, and farmer's income is very low. Because of population pressure and the need for sustained production, a suitable farming system is imperative when these hillslopes are developed.

Major Soil and Water Conservation Works

Extension of Soil Conservation on Cultivated Land. The principal soil conservation treatments on cultivated slopeland are bench terraces (Figure 1), hillside ditches, individual basins, orchard terraces, stone barriers, hexagons, drainage systems, cover cropping, mulching, etc. To reduce erosion of surface soil, fertilizers, seeds, fruit trees, and food are subsidized. Cash or low-interest loans, labor, machine services, etc., are provided as incentives to small farmers for carrying out the work (*3*).

Reforestation and Forest Protection. The Shihmen Watershed Administration, in cooperation with the concerned agencies, provides farmers with free tree seedlings for planting on their own land and supervised forest cutting in the watershed (Figure 2).

Highway Side-Slope Stabilization. Road construction in mountain regions accelerates soil erosion because, during and after construction, large areas of cut-and-fill slopes are exposed. Construction often causes landslides also. Vegetation (staking and wattling) or retaining walls are generally used for highway or mountain road side-slope stabilization (Figure 3).

Landslide Treatment. According to a recent survey, the reservoir has 976 landslide sites within its watershed area, and sedimentation is a serious problem. Hence, the administration has been making efforts to promote watershed management work to reduce sediment.

Landslides occur due to the weakness of parent rocks, especially during new highway and mountain road construction during the typhoon season (from June to September). Various treatments are being adopted, such as retaining walls, buttresses, piling, and similar methods (Figure 4).

Stream Erosion Control. Because of natural conditions in Taiwan, streams are generally short and flow is rapid. Consequently, stream erosion control within the upper watershed is the most effective way to reduce the sedi-

Figure 1. Bench terraces and bahiagrass on risers.

Figure 2. Reforestation in the Shihmen Reservoir watershed.

Figure 3. Road side-slope stabilization (vegetation and retaining wall).

Figure 4. Landslide treatment.

Figure 5. Stream erosion control.

Figure 6. Check dam on main stream.

Figure 7. Check dam construction in tributaries.

ment content of the flow. The most common measure used in this watershed is the construction of check dams. Other types of stream erosion control structures include submerged dams, submerged sills, bank protection dikes, and stream regulation works. Usually, a series of step-like check dams is needed for effective stream erosion control within a critical area (Figure 5).

Check Dam Construction. In order to reduce the silt that washes down to the reservoir during the rainy season, check dams were built on the main streams and tributaries. There are three check dams on the main stream at present: (1) Yi-Hsin check dam, storage capacity 8.2 million cubic meters; (2) Pa-Lin check dam, storage capacity 10.4 million cubic meters; and (3) Yung-Hwa check dam, storage capacity 12.4 million cubic meters (Figure 6).

Ninety-one small check dams were built in tributaries for preventing sediment and debris from flowing into the reservoir (Figure 7).

Gully Control. A gully on slopeland was selected for treatment to prevent growth of the gully (Figure 8).

Aerial Survey. To determine changes in landslide areas, cover crop use on the slopeland and land use in the watershed, as well as for use in planning, an aerial survey has been made every 3 to 5 years.

Extension Education. Most of the farmers in the watershed are aborigines. They lack knowledge of soil and water conservation and agricultural techniques. The administration held farmer training classes, field days, home visits, and demonstration plots to illustrate how to practice soil conservation and increase agricultural production, as well as to help farmers in marketing, etc. (Figure 9).

Natural Environment

Most soils in the Shihmen Reservoir watershed are red or yellow and gravelly. Average annual rainfall is more than 2,000 millimeters. The heavy rainfall is in May to September, during the typhoon season. Average annual temperature is about 20 °C. The minimum temperature is below 14 °C in January. The maximum temperature is about 27 °C in July and August.

Total area of cultivated land in the Shihmen Reservoir watershed is 2,527 hectares. This includes 1,263.18 hectares of orchards, 614.13 hectares of paddy fields, 505.64 hectares of upland crops, 137.73 hectares of tea farms, and 3 hectares of nursery.

Figure 8. Gully control.

Figure 9. Extension education (demonstration plot).

Figure 10. Tea plantation in the low altitude.

Figure 11. Fruit trees (pear) planted in the high altitude.

Present Cropping Systems

Most farmers in the watershed are engaged in small farming systems in the low altitudes. They grow rice (*Oryza sativa*), tea (Figure 10), sweet potatoes, oranges, etc. Fruit trees [pears (Figure 11), apples, and juicy peaches], bamboo, or pine (*Pinus spp.*) trees are grown in the high altitudes. Only rice and sweet potatoes produce two crops per year; the others are perennials. Continuous cultivation of slopes to only one crop not only depletes soil fertility but also creates soil erosion. New techniques must be introduced to small farmers, such as better crop rotations, multiple cropping, and cover cropping. These techniques benefit erosion control and fertility maintenance as well as crop production.

Future Prospects

Because of the increasing population and the limited area of arable land in Taiwan, farmers have begun to cultivate steep areas, causing serious erosion that menaces agricultural production and the stability of watersheds. Soil conservation and suitable farming systems must be adopted. The work that must be undertaken is summarized as follows:
  • Fruit trees planted on steep slopes must be established with soil con-

Figure 12. Diversified farming (crops, fishery, and duck raising).

servation works, such as hillside ditching, bench terracing, drainage systems, and cover cropping, bahiagrass (*Paspalpum notatum* Flücggs) or clover, for example (Figure 1).

• Paddy fields must be converted to vegetable or flower production. Due to overproduction, the income from rice is lower than from other crops. The government encourages farmers to grow vegetables, flowers, or upland crops instead of rice in the paddy fields.

• Orchid cultivation must be developed. There are many wild Chinese orchids, azaleas, and begonias in the watershed. These should be collected and propagated or used as crossing material to improve varieties.

• Mushroom culture must be developed. Low temperature and high humidity in the high altitudes make the watershed suitable for mushroom culture.

• Diversified (integrated) farming must be implemented. The altitude and climate of most areas in the Shihmen watershed are suitable for livestock and crop production. The farmers may plant grass on risers as pasture for livestock and poultry. In some areas of low altitude, farmers raise swine, goats, dairy cattle, rabbits, and deer.

Conclusion

The Shihmen watershed has 2,527 hectares of cropland and 69,723 hectares of forestland. Because of fertile soils, plenty of rainfall, and optimum temperature, there is the potential to develop agriculture and forestry. However, the farmers grow only single crops, such as tea, rice, sweet potatoes, oranges, and bamboo, in areas of low altitude and fruit trees (pear, peaches, and plum), bamboo, and pine trees in areas of high altitude. For the future, the use of hillslopes for diversified (integrated) farming is being emphasized in this watershed (Figure 12), converting paddy fields from rice to vegetables or flowers and developing mushroom production as well as orchid and other horticultural production, all in order to increase farmers' income.

REFERENCES

1. Chu, Y. Y. 1987. *An introduction to soil and water conservation in Shihmen Reservoir watershed*. Shihmen Reservoir Administration, Lung-Tang, Taiwan.
2. Chu, Y. Y. 1988. *Studies on farming systems in Shihmen watershed*. Taiwan Agriculture 24(4): 61-66.
3. Sheng, Ted C. 1986. *Watershed conservation*. Chinese Soil and Water Conservation Society, and Colorado State University, Fort Collins.

A TRANSPORTATION SYSTEM FOR HILLSLOPE CONSERVATION FARMING IN TAIWAN

CHIN-TEH HSIEH

The goals of conservation farming on hillslopes are to increase mechanization and to minimize labor cost. Therefore, the construction of farm roads is considered an important task in the development of conservation farming. Because of the steep topography and poor geological and climatic conditions, farm roads need to be carefully designed to include suitable soil and water conservation practices. This is necessary to provide uninterrupted transportation, along with very little soil loss.

Transportation System Design

A complete farm road system is essential to connect spaces between tree rows within the farm areas and to connect the major highways outside the farm (Figure 1). In addition to increasing farm mechanization, this road system can provide a means to transport farm materials and produce using various vehicular sizes, instead of relying solely on manual labor. Because of varying topography and farm size, the following combinations of transportation systems are commonly found in Taiwan:

Farming Path. The hillside ditch commonly found on slopelands is built in a broad-based "V" shape (Figure 2). The ditch is about 2 meters wide, with a gradient of about 1 percent. It provides passage for small machines and vehicles. The ditch spacing can be determined using the formula VI=(S + 6)/10, where VI is the vertical interval and S is the slope of the ground surface. Then, the ditch spacing, HI, is HI=(VI/S) x 100.

The base of the bench terraces constructed in the past was usually less than 3 to 5 meters wide. Spacing for vehicular passage was not considered by orchard farmers because machines were not commonly used at that time. After 6 or 7 years of growth, tree crops usually fill in the open space, preventing any machine use.

In order to enhance efficient management, the orchard terrace must be modified to allow convenient machinery access. This can be achieved by constructing an improved farming path using a small excavator (Figure 3). The farming path can be constructed on every other terrace, allowing close proximity to every row of fruit trees. The path is usually 1 to 1.5 meters wide, enough for a small machine to move in and out of the orchard farm while performing field operations.

Grass should be planted on the top and side slopes of the farming path to minimize soil erosion. When a farming path crosses a drainage ditch, a culvert should be constructed or a concrete bridge built over the ditch.

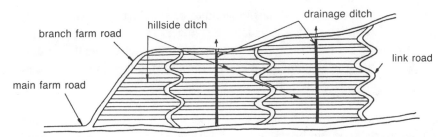

Figure 1. Plan of farm transportation system in hillslope conservation farming.

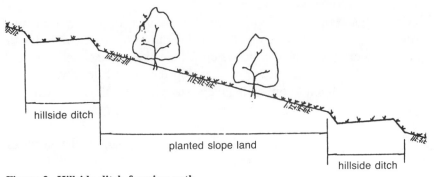

Figure 2. Hillside ditch farming path.

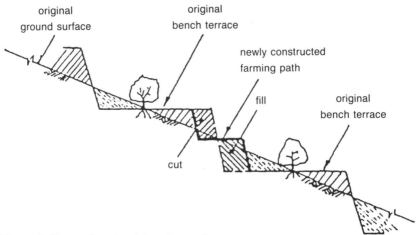

Figure 3. Terraced orchard farming path.

Link Road. A link road connects the farming path with the branch or main farm road. It is usually 2 to 3 meters wide and allows for the movement and operation of small farm machines or small trucks. Because each downsloping hillside ditch is usually 100 meters in length, the spacing of the link road between two down-sloping hillside ditches should be doubled (i.e., not longer than 200 meters). Because the farming path is constructed along the contour line, the link road should run up and down the prevailing slope for better connection and management. The longitudinal gradient of the link road should not be greater than 30 percent. The minimum curvature radius should be 5 meters. For steep-slope farms, the link roads should be angled or "Z"-shaped to reduce the slope gradient (Figure 1).

The location of link roads with respect to the drainage ditches is illustrated in figure 1. Excess water from hillside ditches and bench terraces should not drain toward the link roads. If this cannot be avoided, side ditches should be built to accommodate excess runoff.

Grass should be planted on link roads as soon as they have been constructed to prevent soil erosion. The road surface should be covered with graded gravels or concrete on steep slopes. Side ditches are desirable where excess runoff occurs. Curved or reverse-sloped road surfaces covered with concrete, in addition to protecting the surface of the link roads, can also enhance drainage. Adequate culvert drains should be provided.

Farm Road. A farm road connects link roads in the farm to the highways or village roads. It should be 4 to 5.5 meters wide, allowing for the passage of bigger trucks than can travel on link roads. The maximum vertical gradient should not exceed 15 percent. The minimum curvature radius should be about 10 meters. Density of the farm roads varies according to the local topography. In 1985, a survey of 11 developed locations indicated that the average density of farm roads was about 19 meters per hectare, whereas the expected target is about 29 meters per hectare.

Areas of slippage or potential landslides should be avoided when planning farm roads. A balance should be maintained between cut and fill. Concrete or stone-lined side ditches should be used on steep gradients and poorly structured or highly erodible sections of the farm road. When sediment from unstable upslopes fills the side ditches, L-shaped ditches should be used instead.

Where a drainage ditch crosses a farm road, culverts should be constructed at 150-meter intervals to alleviate the large quantity of runoff water from the side ditches. The culvert size should be enlarged 30 to 50 percent for heavy upstream sediment or litter load.

To prevent landslides, side slopes should not be too steep. The downhill side slopes of a farm road (fill) should be within 1:1.25 to 1:1.5 (height:base ratio); whereas the uphill side slopes (cut) should be within 1:0.5 to 1:1. The uphill side slope should be cut like a terrace if it exceeds 5 meters in height. For unstable side slopes, suitable grasses should be planted to provide soil erosion protection.

Conclusion

Although hillslopes are vulnerable to natural calamities, they are targeted for development because of Taiwan's high population pressure. In the planning and construction of the transportation system, it must be remembered that soil conservation is essential to the development and utilization of hillslopes.

REPORTS OF
DISCUSSION GROUPS

8

PLANNING AND STRATEGY

JAMES R. MEIMAN and TED C. SHENG

Three planning and strategy group
identified 18 different items of concern. Using the nine key factors identified by C. C. Koh and associates in their keynote speech, the group selected
four factors on which to concentrate: (1) government support, (2) integration, (3) incentives, and (4) local involvement. For each factor, Taiwan's
experience was discussed first. Then, the experiences of other countries
were compared. A summary of the key points on each of these four factors
is provided in the following paragraphs

Government Support

All members of the group agreed that firm and continuing support was
needed for a successful soil and water conservation program. This support should be provided in the form of financing and policymaking. The
group focused on how to obtain this support. Important approaches that
were identified include: linking conservation to the entire agricultural system;
working with groups, such as professional societies, nongovernmental
organizations, and the public at large; using all forms of media; briefings
and field demonstrations, especially for top officials; taking advantage of
disasters to bring attention to conservation problems; and linking conservation to productivity. All of these approaches assume that whatever programs are being undertaken are being conducted well. Starting small with
a well-planned and well-executed program is the best basis for future growth.

Agency and Program Integration

The base for an integrated approach is a unifying policy within and among the agencies involved. Joint planning must be carefully integrated both vertically, from agency head to farmer, and horizontally across agencies. A multifunctional approach should be used in planning, budgeting, executing, and monitoring. This can be accomplished by designating a lead agency, the agency with the most at stake in good land use results within a given watershed. Within this lead agency, interdisciplinary teams should be able to execute a set of core functions. Other functions can involve other agencies, but always under the mantle of the joint planning and monitoring concept.

Incentives

There was a wide diversity of experiences and opinions within the group concerning incentives. Among the various types of incentives, there was a general consensus that the most workable include: lowering the price of inputs, increasing the price of outputs, providing services, low-cost loans, and cost-sharing. The first two types of incentives are applicable to agricultural production in general. The other incentives have been widely used for conservation work. Although Taiwan has used cash incentives effectively, representatives from several countries reported bad experiences with the technique. Some preferred to emphasize the provision of services, especially those that would build local community organizations that could then draw on other available resources. Taiwan has used the provision of roads to link individual farms with markets as an incentive for conservation farming.

Local Involvement

Taiwan began with a collection of targeted baseline data on biophysical and socioeconomic conditions. Areas of 50 to 200 hectares were selected, and discussions of problems and solutions were initiated with small groups of farmers (10-20) and farmers' organizations. Promoting concentrated crop development and providing design and building materials for the link roads were powerful forces for bringing farmers together in joint planning. A training program for farmers was developed concurrently as planning progressed. The planning and strategy group agreed that this type of approach can be very successful in many different settings. Among the essential factors that should be included are baseline survey data, selection of target areas based on farmers' interest and productive potential, education of farmers and the general public about available programs, joint planning with farmers, involvement of local organizations and leaders, and use of competition and rewards.

Conclusions

In conclusion, the group recommends that planning and strategy be given greater emphasis in future meetings. Even these four factors could not be given the detailed level of consideration required. Moreover, there are many other elements of planning and strategy that we did not discuss. Among this latter group are such items as the management of integration at each of the various levels of government; the design and implementation of training and public education programs; and the application of a flexible and dynamic planning approach that emphasizes a learn-by-doing attitude, which encourages continual feedback and adjustment.

FARMING SYSTEMS
AND INFRASTRUCTURE

RAVI SANGAKKARA

Afarming system on hillslopes envisages the development of a sustainable unit that produces agricultural commodities chosen by the farmer, with judicious management of soil and water. In achieving this, the decisions of the farmer are very important because they involve the needs and welfare of the family.

The principles of developing viable hillslope farming systems involve the farmer, the land, and government policy. However, because the farmer ultimately puts all decisions into practice, his role and the factors that enhance his capacity to better farm his hillslope land are the main considerations. In some instances, national and regional goals and priorities may take preference over farmer requirements and choice.

Hillslope farming requires specialized knowledge of the systems and of socioeconomic factors involved. It is usually more difficult than farming less sloping land. In countries with limited forest reserves, these systems are established at the expense of forest cover. Poor management of the hillslopes leads to erosion, flooding, and environmental degradation. Hence, the government has a direct role in planning the policies of hillslope farming in a country. Good watershed management policies, such as those in Taiwan, are a prerequisite to sustainable hillslope farming.

Research and Extension

The primary factor required by farmers is guidance in principles of successful hillslope farming. This is achieved by a good extension network, the objective of which is to convince the farmer that the recommended guidelines will provide him with an economically viable, sustainable system. This can be achieved through discussions, demonstration plots, and visits by the extension worker.

Research is a prerequisite to a good extension program. The research program needs to identify farmer problems and to carry out on- and off-farm research projects. Farmer participation at the planning, implementation, and interpretation stages is essential.

To develop a good research program, the government should provide financial and institutional support. Collaborative research projects between institutions and development of long-term case studies and multidisciplinary programs should be initiated.

Research and extension activities should be enhanced by the establishment of farmer cooperatives (as is done in most developing countries), development of roads to markets, establishment of retail outlets, and availability of necessary inputs and required support services (e.g., facilities for repairs, etc.) at reasonable prices to the farmers. In addition, to prevent migration, schools, health units, social activities, and, in some countries, security need to be provided

Selection of Farming Systems

The opposite extremes of agriculture on hillslopes are national forests and clean, open farming. While national forests play an important role in maintaining the environment, they are not agriculturally productive and in most developing countries are considered as locking up useful land. The other extreme of clean, open farming on hillslopes is common in developing countries, but this land use is seldom suitable, owing to problems of erosion, loss of forest cover, and changes in the environment.

In this context, agriculture on hillslopes should combine the beneficial aspects of these two extremes. Programs of conservation farming and agroforestry are the most appropriate farming techniques for hillslopes, especially in the developing world where there is tremendous pressure for increased food production. In contrast, in the developed world, silvicultural systems can be used on the hillslopes, along with other perennial systems.

Whereas annual systems provide food requirements, the development of perennial crop systems, such as orchards, also help conserve the resources of the steeplands while producing a crop. The benefits of these systems are amply demonstrated in Taiwan.

Many farming systems have been recommended for hillslopes. However, the adoption of a system will depend primarily on the resources and infrastructure available. Hence, the decision to adopt a proven method, such as alley cropping, mixed systems, agroforestry techniques, or conservation farming, will depend on the situation at a given site, and guidelines must be specific enough to reflect this.

Incentives and Other Assistance

Subsidies provide assistance to the poorer farmers who generally farm hillslopes. These subsidies can take the form of inexpensive inputs and reasonable prices for products. Development of forest farming systems, where necessary, will also help in achieving the objective.

International organizations play a vital role in financing, policy planning, training, technical assistance, and research on agricultural and socioeconomic aspects. Workshops, such as this one, also can play a role in elucidating the principles of hillslope farming systems.

SOIL AND WATER
CONSERVATION

S. A. EL-SWAIFY and W. C. MOLDENHAUER

This discussion group recognized the increasing global concern with soil erosion problems, particularly in tropical steep lands. Considerable evidence indicates that natural resource degradation in many countries is nearing the point of no return. There is urgent need, therefore, to sensitize and secure commitments from all members of the international community to adopt wise, productive, sustainable, and protective land use practices to ensure the welfare of future generations.

The necessary elements for planning and implementing effective conservation for sustainable agriculture on hillslopes were summarized by S. A. El-Swaify (pp. 93-100). These elements are technological, economic, social, and political. Technological elements begin with appropriate selection of land uses and management alternatives based on inherent characteristics of the site. Important inherent characteristics include climate, soils, and topography. Management alternatives pertain to cropping systems and land and water management. All of these elements must be integrated—in a favorable socioeconomic-policymaking environment—if effective implementation of conservation-effective land use systems is to be realized.

For the most part, a climatic inventory is lacking in areas where it is most needed. Data is needed on drop size and intensity of rainfall and on the influence of altitude, geographic distribution, and slope aspect. Depending on the climatic regime, water should be retained at certain times and disposed of at other times. Unlimited infiltration through ponding leads to soil nutrient loss, especially nitrogen and certain pesticides, by leaching below the root-zone and, ultimately, into groundwater. Safe transport and disposal of runoff is a difficult problem, particularly in developing tropical countries where farms are small, waterways are commonly owned and occupy valuable land, and practices performed by each farmer affect the other occupants within the catchment or basin.

Understanding the soils of the area is essential to evaluate their suitability for specific cropping systems, to assess vulnerability to erosion, and to predict the effects of land shaping, earthmoving, or erosion on productivity. On steep lands, we need to determine productivity changes brought about by terrace construction and erosion. We need to know which soils will store large amounts of water and which will not. We need to assess the danger of mass movements, such as slips and landslides. Soil information needs to be interpreted beyond soil profiles to real-scale landscapes.

Concerning topography, most participants agreed that our quantitative knowledge of the effect of slope length and steepness on erosion is nearly nil for steep lands. Some in the group thought soils were more important to erosion than slopes. Rules, regulations, or even guidelines on what constitutes "steep slopes" are not universally agreed upon. For instance, in Taiwan, farming is not allowed above a 55 percent slope, and slopes of 30 percent or less are considered safe. In Thailand, land over 55 percent steepness is now being used in farming, but the law states that land above 18 percent must be kept in forest. In New Zealand, where landscapes are geologically young, mass movements are perceived as a continuous threat regardless of land use.

What is the influence of cropping system on soil erosion? Are agroforestry systems, such as alley cropping, proven, safe practices for steep slopes? Participants raised a number of questions on these issues. Probably the two most frequently asked involve competition between the tree and crop components of the system (for water, nutrients, and sunlight) and the quantitative erosion protection imparted by alternative systems on steep slopes. Alley cropping, if implemented correctly, prevents complete canopy closure, but not competition for water. Many countries use alley cropping on 30 to 40 percent slopes, and, in Nepal, on even greater slopes. Despite these common perceptions, no relevant, hard data is available for such slopes.

Management alternatives include land management (land shaping and terracing), water management, and integration. Conference participants from the Philippines and Thailand emphasized that it is essential for the farmer to see a benefit from conservation measures. To the contrary, many have seen their crop yields decline from exposing less favorable subsoil materials during the land shaping and terracing operations. This is one of the strong arguments for integrating good land husbandry with engineering measures. Terracing labor costs may be too high in certain developing countries. Maintenance of engineering structures is a major problem. Often, farmers are not consulted about alternatives or informed about maintenance needs. Farmers usually won't maintain terraces that are forced upon them. Major land shaping and terracing projects need both community and government participation. One example of successful terracing is practiced in Taiwan. Here, terraces are constructed so that they can be used for transportation of farm products, which is very important to the farmer.

Concerning water management, it is critical to keep in mind that runoff will always occur. This excess water needs to be safely disposed of and, where necessary, captured and used for supplemental irrigation (e.g., in seasonally dry periods). Where appropriate, stored water may also be used for such other income-producing activities as aquaculture (fish ponds). If runoff water is heavily laden with sediment, then storage ponds must be cleaned periodically to restore adequate storage capacity. In Taiwan, there was little evidence of sediment movement in excess runoff after effective conservation systems were implemented.

Integrating farming system components is a necessity in multifarm situations. Consideration must always be given to farmer opinion and needs. Short-term as well as long-term benefits of effective conservation need to be emphasized. A sampling of the conference participants' greatest concerns emphasized participation by the farmers (Lesotho), strong policy by the government (Thailand), land tenure (Philippines), economic gains (Taiwan), strong government support (several delegates), and education of policymakers (most delegates). In the Philippines, intervention schemes were primarily top-down and emphasized only long-term benefits, which didn't impress the people. Examples abound in many countries of farmers who have abandoned their land in expensively established development/conservation projects.

Monitoring is another crucial though often neglected element of project implementation. Without it, it is difficult to ascertain whether project objectives have been achieved. Taiwan appears to be an example where monitoring is given appropriate emphasis.

Based on the deliberations and discussions among members of this discussion group, therefore, the following elements are needed to ensure conservation-effective land use: a good land resource inventory, a clear national policy on land use priorities, adequate land tenure systems, reduced fragmentation of land, reduced cost and risk of adopting improved technology, effective education and extension services, enforcement of land use policies, sufficient incentives, meaningful involvement of farmers at all levels, and a strong commitment to monitoring.

TECHNOLOGY TRANSFER

MAURICE G. COOK and KEITH FAHRNEY

Transferability of technology is site-specific. In a broad sense, concepts may be transferred; however, specific techniques often need adaptation to local environments/situations. Technologies are not like, as Jan Bay-Pettersen put it, "suit cases that can just be picked up and put down in a new location."

Hillside ditches with grass cover, as practiced in Taiwan, were suggested as an example of technology with good potential for transferability because they are inexpensive and easy to construct. In Taiwan, conservation improvements are viewed as a package of technologies, such as transportation, irrigation, and the development of waterways. The fanya juu terrace was mentioned as a low-cost technology suitable for areas that are capital-poor but rich in human resources. Drip irrigation systems were discussed as possible technology for transfer to sloping land, with certain limitations. This technology is considered too complex for many developing countries, and recent trends are toward simplification. Taiwan's experience in conservation education was offered as an example of an effective technology for transfer. Forty years of formal and informal education have made conservation development programs possible. Formal education includes vocational agriculture schools and university programs. Informal education has been accomplished through township meetings, farmers' organizations, and extension services.

Specific barriers to the adoption of technologies that were identified by the discussion group included lack of education, absence of economic incentives, land tenure issues, and international trade agreements. The absence of economic incentives was considered to be the most serious constraint.

Solutions to the lack of education must involve farmers, the general public, and policymakers. Farmer education can be accomplished through formal and nonformal programs, extension, and field demonstrations. Active, concerned groups can raise the environmental awareness of the general public and of policymakers. Public concern over water quality, natural disasters, and environmental degradation can be used to encourage adoption of soil and water conservation practices. Conservation and concern for the environment may be (at least partially) a function of economic development, so conservation groups are not likely to be effective in areas with subsistence-based economies.

Economic incentives can help to assure adoption of conservation technologies. These incentives depend upon national priorities, as defined by political bodies. Examples of incentives include cost-sharing, low-interest loans, price supports, and market stabilization schemes. Cost-sharing to finance conservation improvements is effective in both Taiwan and the United States, but, so far, it appears to be less effective in Malaysia. Low-interest loans can be provided by either the government or the private sector. Market stabilization usually requires a government with sufficient economic resources and political support for the farmers.

Land tenure encourages conservation and long-term interest and care for the land. This is exemplified by the situation in Malaysia, where farmers with long-term leases adopt conservation measures, but squatters in mountain areas practice shifting cultivation. In Taiwan, farmers who first lease government land may later be granted title after implementing adequate conservation measures.

Prediction of the transferability of conservation technologies can reduce costs and expedite development efforts. Modeling can be useful for identifying general components of agricultural systems. However, consideration of local variables is essential to predict transferability. Pilot studies are recommended prior to large-scale implementation of new technologies.

Transferability may be internal (depending upon characteristics of the technology itself, such as cost, risks, and complexity) or external (a function of more generalized components of the system, including cultural values, market prices, etc.). The ultimate test of transferability is farmer adoption; however, new technologies generally reach farmers only by filtering through the perspectives of researchers and professionals. Farmer-to-farmer extension may have potential under certain circumstances.

Case studies of past successes and failures of technology transfers can help to improve future performance. Failures are often more informative than successes, but failures are seldom documented. Examples of institutions that are successful in transferring technologies would be helpful. A description of the structure and functions of the Chinese Soil and Water Conservation Society, for example, would help determine the appropriateness of such an institution as a vehicle for conservation technology transfers in other countries. Appropriate mechanisms for transfer of technologies between institutions in developed and developing countries need to be explored.

Media promotion of soil and water conservation (integrated with related environmental concerns) aimed at policymakers and the general public can enhance the success of technology transfer. Sample brochures and videos should be developed in a broad, generic style to allow for modification to suit regional and local emphasis. Organization through international conferences and workshops, such as this International Workshop on Conservation Farming on Hillslopes, can be vital to our local efforts in striving to realize conservation of our soil and water resources.

THE TAIWAN EXPERIENCE:
A WORKSHOP SUMMARY

TED C. SHENG and JAMES R. MEIMAN

Taiwan has developed sophisticated and effective methods for conservation farming on hillslope land. As such, the nation represents an advanced stage of evolution in hillslope farming techniques. The experience of Taiwan can be valuable to developing countries both in illustrating a national evolution in hillslope farming, from subsistence to targeted commercial enterprise, as well as providing practical examples of the policies and techniques that are required to develop sustainable economic enterprises on hillslope land. Much of the discussion at the workshop involved participants from 23 countries probing for these policies and techniques.

The overriding message of the 1987 conference in Puerto Rico ("Conservation Farming on Steep Lands") was the critical importance of beginning soil and water conservation by on-site land husbandry, but the message from the Taiwan workshop is that, although on-site land husbandry is absolutely necessary, it alone is not sufficient for a successful hillslope conservation farming program.

An examination of the Taiwan experience suggests that successful conservation farming programs must deal with increasingly complex systems, beginning with the site-specific and eventually reaching the macropolicy issues of pricing and marketing. Furthermore, there appears to be no straightforward path to success other than the flexibility to adapt as we learn from our actions. Admittedly, Taiwan was in a somewhat unique position to follow this route because, when it started conservation farming some 35 years ago, it had strong government support, funding to begin a comprehensive program almost from the beginning, and no entrenched

313

bureaucracy. The gradual evolution of that program is described later.

In addition to stimulating papers and poster sessions, two special features of the workshop involved the emphasis on infrastructure and the excellent organization of the field tour.

Infrastructure, such as roads, machinery, and irrigation, often is very necessary for modern farms on hillslopes. It was rare, however, in the previous soil conservation workshops or conferences for the subject of infrastructure to be included. This workshop not only had a special session on infrastructure, including several papers on mechanization on slopelands, transportation systems, and drip irrigation, but also demonstrated, in the field, various farm paths, means of transportation, sprinkler irrigation, and use of small machines for spraying and other operations. In addition, an exhibition of farm machinery for hillside farming developed in the last 2 decades in Taiwan was also included in the program, and it generated much interest and attention.

The highlight of the workshop was the 2-day, mid-workshop tour. Not only was it well organized and proceeded almost flawlessly, but it also was very worthwhile to the objective of the workshop. For instance, at the first stop in Mioli County, participants had a chance to examine closely a young orchard with conservation treatments, irrigation installations, and mechanization operations. At the second stop, a vast area (some 5,500 hectares of slopeland) developed in the last 2 decades, proper conservation measures and various mature orchards were displayed. It can be seen that the project was successful because farmers are vigorously tending the crops and maintaining the conservation structures. At the last few stops in the Pakua Mountain area, participants had an opportunity to see good land use in the watershed area before visiting the downstream torrent control structures for protecting nearby villages. The tour was supported by a beautiful guidebook.

Evolution of Taiwan's Program in Conservation Farming

For the last 35 years, Taiwan's program in conservation farming has experienced a dynamic evolution. This resulted partly from the rapid changes in its socioeconomic conditions, but it resulted mainly from continuous efforts to seek the best farming solutions to fit the needs of the people. This evolution has involved (1) changing from individual farms to an integrated and group approach, (2) merging erosion control and farm management, and (3) switching from labor-intensive to labor-saving practices.

When Taiwan started its soil conservation program in the early 1950s, extension work concentrated on protecting individual farms here and there.

Although this approach met with some success, the impacts were never great in a region or in a watershed. For this reason, in the mid-1960s, the government initiated a program to channel more resources into integrated development of the slopelands, involving groups of farmers in pilot projects. This approach proved popular and fruitful, and the program has been rapidly expanded nationwide. Up to the present, a total of 137,000 hectares, or approximately 45 percent of the area actually farmed on slopeland, has been placed under this integrated soil conservation and land use program.

In the early years of the program, erosion control practices were emphasized, such as terracing and waterway installations. With the new policy in the mid-1960s, soil conservation and land use began to merge together with concentrated crop development and marketing arrangements. Gradually, infrastructure needs, such as farm roads, minor irrigation, crop storage, and farm machinery for slopelands, became an integrated part of the program. As a result of all of these factors, most of Taiwan's hill farms are now modernized and producing high-value horticultural crops.

In the early decades, labor-intensive treatments, such as bench terraces, were emphasized for soil conservation. Because of industrialization, shortage of labor, and land use changes from food crops to permanent fruit trees on the hillslopes, simple structures, such as hillside ditches and orchard terraces (both are essentially narrow terraces built at different intervals), have been used extensively in recent decades as primary conservation treatments. They are not only used to intercept runoff but simultaneously as farm paths, which greatly facilitates farming practices and saves labor. In addition, grasses [mostly bahiagrass (*Paspalum notatum*)] are planted as cover crops and also used for mulching material. Thus, erosion has been minimized.

Keys of Success in Taiwan's Conservation Farming

During the meeting and field trips, the success stories of Taiwan's conservation farming were vividly explained and generated considerable interest among the participants. In the keynote paper, C. C. Koh and associates identified nine key factors in conservation farming in Taiwan:

1. Field-oriented organizational structures.
2. Firm government support.
3. Increased professional training and educational opportunities.
4. A successful extension program with a pragmatic approach.
5. Proper incentives.
6. An integrated approach.
7. A joint planning framework.

8. An improved data base derived from island-wide and project-oriented slopeland survey efforts.

9. Continuous endeavors to provide practical solutions and effective practices to identified problems.

Four of these factors received special attention during the discussions and field trip.

Excellent Government Support. Since the beginning, there has been strong government support for the program. The Taiwan government has had a clear and consistent policy in conservation farming and watershed protection. Special institutionalized agencies, such as the Mountain Agricultural Resources Development Bureau (MARDB), and several watershed protection organizations were created. The Taiwan Forestry Bureau was strengthened. Each of these agencies was given clear responsibilities for various aspects of the work. Also, from the mid-1960s, the government supported many universities and colleges to establish B.S., M.S., and Ph.D. programs in soil conservation, watershed management, and forest hydrology. A steady supply of trained manpower was ensured. In recent years, the overall government budget for conservation and watershed protection has amounted to $100 million annually. For a small island nation, this is a very high investment, compared with that in other developing countries.

Integrated Approach. Taiwan adopted an integrated approach for conservation farming and slopeland development as early as the mid-1960s. The integration of soil conservation with crop development and infrastructure in one package has greatly promoted the work on the steep slopes of the island. Technical services and incentives are given to all kinds of work. Both at the planning and implementing stage, close coordination among various government bodies was obtained, with MARDB as the lead agency.

Involvement of Local People. To pursue conservation farming in an area, a local development committee is usually organized. Seven to nine farmers are elected as board members to be involved in planning, implementation, land acquisition, and local funding. All of the work is designed to fit farmers' needs. Using a government master plan as a base, the work is carried out voluntarily by local people. Local organizations, such as farmers' associations and local government, are actively involved in the program.

Continuous Endeavors for Practical Solutions. Throughout the evaluation of the Taiwan program, there was what might be called a "learn-by-doing" approach. Several examples were observed or reported on at the workshop.

When it was evident that hillslope-adapted machines were key to efficient hillslope farming, a research program was initiated that resulted in a fleet of practical and small machines for hillslope agriculture. When the traditional bench terraces were found unsuitable for modern orchard farming, existing terraces were modified and a shift was made to hillside ditches for mechanization. A third example of flexibility relates to the use of forest-land. When it was found that some of this land was occupied by farmers and needed for agriculture, a policy was established to permit conversion to agricultural use if the farmer used the land according to a new classification and treated the land properly with conservation practices. Each of these examples reinforces the far-sighted and flexible approach that seeks innovative solutions based on practical considerations.

Experience from Other Countries

The papers from countries other than Taiwan illustrated the great diversity in biophysical and socioeconomic conditions under which hillslope farming is conducted. Each of these presentations emphasized the site-specific nature of problems and solutions. At the same time, they also reinforced the general principles inherent in the Taiwan experience.

Among the many and varied issues discussed in these papers were the basic issue of when and how much hillslope agriculture should be encouraged; the necessity for locally adapted land classification schemes; the use of information systems as a base for program targeting; the special problems related to forest clearing; the utility of climate and soil-based cropping system classification; crop diversification versus monocropping; tree-crop farming systems, alley cropping, and other agroforestry practices; the much neglected role of livestock; the issue of slope limits for effective vegetation strips; the variety and effectiveness of extension approaches; the need for better methods and data to predict soil erodibility; the question of how to get effective farmer involvement; the analysis of conservation in the context of farmer investment opportunities; risk as a factor in conservation investment; and the integral relationship between soil productivity and erosion. While this list is neither exhaustive nor new, it illustrates the extreme complexity of hillslope conservation and, more importantly, that those working on hillslope systems are aware of this complexity and attempting to deal with it.

Some noteworthy experiences and trends in other countries are highlighted as follows:

• In Australia, conservation farming is seen as an integral part of a total catchment management in that planning and implementation are on a catchment basis, involving all relevant departments, authorities, companies, and individuals with responsibilities for management of land within catchments. The objective is to achieve both resource protection and sustainable production.

• Organizing soil conservation programs on a watershed basis is also stressed and gaining importance in India, as shown in the case presented for the State of Kerala.

• An upland farming system project in Indonesia recently showed that technology developed in lowland areas is hardly suitable for uplands, especially those requiring high inputs and complicated management. Livestock is recommended to be included in the hillslope farming because livestock provides cheaper organic matter and draft power and contributes to farm income.

• South Korea's experience on slopeland reclamation is that for each soil type many kinds of land use can be recommended; the most suitable one must be determined by economic, social, and political considerations. In addition, for hillslope farming to be successful, climatic zoning and soil improvement are essential.

• In Malaysia, though hillslopes are mostly planted to tree crops, erosion does constitute a serious problem during land clearing and when the crops are immature. Conservation work, such as bench terraces, individual basins, or cover crops, is necessary. Farm transportation systems also are required for these hillslope farms.

• Integration of traditional conservation measures (level bench terraces) and modern practices (simple structures and biological measures) is necessary in Sri Lanka to plan and implement land use and conservation work in a watershed. The former is for conventional crops, such as rice, while the latter is for developing tea, coffee, and other hillslope plantations.

• Thailand's experience with hillslope development is somewhat different from the others. Because of the rapid destruction of forest resources, especially in the northern region, the current government policy is to restrict migration to the hilly areas, to develop forest resource potential, and to emphasize watershed protection. Land suitability classification, conservation structures for arresting erosion, woodlot establishment, and increasing production on existing cultivated slopes are emphasized much more than expanding new areas for hillslope farming.

Conclusion

In addition to the four key factors mentioned previously, what else is transferable from the Taiwan experience? One is struck by the perspective of balance. Emphasis is placed on both on-site work and the integration of sites within the concept of the watershed; the watershed is used as the planning unit even though application is implemented on a site-by-site basis. Similarly, there is no fruitless debate about vegetative methods versus structural measures; both are combined effectively. Neither is the top-down or bottom-up approach overemphasized; one finds effective participation from both directions. Attention is given to both the broad policy concerns and the details of specific treatment measures. There is a careful harmonizing of meeting the farmers' need for increased productivity and the need to protect the soil and water resources.

Finally, and perhaps most importantly, one cannot help but be impressed by the hard work, dedication to detail, and persistence of the workers in Taiwan at all levels. These traits were obvious in the conduct of the workshop and associated field trip. This attitude pervades the Taiwan experience.

It is difficult to summarize succinctly a workshop involving more than 160 participants from 23 nations, but perhaps one participant came closest when he said, "Now I see hope for hillslope development."

CONTRIBUTORS

Nazeer Ahmad
University of the West Indies
Trinidad, West Indies

Pervaiz Amir
Badan Penelitian Dan Pengembangan
 Pertanian
Salatiga, Indonesia

A. Barus
Centre for Soil Research
Bogor, Indonesia

E. K. Biamah
University of Nairobi
Nairobi, Kenya

J. D. Cheng
Department of Soil and Water
 Conservation
Chung-Hsing University
Taichung, Taiwan

Pi-Wu Chien
Mountain Agricultural Resources
 Development Bureau
Nantou, Taiwan

Yu-Yung Chu
Shihmen Reservoir Administration
Lung-Tang, Taoyuan, Taiwan

Maurice G. Cook
North Carolina State University
Raleigh, North Carolina

Ai Dariah
Centre for Soil Research
Bogor, Indonesia

S. A. El-Swaify
University of Hawaii
Honolulu, Hawaii

Keith Fahrney
University of Hawaii
Honolulu, Hawaii

S. Fujisaka
International Rice Research Institute
Manila, Philippines

Teruo Fujiwara
Yamaguchi University
Tokiwadai, Ube City, Yamaguchi, Japan

Mitsuo Fukada
Yamaguchi University
Tokiwadai, Ube City, Yamaguchi, Japan

D. P. Garrity
North Carolina State University
Raleigh, North Carolina

B. S. Ghuman
International Institute of Tropical
 Agriculture
Ibadan, Nigeria

Earl H. Grissinger
Agricultural Research Service, USDA
Oxford, Mississippi

J. S. Gunasekera
Soil Conservation Society of Sri Lanka
Anniewatte, Kandy, Sri Lanka

Albert R. Hagan
University of Missouri
Columbia, Missouri

Ghulam Mohd Hashim
Agricultural Research and Development
  Institute
Kuala Lumpur, Malaysia

J. G. Hawley
Division of Land and Soil Sciences
Palmerston North, New Zealand

R. Howeler
Centre International de Agricultura
  Tropical
Bangkhen, Bangkok, Thailand

Chin-Teh Hsieh
Mountain Agricultural Resources
  Develop Bureau
Chung-Hsing Village, Nantou, Taiwan

Mou-Chang Hsu
Mountain Agricultural Resources
  Development Bureau
Nantou, Taiwan

Su-Cherng Hu
Council of Agriculture
Taipei, Taiwan

J. P. Jaiswal
North-Eastern Hill University
Medziphema, Nagaland, India

Somjate Jantawat
Kasetsart University
Bangkok, Thailand

In Sang Jo
Rural Development Administration
Suweon, Republic of Korea

T. C. Juang
National Chung Hsing University
Taichuing, Taiwan, R.O.C

B. T. Kang
International Institute of Tropical
  Agriculture
Ibadan, Nigeria

M. L. Khybri
Central Soil and Water Conservation
  Research and Training Institute
Dehradun, India

C. C. Koh
Council of Agriculture
Taipei, Taiwan

S. W. Lee
Council of Agriculture
Taipei, Taiwan

Mien-Chung Liao
Council of Agriculture
Taipei, Taiwan

Taneu Liao
Council of Agriculture
Taipei, Taiwan

Jiann-Jang Lin
Mountain Agricultural Resources
  Development Bureau
Nantou, Taiwan

Yuan-Lin Lin
TSU-THAI Associates, Inc.
Taipei, Taiwan, R.O.C.

James R. Meiman
Colorado State University
Fort Collins, Colorado

L. Donald Meyer
Agricultural Research Service, USDA
Oxford, Mississippi

William Moldenhauer
World Association of Soil and Water
  Conservation
Volga, South Dakota

Dimyati Nangju
Asian Development Bank
Manila, Philippines

Soon Leong Neoh
Neoh Choo EE & CO SDN.BHD
Penang, Malaysia

G. Balakrishna Pillai
Kerala Agricultural University
Trivandrum, Kerala, India

S. Putthacharoen
Kasetsart University
Bangkok, Thailand

Sanarn Rimwanich
Ministry of Agriculture and Cooperatives
Bangkok, Thailand

U. Ravi Sangakkara
University of Peradeniya
Peradeniya, Sri Lanka

V. K. Sasidhar
Kerala Agricultural University
Trivandrum, Kerala, India

Ted C. Sheng
Colorado State University
Fort Collins, Colorado

Soleh Sukmana
Badan Penelitian Dan Pengembangan
    Pertanian
Salatiga, Indonesia

H. Suwardjo
Centre for Soil Research
Bogor, Indonesia

D. B. Thomas
University of Nairobi
Nairobi, Kenya

Pen-yu Tu
Chinese Soil and Water Conservation
    Society
Taipei, Taiwan, R.O.C.

V. Vichukit
Kasetsart University
Bangkok, Thailand

K. Viswambharan
Kerala Agricultural University
Trivandrum, Kerala, India

W. A. Watkins
Soil Conservation Service of
    New South Wales
Chatswood, N.S.W., Australia

Chia-Chun Wu
University of Mississippi
Oxford, Mississippi

Huei-Long Wu
Council of Agriculture
Taipei, Taiwan

Ju-shiung Wu
Mountain Agricultural Resources
    Development Bureau
Nantou, Taiwan

INDEX